"Our affair belongs to the past."

Seth's tone was concerned as he opened the car door. "So do we have to be enemies? Karis, I'm trying to help. A kidnapping is one hell of a nightmare, especially for a girl on her own in a strange country. Wouldn't talking about it make you feel easier?"

"I suppose it would," Karis agreed, half seduced by a need for his sturdiness. "But—"

"So please, get in the car."

With misgivings Karis climbed in. By talking to Seth she would involve him, which meant the situation would end up under his control. He wouldn't domineer; he would simply slide into the role of ship's captain.

"If I explain about the kidnapping," she told him sternly, "you're to be just an audience, period."

His smile was in full bloom. "That's all I ever intended to be."

ELIZABETH OLDFIELD began writing professionally as a teenager after taking a mail-order writing course, of all things. She later married a mining engineer, gave birth to a daughter and a son and happily put her writing career on hold. Her husband's work took them to Singapore for five years, where Elizabeth found romance novels and became hooked on the genre. Now she's a full-time writer in Scotland and has the best of both worlds—a rich family life and a career that fits the needs of her husband and children.

Books by Elizabeth Oldfield

Don't miss any of our special offers. Write to us at the following address for information on our newest releases.

Harlequin Reader Service
901 Fuhrmann Blvd., P.O. Box 1397, Buffalo, NY 14240
Canadian address: P.O. Box 603,
Fort Erie, Ont. L2A 5X3

ELIZABETH OLDFIELD

touch and go

Harlequin Books

TORONTO • NEW YORK • LONDON
AMSTERDAM • PARIS • SYDNEY • HAMBURG
STOCKHOLM • ATHENS • TOKYO • MILAN

For my sister-in-law Margaret who
lives on a light station,
off British Columbia

Harlequin Presents first edition November 1987
ISBN 0-373-11030-8

Original hardcover edition published in 1987
by Mills & Boon Limited

CHAPTER ONE

SETH would know what to do. Cool and clear-thinking, Seth Mauroy always knew what to do. Damn him. Karis flung a fierce glance at the telephone, then sighed. All her instincts rebelled against appealing for his help, yet what alternative was there? Who else could she ring? Her stepfather's enthusiasm for socialising might have brought battalions of people trotting in and out of her life during previous visits to Bangkok, but they were acquaintances at best. Seth was not an acquaintance. She knew him well—in all manner of ways. Correction, *had* known him well. The past tense was required. For six months there had been no contact between them.

Karis thrust a hand through the ash-blonde hair which met her shoulders in a swinging, geometric line. Should she contact him now? If she did, how would he greet her? Not with whoops of joy, that much was certain, for mere weeks after visiting her last year he had been seen swanning around with a Thai maiden of aching beauty stuck to him like cling-film. Seth, it appeared, had recovered in double quick time from the fiasco of what she supposed could be described as no more, no less, than an extended holiday romance. But hadn't she also recovered? With determined steps Karis strode across the living-room to lift the receiver. This agony of indecision smacked of the juvenile, and at twenty-four she was an adult. An adult who, on this occasion, needed advice. Seth could advise her. It was as simple as that.

She dialled the number, and was in the throes of

rehearsing a controlled approach which would contrive to sound both pleasant yet aloof, when the phone at the other end of the line was abruptly grabbed up.

'Seth Mauroy.'

The identification bristled with highly charged emotion. He sounded impatient, restless, and it did not need two guesses to know he had been standing over the telephone willing it to ring. Why the urgency? Had one of his achingly beautiful Thai maidens promised to get in touch?

With her rehearsal cut short, the controlled approach emerged as a pathetically lumpen stutter.

'It's—it's me. Karis,' she mumbled.

'Karis?' There was a pause. 'Karis who?' he enquired.

Her deep blue eyes hardened, her spine stiffened into indignant steel. How many women called Karis did he know? And this from a man who had once claimed he could recognise her voice before she had completed one syllable, and then only if telepathy had not already advised she would ring. Seth had not only recovered from their affair, he seemed to have forgotten she had ever existed!

'Karis Buchanan,' she said spikily. 'I'm calling about Leon. You see, we were supposed to be dining out this evening, but he hasn't come home.'

'And what do you expect me to do—fill in because you've been left in the lurch? Odd, I understood my days of "have tuxedo, will escort" were over.'

The sardonic reply had her scowling. Seth made it sound as though she had phoned to proposition him in a roundabout kind of a way. As though he imagined she had spent the last six months sobbing into her pillow, and now interpreted this call as a puerile attempt to start stitching their relationship together again. The arrogance of the man!

'All I want——' she began.

'I wasn't aware you were visiting Thailand,' he interrupted, in a tone which accused her of creeping into the country on the sly and totally destroying the population balance. 'When did you arrive?'

'Three days ago.'

'Taking a break from the mums with tums?' he asked drily.

'Yes.' She was curt. Her aerobics studio had always been an emotive issue between them and Karis had no intention of discussing it now. 'Leon said he'd be back by seven at the latest because he'd booked a table for eight o'clock, but now it's nearly ten and there's still no sign of him.'

Seth gave an audible sigh, and began speaking as if she were saddled with an I.Q. which would have a struggle to reach the low forties.

'Allow me to wise you up on some facts of local life. Bangkok may be called the City of Angels, but that doesn't stop the traffic from being devilish. People have been known to pass from youth to middle age to damn near senior citizenship while they're trapped in jams—if the exhaust fumes don't asphyxiate them first. Chances are your stepfather's stuck in the middle of a snarl-up somewhere.'

'At this time of night?' she protested.

'It's possible. Or there may have been an accident. I don't mean involving Leon, but a collision in the city centre, even roadworks come to that, can clog up streets within a two-mile radius. Regrettably the police often move at a speed which resembles somnambulance, so sorting things out can take forever.'

'Perhaps I should ring the police?' Karis suggested, resenting his tone of measured impatience.

Did he think she hadn't already considered the

abysmal traffic? Did he believe her incapable of making a rational assessment of the situation? She might not have lived most of her life in Thailand like him, but she had grasped the basics.

'Leon was due in at seven and it's not yet ten? They'd hardly send out tracker dogs on the strength of him having been absent less than three hours,' he scoffed.

'But——'

'Don't worry, Leon won't have come to any harm. If anyone knows their way around, it's him.'

'You don't understand. He only——'

'Have to go,' Seth went steamrollering on. 'I'm expecting a call at any moment and need the line free. It's important. 'Bye.'

The phone went dead. So much for Frenchmen being gallant! Karis thought, dropping the receiver back on its cradle with a petulant clatter. Admittedly Seth Mauroy was only half French, but his degree of gallantry had been nowhere near fifty per cent. On the contrary, he had off-loaded her with bruising haste. She stalked across to slide open the glass doors which led out on to the balcony. What did she do now? With a sigh, she rested her elbows on the wide stone ledge of the balustrade and gazed out into the darkness. By day the view from the tenth-floor apartment was a depressing urban sprawl, flat-roofed 'shop-houses' being the city's main feature, but when night fell the drabness was obscured and touches of wonderland revealed. Elegant, gold-encrusted spires rose spotlit in the dark, the magnificent scarlet and green roofs of the Grand Palace were visible, and even the workaday Chao Phaya river took on the mystique of a metallic jet snake, sliding silently through the slums and shanty towns of the metropolis.

Karis hooked a strand of fair hair back over one ear.

Tonight she was too busy fretting over her stepfather's disappearance and that exasperating phone call to marvel at the sights. Damn Seth again. A year ago he had been spouting vows like, 'If you ever need me just call and I'll be there'. What price those vows now? OK, their relationship was defunct, any reason for him to slay dragons on her behalf had been nullified; but she didn't want him to slay dragons. Never had. All she wanted was for him to have had the courtesy to hear her out. Surely then he would have understood there was a solid basis for her fears?

Yet even if Seth had agreed Leon's absence required attention, would he have cared two hoots? Probably not, she thought scathingly. His antagonism had never been brought out into the open, but she well remembered the tightness which had gripped him whenever her stepfather had been around. If some calamity had befallen the older man Seth was not the type to play hypocrite and pretend to wallow in inconsolable grief. Some calamity? What calamity? Had Leon been mugged and left unconscious in a dark alley? Knocked down by a hit-and-run driver? Felled by a heart attack? Her blood ran cold. Eighteen months ago her mother had suffered a coronary and died within hours; could history be repeating itself? No. She was being morbid, over-imaginative.

Karis fidgeted with the sequinned lapel of her black silk jacket. Worn over a camisole top and with matching trousers, the jacket was reserved for special evenings. Leon, in his effusive way, had insisted this was to be an *extra* special evening, which was why for two and a half hours she had been decked out glamour-girl fashion, with eyelids gilded, lips glossed, and hair brushed to a sheen. The point of the lapel was straightened again. More and more she felt like a Cinderella whose Fairy

Godmother had ceased waving her wand midway. What had happened to Leon? She could not go to the ball without him. Though now she didn't want to go. Any glow of anticipation had faded, together with her appetite. All she wanted was for him to return. Karis frowned, thinking how her stepfather was one of the 'hail fellow, well met' variety, never happier than when chatting with someone over a drink. He couldn't have met a group of his cronies and forgotten the time to this extent—could he?

The sixty minutes which followed dragged like sixty years. Ears straining for the whirr of the elevator, the sound of homecoming footsteps, she paced around the apartment, but Leon did not appear. When the clock struck eleven, Karis decided she had to do *something*. To hell with Seth's ridicule, she would report the matter to the police. She did not want Interpol alerted, but didn't it make sense for them to have a note of her stepfather's name, just in case an accident had befallen him?

Having reached a decision, next she needed to put it into action. Back home reporting the matter to the police would have been a straightforward question of a telephone call. Not so here. Her Thai was non-existent, and she had already discovered the pitfalls of speaking blind with people whose English was limited. An eagerness to please meant the locals would give chirpy assurances of understanding when, in reality, messages were being garbled, turned inside out, stood on end. Would the police be similarly unreliable? Maybe not, for there were special 'Tourist' officers on the force— linguists trained to advise foreigners—yet what were the chances of one taking her call at this late hour? Karis sighed. Her best bet was to go to the constabulary headquarters a few blocks away, and speak with someone face to face. Only then would she be able to verify the facts had been properly logged.

After scribbling an explanatory note in the hope of Leon's return during her absence, she collected her bag and went down to street level. In seconds a *tuk-tuk*, a little open three-wheeled taxi, chugged up. The normal routine was to haggle at length over a price, but tonight Karis simply quoted her destination and climbed aboard. With an Oriental mix of panache and disdain, the driver swerved in front of a truck, skipped a red light and charged towards the police station in a manner reminiscent of a charioteer. The roads were busy, but the traffic flowed. There was no sign of any hold-up. So much for Seth's theory! It had been a throwaway theory, she thought caustically, and a throwaway phone call. Most unsatisfactory. If he hadn't been in such a rush to cut her off she could have asked the name of a policeman friend of his. The man, a high-ranking officer at the police headquarters, spoke excellent English, and would be the ideal person to approach.

'That way,' Karis said on impulse, flapping her hands to denote a diversion.

Seth might have no time to spare for her over the telephone, but he would be forced to spare time if she landed on his doorstep. After all, she only wanted a couple of minutes in which to jot down the policeman's name, because even if he wasn't on duty at least asking for him would give her mission an added air of importance. Two minutes were not much to ask—or were they? A look at her wristwatch showed it was nearing eleven-thirty. Would Seth be in bed? If so, he would not appreciate her disturbing his sleep, or any other activity for that matter. Huh! Serve him right if she did put the kibosh on an ecstatic union. That would even the score for the 'Karis who?'.

His home was an old teak house which overlooked a

klong, a canal, in a charming backwater of Bangkok. Lovingly restored by the wealthy American who had been its previous owner, the house contained the latest refinements for modern living, yet with no loss of its intrinsic Thai nature. One of Seth's hobbies, his *only* hobby, was collecting treasures on his travels around south-east Asia, and the pale caramel teak of the high-ceilinged rooms made a stunning setting for his oyster-shaded carpets, delicate watercolours, the hundred-year-old chandelier he had had shipped over from Korea in pieces and painstakingly rebuilt. Once Karis had been as enchanted with the house and its contents as she had been with their owner; but at the sight of lights blazing behind the richly carved shutters her pulse tripped. Everything looked familiar, yet was ... alien.

'Would you wait here, please?' she asked the taxi driver, miming how she would be gone just milli-seconds, but a healthy collection of *baht* needed to be pressed into his palm before he would agree to stay put.

A second time that evening Karis started to rehearse a speech and a second time was thwarted, for as she mounted the shallow flight of wooden steps which led to the verandah, the front door swung open. Her immediate impression was of a tall, loose-limbed silhouette, but a moment later the image solidified. It became a man in dark trousers and shirtsleeves, whose raven-black hair was tousled across his brow.

'Another visitor, isn't this my lucky day?' he drawled, and heavily-lashed hazel eyes, once used to transmit tenderly intimate messages, swept over her like all-seeing, all-censoring searchlights. Seth folded tanned forearms and lounged back against the door jamb. 'Earlier this evening Kovit bursts in, blubbering about a disaster which I'm expected to solve, and now——'

'I don't expect you to solve anything,' Karis told him,

irritated because a pang had struck somewhere in the region of her heart. How satisfying it would have been if the past six months had dwindled him, made him lacklustre, but alas, Seth Mauroy remained a charismatic and extremely collected individual. With his dependable cleft chin and intelligent brown eyes, he emanated both calm and an aura of strength. The combination was compelling. Members of both sexes showed a tendency to gravitate towards him whenever a shoulder was needed to cry on. And Seth's shoulders were broad. 'The only reason I'm here is to ask for the name of that police officer you know, the one who deals with your explosives certificates,' she pressed on, her briskness making it plain she required his assistance in a most minor way. 'I'm going to the police station and——'

'I take it Leon's still A.W.O.L.?' he interrupted.

'He is, or rather he was when I left the apartment. Could you tell me the officer's name, please?' she demanded, aware of a surge in the noisy chug of the *tuk-tuk* waiting at the kerbside. Already the driver was growing impatient.

'Sivapatarakhampol.' Thai names have a habit of sounding like the alphabet spelt backwards, but Seth had spoken quickly—on purpose, judging from the amusement fluttering around his mouth. Although English was his mother tongue, he possessed equal fluency in French and Thai. 'But aren't you being a touch neurotic? Bringing in the storm-troopers at this stage seems——'

'Neurotic!' Karis exclaimed.

'It must have crossed your mind that Leon may well have an excellent reason for reneging on your dinner date?' A brow lifted. 'And I'd be obliged if you wouldn't heave your breasts at me.'

Whether that was its intention or not, the request

ensured she became instantly hot and bothered. Because their relationship was over, she had assumed Seth would treat her as neutral, as sexless. However, his plea, combined with the glint in his eyes, was proving the assumption wrong.

'But——' she blurted, then dried up, aware of having too much in common with an apoplectic tomato.

'But what?' he prompted. 'Now take it slow and easy, and tell your Uncle Seth.'

Karis glared. 'But it wasn't just a casual arrangement. Leon had arranged what he called "a night to remember",' she informed him coldly. 'You know how particular he can be, ordering the wine beforehand, stipulating which table? Well, he'd done all that. He finished his calls early, came home, laid out the clothes he intended to wear. Then he explained that he needed to go out, but that he'd be back in good time to shower and change. Apparently he'd run into a business contact and they were meeting up for a quick, early evening drink.' The chug of the *tuk-tuk* peaked to a sudden climax, and she spun round to see it vanishing into the night. 'Damn!'

'Which business contact?'

'He didn't say,' she replied, wondering what the chances were of alternative transport coming along. She swivelled to him. 'I thought perhaps you might have an idea.'

'Not me. Since our commercial dealings were severed Leon's path and mine don't cross too often.'

'You can't suggest where he might be?'

He thought for a moment. 'Possibly,' he admitted, the word sounding as though it had been prised from him. He rubbed a hand over his face in a gesture of weariness, then said unenthusiastically, 'I guess you'd better come in. Before you rush pell-mell to inform the authorities, there are one or two facts you ought to know. It's your choice,' he said, when he saw her hesitation. 'If you prefer to remain in ignorance and make a fool of yourself, don't let me stop you.'

Karis bridled, then, with a look which stabbed like a dagger, right between the shoulder blades which lay beneath his white poplin shirt, went with him across the verandah.

Walking into the house felt suspiciously like coming home; a sensation which did little for her peace of mind. Karis sneaked a look around. The ivory elephant still occupied its niche in the hall, the pot plants continued to spread themselves in leafy splendour, his display of brass weights glistened for ever bright. In the airy living-room, the huge, pale green celadon lamps and the Chinese altar table which did duty as a drinks cabinet seemed like old friends. The wall pinned with exotic painted kites brought back memories, too. Only a gloriously squashy sofa and armchairs in soft cream leather were new. Once she would have complimented Seth on his taste and he would have been pleased; on this occasion she remained silent. Seth indicated that she should be seated, and sank down opposite. When they had been speaking outside his face had been in shadow, but now she was surprised to see how tired he looked. Lines were etched around his eyes, there was a tension in the set of his jaw. Seth never cracked under pressure— and as he was managing director of a Western explosives company competing in the cut-throat Oriental market-place the pressures on him were severe—he merely bent a little, yet this evening there were signs of a definite sag. Could that important telephone call he had mentioned indicate some kind of a crisis?

'Sorry if I'm intruding,' politeness insisted she said, but when all her apology received was a shrug, an offhand one at that, Karis wished she had saved her breath.

'I might be speaking out of turn here,' he said, tossing aside silk cushions as if they were sandbags purposely placed there to offend, 'but Leon has a girl-friend—a woman friend, she's in her forties.' He cast her a cautious look. 'Has he ever mentioned her?'

'No. Should he?'

'He's known her for years.' There was a pause, then he added, 'Rumour has it they're close. Close as in . . . sleeping together.'

'Oh.' Now it was Karis's turn to shrug. With such a glaring gap in her knowledge being pointed out, what else could she do? It was possible there were other gaps. Very possible. Karis had first met her stepfather little more than two years ago and, owing to his being a Bangkok resident while her home was in a small Kentish town, had been in his company rarely. Indeed, add up the time they had spent together and it amounted to nothing more than weeks. In Leon's case, however, time had never seemed much of a criterion. He possessed an open, friendly manner which, combined with the fact he had brought her mother long-overdue happiness— albeit for a tragically brief time—guaranteed that Karis felt nothing but warmth towards him. Yet in this situation warmth was no substitute for knowledge. And Seth's knowledge of her stepfather went back a long way. She tilted her head to one side. 'You think maybe that's where he is tonight, with this woman?'

'It's a possibility. If Monika needed him——' A long-fingered hand demonstrated a lemming-like rush to obey.

'But if there's been an emergency and he had to go and see her, why not ring and tell me?'

'Perhaps he prefers to keep Monika a secret? She's a

German blonde, chic and soignée. Also she lives in an out-of-the-way house beyond the airport which may not have a telephone.'

Karis frowned. The notion that her stepfather had deliberately kept quiet about this friendship was unwelcome. Yet he had—and for no reason at all. *She* had not expected, nor wanted, him to mourn persistently, yet since her mother's death he had shown a dogged devotion to her memory. His apartment was littered with her photographs. His letters made constant reference to his 'beloved Ruth'. His grief had always seemed genuine, but now she wondered if, misguidedly and for her sake, he could have been displaying an excessive zeal? Leon rarely did anything by half. And having committed himself to the role of sorrowing widower, he could find it tricky to extricate himself and declare an interest in another woman—to his stepdaughter, at least.

'If he is with Monika, it's possible he could stay the night,' she hazarded, and received a nod. 'In which case I ought to wait until the morning before I do anything?'

'I'd wait until tomorrow midday.'

'Midday?' Karis asked doubtfully.

'When a man and a woman wake up in bed together, they do occasionally feel the urge to make love. Or have you forgotten?' One of Seth's most appealing, or most exasperating, assets—depending on which way you looked at it—was a mobile mouth. With just a twitch of a lip all manner of things could be inferred, and his lip had twitched a moment ago. 'That can take time, depending on how thorough you are. Then there's always the——' he broke off as the telephone on the leather-topped writing desk shrilled '—traffic,' he dashed off, in the split second before he leapt to his feet.

A personal state of emergency had been declared.

Raking a hand through his thick dark hair, Seth set off across the room. With brow grimly furrowed and a fevered look in his eyes, it was clear just one thing mattered—answering the telephone. Left abandoned in his wake, Karis did not need to be told the call superseded in total any paltry problem *she* might have.

'Could you tell me the policeman's name again?' she put in swiftly, hoping to snatch up a remnant of his attention.

'Wait until tomorrow, midday,' he flung back.

'But all I want is——'

'Tomorrow.'

'Can't you just——?'

'Leave it,' he ordered, flicking a hand towards her as though she were a pesky fly.

Karis swept from her chair. Her host barely noticed. Neither did he notice the resentful stomp of her heels as she headed for the door. He might not have said, 'Don't call me, I'll call you', but it was implicit. With more pressing matters to deal with, he now regarded her as a pain in the lower back. Ditto! she thought, and cast him a blistering glance.

Seth had reached the telephone. 'Yes?' he demanded, gripping the receiver in a taut fist. There was a moment when he listened intently, then all of a sudden the tension, the grimness, vanished and his face was wreathed in smiles. 'You have? Where was it? Thank God!' He let out a breath of relief. 'Who found it?' he questioned, beaming across at her.

Karis gazed glacially back. She was not prepared to be included in his happiness. Those smiles had nothing to do with her. What was more, she intended to have nothing further to do with *him*. Pivoting on her heel, she marched out on to the verandah. What had she achieved in coming here this evening? An irritating zero.

Appealing for his aid had been a complete waste of time. To hell with Seth Mauroy, she thought, as she ran down the steps. She would have been far better off going it alone.

CHAPTER TWO

WHEN she awoke the next morning and discovered her stepfather had still not returned, Karis felt very much alone. All her worries marched back into her head and tramped up and down, this time wearing hobnailed boots. The suggestion that he might be with the German woman gave precarious comfort, because she didn't *know* that, did she? Her brow puckered as she cut herself a slice of papaya from the fridge. Even if Monika didn't own a telephone, there must be public callboxes on the way to her house. Why hadn't Leon used one of those? She gave her head a little shake. That he should disappear without a word was uncharacteristic, wrong, scary. She was not an alarmist, but . . .

Karis spent the morning learning each and every nuance of the phrase 'to be like a cat on a hot tin roof'. Attempts to distract herself by cleaning the cooker, washing the kitchen floor, even undertaking a strenuous dose of aerobics, did not work, for whenever her antennae picked up the murmur of the elevator all action stopped dead. Breath caught in hope, she waited. Please let it be Leon. Please. Please. Please. Sometimes footsteps did approach the apartment, but without exception they continued past. She returned to her tasks, destined to leap to full alert at the next noise. But if sounds made her edgy, rampant imaginings made her even edgier. Where was he? What had happened? Why no news? Midday took on the dimensions of a deadline. Fingers curled into her palms, Karis waited. And waited. Midday arrived— her stepfather did not.

At one minute past noon she tucked her pink muslin blouse tighter into the waistband of her skirt, and opened the door into his study. Since the previous evening her strategy had been readjusted. Before she contacted the police, other avenues needed to be explored; like ringing around some of Leon's friends. Names had been dredged up from among the battalions of partying souls. She recalled a Wilfred Green, or was it Brown? Two Texan brothers, Hank and Pete—something. Unfortunately there was no address book in the living-room to help jog her memory, but perhaps there would be one in the study? Yet it was with misgivings that Karis began searching around. Her stepfather, she knew, would not be pleased. Despite the circumstances insisting on her entry, he might well regard it as an intrusion. Easy-going in every other way, he had strict rules concerning the small room from where he operated his clutch of agencies. The study was *his* domain, a private haven which the silver-haired businessman jealously guarded.

Karis soon discovered its contents were also guarded. There was no address book, no list of numbers beside the telephone, not a single scrap of paper lying around. She tested the metal filing-cabinets, but found every drawer in all three securely locked. With a sigh of frustration, she headed for the door. Now there seemed nothing else to do but to wade into the telephone directory, and hope she struck lucky with a Wilfred Green, or Brown. She was leafing through the pages when another idea surfaced. Why not attempt to make contact with one of her stepfather's buddies through the golf club? As a devotee of the game, and a frequent user of the bar and restaurant facilities, he was well known there. Karis began to look for the number. If she rang and asked the switchboard to connect her with someone—anyone—

who knew Leon, surely there would be a response? It seemed worth a try.

Engrossed in her search, the shriek of the telephone almost shot her out of her skin. Instantly her spirits soared. This was Leon— at last. It had to be. And if he confessed he had spent the night making hay with his German fräulein, she would merrily strangle him!

'Leon?'

'Hello, Karis.'

The line was crackly, his usually booming voice faint, but it *was* him. Relief started deep inside, rippling outwards in ever-increasing circles until she felt limp all over.

'Where are you?' she demanded. 'What have you been up to? Are you all right?'

'I'm fine,' he said, then hesitated. 'That's not quite true. You see, I've——' there was a second hesitation '—actually I've been kidnapped.'

Karis's brows dipped down. The connection was poor, all kinds of extraneous noises were coming through, but he hadn't really said 'kidnapped', had he? No, his speech must have been distorted. She pressed the receiver closer to her ear.

'Could you repeat that?'

'I've been kidnapped.'

'Kidnapped?' she echoed, in stunned disbelief. He *had* said 'kidnapped'. In fact, he had shouted it.

'Yes. I was on my way back to the apartment yesterday evening when a couple of fellows, scruffy types, loomed up out of nowhere. Gave me quite a fright, I can tell you. One grabbed my right arm, the other my left, and before I could say a single word I was being frogmarched towards a car which had driven up alongside. Wallop!—I was bundled inside. They pushed me down flat on the back seat, covered me with a blanket, and I heard an ear-splitting squeal of tyres as we skidded away from the kerb.'

Karis half snorted, half laughed. Leon was an accomplished raconteur, and if there was a tale to be told had no qualms about increasing its impact value by aid of a sleek remodelling job. But kidnapped? If this was his idea of a joke, she did not find it amusing. Not when it came on the top of all her anxious hours.

'You think I don't know the truth?' she chided.

'What do you mean?'

'That you've spent the night with Monika someone or other. Look, Leon, I presume you imagine I mind, but I don't. If you've found someone new, I'm delighted. What doesn't delight me is the way I was left dangling. A call to say our dinner date had been cancelled wouldn't have taken more than two minutes.'

'But I couldn't,' he protested. 'Believe me, I have been kidnapped. One of the men wants to speak to you. Hold on.'

In bewilderment, Karis held on. There were mumblings in the background, then a foreign voice began to quote lines sing-song fashion.

'We are holding Mr Thorburn captive and we demand a ransom for his return. If the money is not paid he will be shot.'

'Shot?' she croaked.

'Shot. Here is what you are to do.'

Numbly she listened as the man detailed how, at an appointed hour the next day, she was to make her way to a busy part of the city. There someone would be waiting. When they approached and said Leon's name, that was her signal to hand over a large amount of cash.

'Once the money is in our possession, Mr Thorburn will be released. A warning,' the man finished up. 'You are not to contact the police. If there is any interference, if at any point we suspect we are being spied upon or followed, then beware. Any kind of monkey business which results in us not receiving the ransom means you will not receive Mr Thorburn. Is that understood?'

'Yes.' It was a small word, said in a small voice. Karis's stomach tipped over and she shivered. This was no joke. The voice might be heavily accented, the line poor, but the message was clear enough. And deadly. 'Yes,' she repeated, louder.

'No police.' Leon was back on the line now, almost begging. 'For my sake, Karis, it's essential the authorities aren't brought into this. Or anyone else. Involve other people and there could be slip-ups. We can't afford that.'

'You haven't—haven't been hurt?' she faltered, fear jamming her throat.

'Oh no, don't worry on that score, pet. These men aren't vicious, just greedy. Money's their aim. Please get it. Please co-operate, that's all I——'

Click, the connection was cut. Karis staggered to the nearest chair and dropped down, exhausted. Desperately she attempted to come to terms with what had happened, but nothing made sense any more. The last few minutes felt as if they had been cut out of a movie—unreal, spooky, terrifying. Leon had been kidnapped? Her mind wrestled with images the word conjured up. But kidnapping didn't happen in *her* world. It was a fate reserved for wealthy business tycoons, heiresses, politicians and such. Other people, strangers. She pressed her palms together in a vain attempt to stop her hands from shaking. Her stepfather was not a tycoon, though she supposed he could be mistaken for one. Well built and with the military bearing you would expect of an ex-officer from the Household Cavalry, Leon looked impressive. Didn't he wear monogrammed shirts, handmade shoes, and order his safari suits from one of London's finest tailors? He also had what Seth had once described as a 'cathedral' voice, so he sounded impressive. Was that why he had been whisked away?

Karis scolded herself for digressing. At this stage the whys and wherefores were unimportant. The vital issue was obtaining the ransom money. Although the sum involved amounted to a hefty chunk of cash, astonishingly it was an amount she could raise. For that, if nothing else, she thanked her lucky stars!

By late morning the next day all her transactions were complete. Buoyant on relief, Karis galloped back from the bank. There had been no awkward questions, no undue delays. The cashier had given her neat bundles of notes and, as instructed, she now placed them in a large brown-paper bag. She glanced at the clock. In two hours she must head for the rendezvous, until then a lifetime had to be lived through. As she waited, chewing at a hangnail, her buoyancy deflated. Doubts which had worried her yesterday, and intermittently through a long and sleepless night, plagued her again. Should she ignore the kidnappers' threats and Leon's pleas, and contact the police? Karis was sorely tempted, yet the fear of something going wrong held her back. The hangnail demolished, she sucked at the tip of her thumb. Was making the ransom so readily available the correct way to proceed? She did not begrudge paying—money was only money, and what were pieces of paper in exchange for a life?—but obeying without a single protest, a stab at negotiation, seemed . . . inadequate. At a time when the world at large sought to combat terrorism, she was giving encouragement. Karis frowned, grimly aware that by meeting the kidnappers' demands she might be paving the way for other people to

be abducted. Yet was any other course of action open to
her? Try as she might, she could not think of one.

At the specified time she went to a city-centre
crossroads. On a patch of waste ground a raggle-taggle
fruit and vegetable market had evolved, and she hovered
a little way apart from where customers were discussing,
prodding and bargaining over the produce displayed in
the shade of black umbrellas. As she stood there,
hugging the paper bag to her chest like a long-lost child,
Karis glanced warily around. Was she being watched
from behind the pyramids of watermelons, the heaps of
pineapples? Had a look-out been posted to check she had
told the truth when she had promised to be there entirely
alone? No tricks, the man had warned. But trickery was
out of the question when Leon's life was at stake.

Ceaselessly, the sun beat down. The traffic trundled
by, belching out fumes. Shoppers argued prices at the
fruit stalls. Bangkok is a place of odours, good and not so
good, and the 'sweaty socks' aroma of the durian had
Karis wrinkling her nose. The large rough-skinned fruit
had been banned from hotels and aircraft, and she
heartily wished it had been banned from the streets.
Growing hotter and stickier by the minute, she
continued her surveillance. Rapid mental notes were
made of anyone who came near, in case they suddenly
hissed Leon's name. She was determined to memorise as
much as possible about whoever collected the money,
then if something went wrong—heaven forbid!—an
identikit picture would be stored in her head.

It was a chubby, brown-skinned man in white vest
and baggy grey shorts who eventually spoke to her. He
had been loitering on the corner for several minutes, and
she was surprised when he roused himself and walked
over. That he should have waited there, allowing ample

time for her to note his appearance, seemed remarkably lax.

'Money for Mr Thorburn,' he said, with a tentative smile.

Having anticipated the meeting in fear and trembling, Karis experienced a perverse sensation of anti-climax. She had not visualised being put into a stranglehold by a thug armed with a machete and machine gun, but she had visualised some degree of menace. There was none. The man sounded as inoffensive as a Saturday afternoon charity worker appealing for funds.

'You get no money until I know when he's being returned,' she declared, tightening her grip on the paper bag.

'He come back apartment next week.'

'Next week? That's ridiculous,' Karis protested.

'Next Wednesday, missie.'

'But this is Wednesday! You can't mean you're going to keep him for another week?' She stood firm. 'I insist Mr Thorburn be returned today.'

'No can do.'

'Tomorrow, then?'

'Sorry, missie. He long way away—down south, on island.' She received an embarrassed, apologetic smile. 'Next Wednesday. OK?'

'No.' Karis shook her head, sending the blonde strands swishing. 'I don't care where he is, you must be able to bring him back to Bangkok long before then.'

Amid the general cacophony of city traffic, one noise had begun to dominate. A car horn was being punched at regular and prolonged intervals. Glancing up, Karis realised the din originated from a milk-white Porsche which had stopped at traffic lights across the junction. Behind the wheel sat a man in a dark business suit and pale shirt. He had wound down his window and was waving frantically. Whose attention was he trying to attract? The mirrored sunglasses which obscured his gaze made it difficult to assess. Karis squinted into the sunshine. Could he be waving at her?

Yes. The man in the car was Seth! What did he want? Why all the fuss? With a twist of her stomach she realised she could ill afford fuss, not *now*. But it was too late. The chubby Thai had ceased to smile, and instead was glancing anxiously between the car and her, tying up a connection. Was he imagining she had an ambush planned, that Seth's arrival—even on the far side of the crossroads—represented interference? But interference could result in her stepfather being shot!

Whether Karis thrust the money at the kidnapper or whether he grabbed it was a moot point, but the bag changed hands at speed. Then—whoosh!—the chubby man darted off, weaving a surprisingly nimble path through the crowds. With a sigh of resignation she watched him go. If Leon's return could have been fixed for an earlier date, she would have felt much happier, but next Wedn

esday *had* sounded definite. That the man had taken the money and made a hasty exit was something she could live with—just. But then she really had no choice.

Seth, however, believed otherwise. That became clear when the lights changed and the Porsche skidded across the junction, accelerating down the road in hot pursuit. For a moment the horror of what his action might entail held her rigid, then adrenalin surged.

'No!' Karis yelped, and made chase.

Pure chance had had her pulling casual turquoise trousers and shirt out of the wardrobe that morning, and now she was grateful for their easy fit. Within ten yards, her gratitude extended to her espadrilles. The pavement was an obstacle course; uneven kerbs, broken paving stones, unexplained holes lying in wait, and her flat, rope soles proved to be not so much a bonus as a necessity. Ignoring passers-by who had turned to gape, Karis pounded along.

'Seth, stop!' she shouted, when she caught sight of the low-slung car slewing to a halt ahead, but he was too busy throwing himself out and charging off to hear.

The plump Thai had swerved into a shadowy crack of an alleyway, and he chased in after him. When Karis panted up, seconds later, she followed. Hot and airless, the alley appeared to be a dumping ground for everything from rotting vegetables to fish heads, and smelled even worse than the durian. Underfoot the going was treacherous. Once or twice she slipped, yet each time she managed to recover and power on. Seth was some twenty yards beyond her, while his prey was roughly the same distance beyond him, fat legs going like pistons.

'Seth, leave him!' she yelled at the dark-suited figure, but his pace never slackened.

That Karis exercised religiously and he never did had once been a subject for amused discussion between them; but this pursuit was proof that even if he scorned press-ups and trunk-curls, Seth Mauroy was fit. As the kidnapper reached the far end of the alleyway, so he was gaining on him. Only yards separated the two men now. Heart in mouth, gasping for breath, Karis chased after them. Then suddenly a miracle appeared in the form of a woman entering the alley, a small child hanging on to each hand. The Thai darted past, but as Seth drew level one of the children stumbled. Forced into executing an awkward cha-cha-cha, he lost precious seconds. Karis made ground.

'Don't—don't interfere,' she panted.

'I'll get him.' The assurance was tossed over his

shoulder as he started forward again.

'No, wait!'

A desperate leap and Karis grabbed wildly at the back of his jacket. There was a tearing sound as the lining ripped. Braked in mid-flight, Seth batted backwards in an attempt at release, but she held on.

'You must let the man go.'

'Let him go?' Chest rising and falling, he turned. He snatched off his dark glasses to lock disbelieving eyes with hers. 'Let him go?' he repeated.

'That's what I said.' Throughout the chase a whole host of emotions—alarm, trepidation, fear—had been jostling in her head, but the realisation of how close he had been to jeopardising Leon's life now had her quivering with anger. 'It would be nice if you asked permission before meddling wholesale in someone else's affairs,' she snapped.

Seth glanced towards the end of the alley, itching to resume his chase. 'Meddle?' he questioned, scowling when the fingers clutching his jacket showed a stout refusal to slacken.

'Yes!' she gasped in a breath. 'Why don't you mind your own business? If I'd wanted your help I'd have requested it.' She gasped again. 'However, I didn't, for the simple reason I do *not* want that man to be caught.'

'You don't?'

'No! And must you repeat everything I say?'

Seth held up a finger before his mouth. 'Cool it,' he cautioned, nodding towards the woman and children who had stopped a yard or two away. 'Lower your voice.'

Karis's blue eyes glittered. 'Why should I?'

'Because in Thailand losing your temper in public is considered a social offence.'

'Is it?' she hissed, and in deference to the woman and

children who were frowning, ostentatiously lowered her tone by several decibels. 'Well, I consider poking your nose in where it isn't wanted no great shakes, either.'

'Forgive me. I failed to realise you were running your very own be-kind-to-purse-snatchers week,' Seth replied, loading the remark with as much irony as it would take. 'However, be assured I've got the message now. Many thanks,' he said, when she removed her hand from what had become a crumpled and deeply creased patch of jacket.

'That man was not a purse-snatcher,' Karis insisted, but received scant acknowledgement.

Seth slotted his dark glasses into an inside pocket, took the strides necessary to reach the end of the alleyway, and peered out. A narrow-eyed look left was followed by a narrow-eyed look to the right. Confirmation that his quarry was indeed long gone made him scowl. The woman and children seemed to interpret the scowl as a signal to move on, for as he returned they walked away.

'You must have realised by now that Bangkok has more than its fair share of crooks,' he said, wiping a slick of perspiration from his brow and grimacing at his wet fingers. 'Wasn't it naïve to engage in conversation with a complete stranger, while at the same time gazing blindly around?'

'I wasn't gazing around,' Karis defended. 'I happened to be looking at you! Which considering the noise you were making is hardly surprising.'

'OK,' he agreed. As an admission of guilt, it did not go far. 'But that noise was meant to be a warning that the guy appeared to have designs on your property. And if he wasn't strictly a purse-snatcher, let's amend him to a paper-bag-snatcher. Same difference.'

'It's not,' she protested. She was all set to say more, but a snort of irritation cut her short.

'Forget the definition,' Seth said heavily. 'Just explain the reasoning which insists a thief should be allowed to go free. And don't tell me I didn't see him steal your——'

'You didn't see him *steal* anything.'

'For crissakes, Karis, I was watching! The guy couldn't keep his eyes off your paper bag, though doubtless that was because you were clutching it so tightly. Anyone would have thought you were carrying gold bars.' Abruptly Seth remembered the damage done when she had grabbed him, and his displeasure was transferred. Removing his jacket, he made a slit-eyed examination of the torn lining. 'Just as a matter of interest, what was in the bag?' he asked, picking tetchily at the broken threads. 'And if you dare tell me I've broken the four-minute mile, drenched myself in sweat and had the clothes bloody well torn off my back chasing after nothing more than a pound of bananas which, according to your version, weren't stolen anyway, I'll——'

'No bananas.'

'Thank God for small mercies. Well?' he questioned, when she hesitated.

How did she explain? Or rather, *should* she explain? The payment of the ransom was meant to be a strictly private affair. Telling a white lie seemed the wisest option. But the man beside her had such a frustratingly lordly air that Karis could not resist this chance to knock him off balance.

'I was carrying money.'

'Money? In a brown-paper bag? And when the guy took it you——'

'Lots of money.'

'Lots?' Seth queried gingerly. In the past Karis had sprung things on him, and now he recognised a worrying smugness in her smile.

'Lots and lots.'

'How much is lots and lots?' he demanded.

She knew she was hamming it up, but the moment was too good to squander. Nonchalantly she tossed a strand of blonde hair back from her shoulder.

'One and a half million *baht*,' she said.

CHAPTER THREE

'ONE and a half million *baht*?' Seth repeated, his voice choked with incredulity.

'That's right.' Karis bit back an intense urge to giggle. During their time together the occasions when his sangfroid had been ruffled could be counted on the fingers of one hand, so to have him keeling over was a giddy achievement. 'At today's exchange rate that's almost forty thousand pounds sterling or in the region of sixty thousand dollars, U.S.,' she continued airily.

'Spare me the currency equations, those I can work out for myself,' Seth said, and swallowed. He drew in a deep breath, then blew it out again. 'What I can't work out is how you come to be hawking a fortune around, and then actively encourage it to go missing. I do recollect you possess a certain flair for kamikaze enterprises, but this action seems extreme, even for you.' He swung his jacket back over one shoulder, a finger crooked through the loop. 'Care to give me a clue?'

All thoughts of giggling faded. Knocking him off balance seemed frivolous, self-indulgent in the extreme. Karis felt ashamed. Engrossed in scoring points, she had forgotten her stepfather's plight. Also, having told Seth this much, she had put herself in the position of being forced to tell him more.

'Like I said, the man wasn't stealing. He was supposed to have the money—in a manner of speaking,' she faltered, as the grim realities swarmed back into her head. Despite the heat, she felt chilled. 'It was for Leon.'

'For Leon?'

'Yes, for his release.'

With his free hand Seth massaged the back of his neck, frowning when his fingers met soggy strands of dark hair. 'Forgive me for being a little slow on the uptake, but what are you talking about?'

'Leon's been kidnapped.'

He gave a startled laugh. 'You're joking!'

'I only wish I was,' Karis said despondently.

'But—but who the hell would want to kidnap him?'

'I've no idea. He appears to have been picked off the street at random.'

Seth's brow furrowed. 'Let me get this straight. When Leon went missing on Monday evening, he really was missing? You haven't seen him since?'

'No, though I have spoken to him on the telephone. And to one of the kidnappers.'

'Who are these kidnappers?' He snatched an idea out of the air. 'Crackpot extremists keen to publicise some cause or other?'

'They don't seem to be any special group, and they definitely don't want publicity.' Karis's stamina had begun to drain, and she needed to fight to mobilise it again. 'It's—it's OK, everything's organised. I apologise for being so ungrateful about you coming to what must have seemed the rescue.' She flashed him a fractional smile. 'You weren't to know you were in danger of wrecking everything. If you'd caught the man there could have been . . . problems. Oh, and I'm sorry about your jacket,' she added, when he just stood and looked at her. 'I'll be happy to pay the cost of repairs.'

Seth shook his head, though whether in refusal of her offer or to clear his thoughts was uncertain.

'Correct me if I'm wrong, but as I understand it Leon's been kidnapped, you've just shelled out a ransom of one and half million *baht*, yet you say everything's hunky-dory?'

'No, I said everything was organised.' Karis crossed mental fingers. She wasn't going to think about things going wrong. Not when her stamina had once more begun to glug away like water down a plug-hole. Not when all she wanted to do was find a cool tranquil place where she could lie down and go to sleep. 'It was decent of you to wade in. Thanks. Sorry about the jacket again. Don't forget to send me the repair bill.'

'Hold it!' Seth raised a blocking hand. 'I'm getting the impression this is a farewell speech.'

'It is.'

'For God's sake, you can't just float off into the wide blue yonder! I want an explanation of what's been happening. Don't I deserve one? Maybe attempting to break the land speed record down a back alley in a temperature of over ninety degrees makes barely a ripple in your day, but for someone like me——'

'Aren't you feeling too good?' Karis enquired.

He glared. 'You saucy little bitch! I'm feeling fine. Don't I look fine?' he demanded, in best defensive fashion.

'Well . . . yes.'

It had to be admitted Seth looked in great shape—if bedraggled. Maybe the chase had been fast and furious, but all the evidence indicated he had taken it in his stride.

'Just because I've been around the block a few more times than you, it doesn't mean I'm about to fall to pieces,' he growled.

'I never said you were, but that was a hard run on anyone's terms,' Karis soothed, 'and as you don't take any exercise it would be perfectly understandable if——'

'I *do* take exercise.'

Karis shrugged, disinclined to argue the point. She had been referring to regular work-outs, whereas she knew fine Seth interpreted 'exercise' as a rapid bash around the tennis court or a few lengths of the pool on rare occasions when he could tear himself away from work. Such spasmodic bouts of activity did not count as 'exercise' in her book.

'About this explanation,' she began tentatively. 'I'm supposed to keep everything under wraps, so would you mind waiting until next Wednesday?' She paused, a shadow crossing her face. 'That's when Leon's due home.'

'He's not being released for a whole week?' Seth took hold of her elbow and began shepherding her back along the alleyway. 'Why the delay?'

'I don't know. It doesn't make sense to me, either.'

'What do the police think about it?'

'The police aren't involved.'

The fingers on her arm tightened, jolting her to a halt. 'Not involved?' he demanded.

From the moment his hand had first made contact, Karis had felt itchy. She knew the action was no more than a reflex—as far as Seth was concerned she could have been an old lady he was helping across the road—yet his touch disturbed her. The feel of his skin against hers was an alarming reminder of how *physical* they had once been together. Now, thank goodness, the harsh grip provided an excuse for release.

'Let go of me, please,' she requested.

'Letting go, letting go,' Seth assured her. Restlessly he flexed his shoulders. 'Do you mean the police aren't aware any money has changed hands?'

'The police aren't aware Leon's gone missing.' She began to walk again, picking her way through the garbage she had skied over minutes previously. 'The kidnappers were insistent that under no circumstances should the authorities be involved. The transaction was strictly between them and me.' Karis cast him a glance. 'I don't suppose I should be telling you all this now.'

He was silent for a moment. 'So who have you told?' he enquired.

'Nobody. The kidnappers were adamant that——'

'I realise you haven't contacted anyone official,' he interrupted. 'What I'm asking is—who's been providing moral support?'

'No one.'

'But you can't have——' Seth stopped and started again. 'Are you saying that you've——' He clawed at the knot of his tie. 'Have you been coping with this all on your own?' he demanded at last.

'I do have more between my ears than a smile,' Karis informed him, though no smile was spread there now.

'For heaven's sake, girl, your nerves must be in shreds!'

'They are,' she admitted. Lying down was beginning to seem the only thing to do. 'But I was threatened that if I didn't play it solo Leon might be——' she gulped '—shot,' she got out. 'Besides, even if I'd been free to ask for moral support, who was there? Aunt Connie and her husband were transferred to Islamabad a while back, and I don't know anyone else here, not properly. I've had two holidays in Bangkok, that's all, and then my time was spent either with my mother, or with you. Leon did insist on spinning me around the cocktail-party circuit whenever he had the chance,' she continued quickly, sidestepping thoughts of that all-absorbing love affair, 'but I was introduced to so many people their names barely registered.'

'You could have confided in me,' Seth said, as they

walked from the gloom of the alley on to the sunny street.

'Could I?' she enquired, coating the words in ice.

He took out his dark glasses and placed them on his nose. 'Yes,' he insisted, casting a rueful look over the top before sliding them into position. 'I must apologise for——' he groped for a suitable phrase '——my lack of hospitality the other night, but you caught me at a bad time. Something had gone missing. Company documents.'

'In my case it was *someone*.'

'Touché. You'll be gratified to know I feel appropriately ground down. However, by way of defence I should point out that at the time Leon had only been gone a couple of hours. You could have rung the next day when he didn't show up.'

'Of *course* I could.' Karis spread wide theatrical hands. 'I wonder why it never occurred to me to go in search of your sympathetic ear?'

'I'm ready to listen now,' he assured her soberly.

'Now, right now? Shouldn't you be getting back to your office? Unless things have changed drastically, there must be orders to be given, deals to fix, money to be made.'

'There's nothing that can't wait,' said Seth, as they approached the Porsche.

'Nothing?'

He wrenched open the passenger door with unnecessary force. 'Would you stop trying to kick-start me? Any accusations regarding my addiction to work belong to the past.' He turned a blind eye to her raised eyebrows. 'Likewise our affair, romance, whatever you want to call it, belongs to the past, so do we have to be enemies? Karis, I'm trying to help here. A kidnap is one hell of a nightmare for anyone to have to deal with, never mind a girl on her own in a strange country. Wouldn't talking about it make you feel easier?'

As he had been speaking his tone had modulated. He sounded concerned.

'I suppose it would,' she agreed, half seduced by a need for his sturdiness. 'But——'

'So please, get in the car. We'll go back to my place. Leon's apartment,' he adjusted, when she looked doubtful. 'Wherever you want.' Still she hesitated. 'I give you my solemn oath that whatever you say stays here.' Seth spread a tanned hand across his chest. 'Right here. Look, you don't imagine I'd blab and put Leon at risk, do you?'

'No.'

'Then let's go.' He jerked a thumb. 'In.'

It was with misgivings that Karis climbed into the car. Should she take Seth into her confidence? The idea was inviting. After two days during which the pressure had built up, after two nights with virtually no sleep, she needed an outlet, some kind of release. Bottling everything up had to be bad for her health. And when she thought how those days and nights were only a start to anticipating her stepfather's return, she felt distinctly ill. Was she to spend the week which stretched out until next Wednesday in solitary torment? 'A trouble shared is a trouble halved,' went the saying, and there was no doubt that simply explaining what had happened would be a tremendous relief. Yet ...

She gave Seth a sideways glance as he eased the car into the traffic. Clearly he attributed her hesitation to the fear that in some way speaking out would endanger Leon, but that was not the problem. She trusted his discretion and failed to see how confidences could put her stepfather at extra risk. No, her hesitation came from a different source. Karis licked her tongue over her lips.

By talking to Seth she would *involve* him, which, unless she was very, very careful, meant the situation would end up under his control. He wouldn't domineer, anything but. More, he would slide into the role of ship's captain, steering his craft to safety while she sat below in the cabin, not bothering her pretty little head. He would do it unassumingly, easily and without pause for thought. Taking control was not an ego trip, it was ... the traditional guardian role of the male. But in Karis's view that role was outdated. Unlike Sukanya, his young Thai wife who had died seven years ago, she did not regard herself as a passenger. She was perfectly capable of taking the helm herself, and surviving a drenching from any rogue waves.

'If I explain about Leon, it's on the understanding that all you do is listen,' she told him sternly. 'Nothing else.'

A smile flowered in the corner of his mouth. 'What's the matter? Are you afraid I'll be so overwhelmed with emotion at your plight that I'll clasp you to my manly chest and—*voilà!*—we'll end up enjoying some mutual rest and recuperation?'

Karis gritted her teeth. Trust Seth to imbue her 'keep your distance' warning with sexual connotations. And as for '*we'll* end up enjoying'! He didn't imagine time had stood still and she remained the eager bedmate, did he?

'What I mean,' she retorted, fizzing, 'is that you're to be an audience, period.'

'Take it easy.' His smile was in full bloom. 'That's all I ever intended to be.'

He seemed about to say more—doubtless something irreverent and irrelevant—but abruptly his smile became a frown. Ahead lay a traffic roundabout, where a policeman in a beige military-style uniform was blowing a whistle and making frantic 'move along' signs.

Considering each of the four exits was blocked solid, the officer could be accused of being outrageously optimistic. Seth cursed, executed a hasty left turn, then jammed his foot down hard, cursing again. In avoiding one disaster area, all he had done was tack them on to the tail end of a queue of cars, trucks, taxis, which stretched down the narrow street as far as the eye could see. He wrenched his head around, hoping to escape by means of rapid reversing, but already traffic had drawn up behind. He applied the handbrake and sighed.

'What made you decide to pay another visit to Bangkok?' he asked.

The words themselves were innocuous enough, but his intonation gave the query a detective-to-suspect flavour. Karis shot him a glance. Why the thread of suspicion? He wasn't imagining she had travelled halfway across the world purely in the hope of meeting him again, was he?

'I didn't decide. All I did was comply with Leon's wishes,' she replied, ruthlessly demolishing such bizarre delusions—if they existed. 'This visit was his brainchild. He invited me.'

'Why?'

'Why? Because he thought I might like a change of scene, some sunshine. And because he wanted to see me, of course.'

'But the pair of you have very little in common.'

'We have my mother!' Karis pointed out indignantly.

'And what else?'

'We—well, er——' Smitten by an infuriating mental block, she found it impossible to dredge up another area of mutual interest. 'Leon's good fun,' she defended.

'He's an entertaining bastard, I'll grant you that. Though whether I'd rush to be the guest of someone who can talk the hind leg off several donkeys before breakfast is a different matter.'

Karis gave him a dirty look. After only three days in her stepfather's company she had been beginning to find his jocularity somewhat jarring, but this was not a time for criticism. This was the time for support.

'Is being chatty a crime?' she demanded huffily.

'Not if the chat's easy-come, easy-go, but in Leon's case it isn't. He turns every conversation into a performance, with himself as star.' Tanned fingers drummed at the steering wheel. 'When you've experienced ten years of *Le Grand Fromage* act, you find it immensely wearing. But then acting is what Leon's all about.'

'Who says?'

'I do. Look, you've seen how he tours the room at cocktail parties, as if he's a grand duke or something. It surprises me he's never bought a monocle, that'd be just his style.' Seth's mouth turned down. 'I remember years ago when Sukanya and I were invited to his apartment for dinner. We were met at the door by those two servant girls of his, performing salaams. He had them barefoot and decked out in national dress. All evening they hid behind screens, ready to obey their master's every whim. Leon just needed to click his fingers and up they'd pad bearing gin and tonics on a silver salver. It was like something out of Somerset Maugham.'

'I seem to recall you have a housekeeper who looks after you,' Karis said with frosty precision.

'She cleans the house, makes my meals, agreed. But I'd never expect her to parade around in fancy dress with the aim of impressing my guests. That whole evening was grotesque. He acted the potentate, while those poor girls——'

'Those poor girls enjoyed working for Leon.'

'Rubbish. They humour him because he pays good money.'

Her chin lifted. She supposed she had always known Seth did not like her stepfather, but to hear him articulating that dislike was an affront. In the past he had kept his criticisms to himself, so why air them now? *Now*, when poor Leon was being held captive somewhere, probably at gunpoint!

'Then why did they both weep when they left?' she challenged.

'They've left?'

'They went soon after my mother died.'

'What's he replaced them with, twin butlers?'

'He hasn't replaced them.' Mentally Karis thumbed her nose. 'He told me that after my mother's death he needed solitude, and now he prefers it that way.'

'Old Leon's keeping his apartment spick and span all on his own?'

'He tries,' Karis said loyally. Too loyally, for the phrase was pounced on.

'Only tries? You mean you walked off the plane and straight into knee-deep cobwebs?' Seth chuckled. 'That's why you were invited, to do the spring cleaning. I knew he had to have an ulterior motive.'

'You're nasty, d'you know that! Leon wanted to talk over old times, reminisce about my mother. And considering how devoted he was to her, I don't find that so difficult to understand. He misses her. What could be more natural than to seek comfort by talking about her? Apparently he's tried speaking to people here, but apart from offering trite expressions of sympathy, nobody's interested. He knew I'd listen, so he wrote on the spur of the moment asking please would I visit.'

'The letter came out of the blue?'

'The invitation did, not the letter. We've kept in

touch ever since my mother died. Leon writes on a regular basis.'

Seth peered ahead. The queue remained dormant. Only motorbikes moved. Loaded with everything from buckets of orchids to wobbly mountains of cardboard boxes, they wove impertinently through the inert traffic.

'Strange,' he ruminated, sitting back to resume the wait. 'When Leon held the agency for our detonators we had the devil's own job to get him to commit anything to paper.'

The agency! Karis thought, and Seth's hostility clicked into place. For twenty-five years, during which Cecil Pritchard, the previous managing director, had been in charge, Leon's business methods had never been challenged. Then Seth, who worked on a higher level of professionalism, had taken control. He had been far from satisfied. Exactly why was never specified—Seth had always been tightlipped where the older man was concerned—but she remembered her mother mentioning 'a conflict of interests' in a letter way back. After what appeared to have been lengthy negotiations, the agency had been disbanded, leaving the company to market their detonators themselves. Seth had achieved his aim.

'Well, Leon writes long newsy letters to me,' she announced, needing to champion the underdog.

'What on earth does he find to write about?'

'That's none of your business! And I'm fed up with this Twenty Questions game. Why you need to place his invitation under the microscope and cynically dissect it, I've no idea. Leon wanted to see me, it's that straightforward.'

'Karis, nobody does anything for just one reason,' he said sombrely.

'How profound! You must have read that on the back of a matchbox somewhere. And OK——' she flicked her fingers '—as well as needing to reminisce, maybe he fancied having a female on call to accompany him on his social rounds.'

'He has a female on call—Monika.'

In the turmoil of the day Karis had forgotten about her stepfather's girl-friend, and now it was as if a chair had been whipped out from under her. Silently, she went down with a bump.

'About Monika,' she said. 'Do you think you could put us in touch?' Asking for his help did not come easy, not after she had so forcefully insisted the only thing she required was his ear. She coped by taking an excessive interest in the distant traffic, which at last was showing signs of rumbling back to life. 'I presume she won't be aware of Leon's disappearance, and she ought to be told.'

'The only way to break the news would be to ring Düsseldorf.' Seth waited as the movement dominoed back to their point, then shifted into first gear. Slowly but steadily, he edged the Porsche forward. 'I met a couple of your stepfather's mates the other day, and they mentioned seeing Monika off at the airport,' he explained. 'She flew out of Thailand more or less as you flew in.'

Karis sighed. 'If she's not here, I suppose it's kinder to leave her in ignorance.'

He nodded. 'Giving her the fright of her life long distance ain't cricket.'

The hold-up had occurred within less than a mile of the apartment block, and with the traffic on the move again the remainder of the journey was soon completed. After depositing the Porsche in the underground car park, they travelled up to the tenth floor.

'Ready when you are,' prompted Seth, when they were settled on floral-upholstered rattan chairs in the living-room, tall glasses of Singha beer beside them.

'As you know, two evenings ago Leon and I were due to go out to dinner, but——' Tucking a leg beneath her, Karis launched into her tale. The first part was related in a matter-of-fact fashion, but when it came to the phone call retrospective fear flooded back. Without warning, she felt cornered, bewildered, lost.

'Are you all right?' Seth asked, as her voice quavered. He stretched out a hand. 'Karis——'

'I'm OK, honestly,' she broke in, terrified his quip about clasping her to his chest might be about to come true. Why must he look so concerned? she wondered, with a surge of irritation. Why did he have to say her name in that tender way? Seth was overstepping the mark. Or could she be the one guilty of overreacting? Karis took a drink of beer, and decided she had read more into his solicitude than was there. All he had shown was the normal consideration of one human being for another. She sat a little straighter, and continued her recital. 'Now you know as much as I do,' she said, as she finished.

Seth had been right. She *did* feel better. Nothing had changed, her stepfather was still missing, but the lead which had packed her lungs for the past two days had gone. Breathing was easier.

'He gave no indication as to where he was meeting his business contact?' Seth asked.

She shook her head. 'I presume it was the Golf Club.'

'Not unless the other guy was a member. Leon resigned a while ago.'

'But the Golf Club used to be his second home,' she protested in surprise.

'The place can't be the same without Leon holding

court,' he said pithily. 'The story is he didn't feel he was getting his money's worth, and he was probably right. The club's reckoned to have gone downhill of late.'

Karis sighed. 'Wherever he went on Monday, it's amazing how easily he appears to have been pounced on. I don't understand why a passer-by didn't come to his aid.'

'Because in a mad, bad city people think twice about interfering? Even so, in abducting him like that his kidnappers were taking one hell of a risk. If I planned a kidnap I'd choose somewhere a lot less public. A shadowy car park, for example.' Seth frowned. 'What's happened to his car?' he asked. 'Was he using it the other night?'

'No, it's in the garage being repaired. He either walked to the bar, or took a taxi.' Karis sipped her beer. 'I realise this doesn't help any, but I have the impression the kidnappers are amateurs. Remember what I told you about the phone call? The way Leon described how he'd been accosted in graphic detail? I can't imagine seasoned professionals allowing him to do that. Also, although he wasn't casual, the only time he really sounded uptight was at the end, over the prospect of the police being brought in. And *he* can't rate whoever's got him too highly, not if he refers to them as scruffy types within their hearing!' She gave a brief smile. 'Then there's the little man who came for the money. I'd swear he'd never collected a ransom before. I mean, how dumb can you get, standing there for minutes in full view! Heavens, now I know him as well as my own grandmother.' She nibbled at her lip. 'Trouble is, even though I'd recognise him anywhere, the only description I could give is that he's short, plump and affable—like a million and one other Thais. Which wouldn't help much.'

'The man had no distinguishing features?'

'Just one, a small dark red birthmark beneath his left ear. It was shaped like a teardrop.'

'A teardrop birthmark?' Seth gave her a sharp look, then descended into thoughtfulness. 'Mmm, that's odd.'

'Not really. Lots of people have birthmarks.'

'Even you,' he grinned, tossing aside his gravity. 'Now, where is it? I seem to have forgotten. Would you care to refresh my memory?'

'No, thank you.' He knew exactly where her birthmark was. She was sitting on it! Stony-faced, Karis inspected her watch. 'I'm grateful for your time,' she said, pointedly placing their meeting back on a formal footing where it belonged. 'Talking to you has been . . . therapeutic. From now on I'm sure I shall feel much better. Thank you for listening and——' The telephone rang. Hair rose on the back of her neck, and her stomach clenched and churned. She did not feel better at all. 'Do you think this could be something to do with Leon?' she asked, gazing at Seth in alarm.

'It's possible. Look, you're under enough strain already. Let me answer it.'

She leapt up as he rose to his feet. 'No, no!' she cried, thrusting herself between him and the phone.

'Karis, I needn't let on I know Leon's missing. I could pretend we'd met, you'd invited me up for a drink, and you'd just gone out to, to——' He hesitated, searching for a credible ending.

'*I'll* answer the phone. This is *my* problem and I'll handle it *my* way,' she informed him aggressively.

'OK, OK.' He raised his hands, backing off. 'Don't get those white lace knickers of yours in a knot. Isn't there an extension in the study?' he asked, as she glowered. 'Suppose I listen in on that?'

'No!' she rejected in a fever, then, 'yes!'

The constant ringing of the telephone made it difficult to think straight, but his offer of back-up did seem like sense. Seth strode quickly into the study, then spoke to her through the open door.

'At the count of three, we'll lift the phones together,' he instructed. 'One, two, *three.*'

'Hello,' she said, in a voice she barely recognised as her own.

'Leon here.'

Karis gulped in air. 'How—how are you?'

'All in one piece, so far. Thanks for paying up. It's much appreciated.'

'Leon, the man who collected the money told me you couldn't be released until next Wednesday, but why?'

'I've no idea, pet.'

'You don't—don't think the delay's a——' She stopped short. She had been going to say 'bad omen', but how could she say that? The phrase was not only thoughtless, it would be cruel. Her stepfather had his own imagination to cope with, the last thing he needed was her hinting at dangerous scenarios. 'I'm sure everything will be OK,' she veered off brightly, then remembered his addiction to the social life. 'As soon as you're home I'm going to organise the biggest, best welcome-back party you've ever——'

'My God, you mustn't do that!' thundered Leon. 'I told you before, it's vital no one knows about me being kidnapped. You haven't asked anyone for help, have you?' he demanded.

Karis looked across at Seth. 'No,' she said. 'But once you've been freed I don't see how——'

'The whole matter must remain a secret for *ever.* Unless you want me to fall foul of serious repercussions.'

'I don't. Of course I don't,' she babbled.

'Then mum's the word.'

'Are you being treated well?' she asked anxiously. 'What about food?'

'No problem there. Last night we had jumbo prawns. They were barbecued and served in a hot sauce. You'd have loved them.'

Very much a gourmet, her stepfather often enthused about meals past and present, but to hear him singing praises in these circumstances seemed totally askew.

'I suppose I would,' Karis agreed faintly, then continued, 'are you allowed any exercise?'

'OK on that score, too. Though I don't do all your touching toes stuff. I'm being told to finish now. Cheerio.'

'Will you be allowed to speak to me again before next Wednesday?' Karis shoved in desperately.

There was a pause. 'No.'

It took a second or two to realise he had gone.

'Well?' she asked, putting down the telephone as Seth walked through to join her.

'I'd say you're right about the kidnappers being amateurs. If Leon was in the clutches of a hard-core gang there's no way he'd have been so relaxed. Neither would they have allowed him so much time to yakkety-yak. That call was more than long enough to have been traced.' He reached down to lift his glass from the table and frowned. 'Don't worry, your stepfather's not going to come to any harm.'

'You sound very positive.'

'I am.'

'Why?'

'Gut feeling, and——'

'And what?'

'And Leon did assure you himself he wasn't in any danger as long as the money was paid. It's been paid, so——' Seth swallowed the last dregs of beer. 'I have to go away for a day or two. Will you be all right here? If you prefer to move into a hotel I can easily arrange it. Or you can stay at my house.'

'I'm fine in the apartment, thank you,' Karis told him sturdily. 'Where are you off to this time—Hong Kong, the Philippines, Taiwan? My, you business executives do lead exotic lives!'

'This isn't business. I'm just taking off for a few days.'

Like an Eskimo's ability to recognise eighteen different types of snow, so Karis could recognise variations in his tone. Seth was too glib. Instinctively she knew there was something he wasn't telling her, something she ought to know.

'This is on the spur of the moment?' she queried.

'Mmm.'

'You're taking off in Thailand, or going further afield?'

'Thailand. I intend to climb in the car and follow my nose.'

'Follow it where?'

He set down his glass. 'Why the interrogation?'

'Why the impulse holiday?'

'Because I could use a break. This has been a hard twelve months, both businesswise and emotionally.' His eyes slid past hers. 'A day or two lying on a beach will help recharge my batteries.'

'I don't believe you! This trip has something to do with Leon's disappearance. How dare you?' Karis protested, her temper and her colour rising at the thought of his highhandedness. 'How dare you take it upon yourself to—to tamper with something which is nothing at all to do with you?'

Seth laughed. 'Are you crazy? I'm not tampering, I'm helping—or taking steps towards it.'

'I don't need your help!' she declared. 'I didn't need it

in the past and I don't need it now.'

'That sounds like a battle cry.'

'It's not. It's just that—well, some people are allergic to shellfish, but with me it's men who insist on moving in and taking over.'

He gave a wry smile. 'I don't want to take over, and I'm not insisting on anything. I simply thought you might like to have both Leon *and* the money returned. Was I wrong?'

It was a sneaky, superior, typically Seth-type question. One which did not warrant an answer.

'What do you know that I don't?' Karis demanded.

'Nothing.'

'You must!'

'No. There's just a vague, unformed idea floating around in my head; an idea which could well turn out to be useless. All I intend to do during the next day or so is ask the odd question, see a few people——'

'Oh no, you don't! Leon happens to be *my* stepfather, and——'

Seth became the laconic cavalier. 'Fine. Instead of playing detective, I'll just lay myself down on a white sand beach and vegetate. Goodbye.'

'Um ... no,' she bleated, as he walked to the door. Thoughts swarmed and jostled in her head. Her independence was one thing, turning her back on a chance—no matter how tenuous—of Leon plus the money being returned, was another. Only a dimwit would dismiss a million and a half *baht*. Karis felt like kicking herself. Why had she been so anti? Her outright rejection of his help ranked as nothing less than overkill. 'Couldn't we go together?' she suggested, then could not resist a stab at laying down ground-rules. 'Pool our resources and tackle this thing as a team, as partners?'

Seth turned to face her.

'You're asking to go away with me?' he drawled.

'Please.'

'You want us, once such a dynamic duo, to be alone in Thailand together?'

'Yes, I do.'

His mouth curved. 'You're sure?'

'I am.'

'This is a demand?'

Karis clenched her fists. 'It is!'

He grinned, brown eyes sparkling. 'Then, my adorable chickadee, who am I to refuse?

CHAPTER FOUR

SETH had picked Karis up from the apartment at six forty-five a.m., anxious to get on their way, but in the first hour all the Porsche achieved was a dispiriting fifteen-mile crawl. It had been an inauspicious start. Then slowly, gradually, everything had changed for the better. As the dirty, polluted big-city streets were replaced by suburbs, so they made up some of their lost time. And when the suburbs had petered out into countryside, a canal-patterned, lush countryside of gentle charm, there had been a dramatic increase in speed. Karis looked out of the window and smiled. For much of the morning they had been motoring through rice paddies. Here women in shady straw hats tended shoots of an unbelievably emerald green, while water buffaloes plodded a path nearby. Karis searched the landscape and was rewarded. Thailand is studded with *wats*, Buddhist temples, and among distant palm-trees a stupa gleamed luminous gold in the sunshine. She smiled again.

Despite rising early, she had had a good night's sleep. In consequence, she felt much better. Back to her old self—almost. And, if she was honest, it had to be admitted that Seth's confidence in her stepfather's safety had also helped restore her. Yet although his confidence was comforting, perversely it was also the source of irritation. His description of his belief as a 'gut feeling' did not ring entirely true. Only in matters of love, where he wore his passion close to the surface, was Seth governed by instinct, emotions, impulse. In all other areas of his life he employed the tools of logic and fact. This being so, Karis could not escape the conviction that, although he denied it, some facts were being kept from her now. She sighed, feeling disadvantaged.

So much about this trip left her at a disadvantage. Seth spoke Thai. She didn't. He had travelled the area many times, whereas she was a newcomer. Karis studied the map on her knee. They had driven west out of Bangkok and late morning turned left near a town called Phetchaburi. Presently they were speeding southwards down the long thin peninsula which, given its head and hundreds of miles, stretched down into Malaysia. They weren't going that far. But where were they going? Seth maintained he didn't know their final destination, and wouldn't know until he had spoken to the manager of a tin mine which they were due to reach mid-afternoon. Karis inspected the map again. Leon was supposed to be on an island in the south. Which one? There were many, many islands.

'You think the mine manager might be able to point us in the direction of the man with the birthmark?' she queried.

Seth groaned. She was going over old ground.

'There's a chance, though it's a faint one. But as he's the type of individual who makes it his business to know everybody and everything connected with the extractive industry, I reckon if anyone can help it'll be him.'

Karis frowned at his profile. 'You haven't had any fresh thoughts about where you might have seen the man?'

'For the third time this morning, no! As soon as I do— *if* I do—I promise you'll be the first to be informed. However, as I've been racking my brains for the past God knows how many hours without success, it's clear

the answer isn't going to appear like——' he lifted a
hand from the wheel to snap his fingers '—that!'

What had propelled him into making this journey, so
Seth had explained the previous afternoon, was her
mention of a teardrop birthmark. It had struck a chord.
On first joining his company as a young mining
engineer, he had worked for the technical service
department. In this capacity Seth had travelled the
mines and quarries of Thailand, drilling holes, advising
on blasts, setting off explosives. And somewhere, some
time, he had come across a man with what sounded to be
an identical birthmark. Tie this in with Leon's presumed location, and he had decided a trip south might
prove . . . productive.

Karis had accepted his explanation, yet not without a
fair degree of scepticism. Could such a flimsy clue be
responsible for him blithely deserting the office and
packing his bag? She considered it doubtful. As Seth
himself had said, nobody does anything for just one
reason, and in her view his motivation had to hinge on
something far more substantial.

'You said you remembered the man wearing a hard
hat. What colour was it?' she asked.

'Black, I think, but that doesn't place him with any
particular concern.' She received an impatient glance.
'As I pointed out yesterday, this could be a wild goose
chase. My tech service roaming ended when I became
Cecil Pritchard's right-hand man, and these days I
rarely get to visit customers on site. It must be years
since I saw the fellow. He could easily have moved on by
now. And don't forget that if, by some fluke, we do trace
him, he could turn out to be a different character
entirely.'

'Two people with teardrop birthmarks? You don't
believe that,' Karis protested. 'You wouldn't have

walked away from work unless——'

'I told you, it's a hunch, nothing more.'

She made a tiny moue of annoyance. 'You weren't so negative yesterday.'

'I wasn't so pressurised yesterday,' Seth retaliated. 'Still, whatever happens, I don't intend these next few days to be wasted. Amid our sleuthing, I shall take time off to enjoy myself. I trust you will, too?'

'How am I supposed to enjoy myself while my stepfather's being held a prisoner?' she enquired starchily.

His lower lip quirked. 'I can think of a sure-fire way. Would you like me to show you?'

'Don't bother!'

'Chick, you were well aware this was to be part holiday when you insisted on coming along.'

'A holiday for you maybe, but not for me,' Karis stated.

'But if we're in harness, how do you separate the two? As I was saying, you knew the score when you insisted on accompanying me. And you *did* insist. Great for my ego.' Seth's quirking lip grew into an out-and-out grin. 'It's not every day a young woman feels so strongly about making up a twosome she'll damn near get down on her knees and beg for the privilege! Shall we stop for lunch?' he suggested, finding amusement in the way her stiff back had grown even stiffer. He gestured ahead to where a bungalow restaurant was set back from the road. 'They serve a great *hor mok pla*. Fish curry with vegetables and coconut milk, all wrapped in banana leaves,' he translated, when she looked at him.

After hours of non-stop motoring, the meal provided a welcome change of pace. They ate in the open air, on a lawn which led down to a lazily meandering river. The service was lazy too, but friendly. When the food came it was delicious. Karis relaxed. In the past a shared sense of humour had added sparkle to their conversations, and before long they were exchanging lighthearted comments about the ducks which waddled in and out of the water, about the fire-breathing spiciness of the curry, about a film they had both seen. Abruptly her smile switched off. What was she thinking about? Seduced by the tropical surroundings and Seth's easy-going air, the fact that although they might not be enemies, the two of them were far from friends appeared to have slipped her memory. How could she act like the best chum of a man who had been her lover one month and callously swapped his affections to some other woman the next? That was an error. An even graver one was that she had forgotten all about her stepfather!

'To recap,' she said, wallowing in guilt, 'you reckon Leon might know whoever it was who kidnapped him?'

Seth had chosen a pomelo for dessert, while she had taken a custard apple, and he paused in separating the segments. 'It's just a theory,' he said, with a noisy sigh, 'but if I'm right it would seem to explain a lot. For a start it would mean he wasn't picked off the street at random, which you must agree does seem far-fetched. It would also account for why, during both phone calls, his manner's been so low-key.'

'And if he knows the man with the birthmark, he'll have met him in the same way you did—at a mine or quarry?'

He nodded. 'When Leon sold our detonators he visited much the same places. And, according to my sources, he still keeps in touch.'

'Why? His agency was terminated what—four, five months ago? What's the point in continuing to visit?'

'Contacts. A quarry might seem an odd place in which to push the decorative tiles, solar-heating panels and pool filters which comprise his agencies now, but Leon believes in using his connections. And I mean using.' Seth's lip curled in expressive scorn. 'Over the years he's built up a network of contacts, and he never lets a single one of them go. Your stepfather operates on the basis that to succeed in business all you need is a big personality and highly developed persuasive powers. The quality of the product, or otherwise, barely comes into it. You should see him in action. You've heard of sleight of hand? Leon's perfected sleight of tongue. Five minutes being bombarded with his patter, and the customers are so bloody dazzled they don't know what they're agreeing to buy. Or the price.'

Karis leapt to the defence. 'He's made an excellent living out of his patter, as you call it.'

'Most excellent. Leon enjoys the lifestyle of the ultimate *bon vivant*.' Seth bit into the pomelo and chewed a while. 'His income must have plummeted when we hived off his agency, but obviously he'd saved for a rainy day. Wise man. It's not everyone who can cough up a million and a half *baht* at such short notice.'

'He didn't. I did.'

Seth looked puzzled. 'The bank gave you a loan?'

'No. The money was mine. I had it transferred from home.'

'What!' he exclaimed. He had automatically fed himself a second piece of pomelo, and was now having to speak with his mouth full. 'But where did you get an amount like that, for heaven's sake?'

Karis finished her custard apple and reached for the ice-cold towel which had been provided. 'From the sale of my aerobics studio,' she said, wiping her hands.

The pomelo went down the wrong way. Seth coughed, spluttered, gulped down some water.

'You've—you've sold the studio?' he managed to gasp at last.

'Yes, though not specifically to meet the ransom, of course.'

'You were in and out of that pretty damn quick,' he said tersely.

She affected a casual air. 'I saw no reason to hang around. The transaction was finalised a few weeks ago. When the proceeds came through I needed time to decide what to do, so I stashed them away in a savings account. Good thing, too. It meant there were no problems when I went to the bank in Bangkok. All I did was concoct a story about needing to transfer instant funds for the purchase of an ocean-going yacht, and——' the memory of how simple it had been brought a rueful grin '—and the manager believed me.'

'Wonder Woman to the rescue,' Seth said, clearly impressed.

'Something like that.'

He sat for a moment, digesting the facts. 'With regard to the studio, you—you decided to take my advice?' he enquired stiltedly. 'You cut your losses and ran?'

Karis produced a sweet, sweet smile. 'You don't think I, a mere slip of a girl, could ignore the preachings of a top-flight business executive?'

The comment went ignored. Instead Seth devoted himself to stripping pith from a fresh piece of pomelo. 'If you paid a ransom of around forty thousand pounds, you can't have had too much of a deficit?'

'There was no deficit.'

'You broke even?' His dark brows rose. 'You *are* Wonder Woman!'

'*Avec les* gold tassels.'

'Meaning?' he asked, very much on the alert.

'I dare say this will come as a surprise, if not a

thunderbolt from the blue, but I did far more than break even.' Karis paused, allowing her words to hang in the air. 'Actually I——' she paused again, savouring this second opportunity to knock Seth off balance '—more than doubled my money. Thus I was able to pay off the bank loan, and still walk away with an extremely healthy amount. The ransom made drastic inroads, but it hasn't cleaned me out.'

Her audience let out a long, slow breath of admiration. 'It seems,' he said, 'I owe you an apology. I would've sworn you were on a loser with that studio. I thought you had the wrong location, the wrong formula, the wrong——' He lost patience with himself. 'Who bought it?' he enquired curiously.

'The hotel next door. They were taken over by a national chain who were keen to extend facilities.' Karis pushed back her chair. He knew enough. She saw no point in taking the edge off her triumph by divulging more. 'That was a lovely meal. Let's split the bill down the middle, shall we? The same goes with petrol.'

'How about depreciation on the Porsche?' he threw back. 'Tell me, did you charge bed and breakfast when I stayed with you in Kent?'

'No, but——'

'I understood the arrangement was that we were partners? Partners co-operate, Karis. Which means sometimes I help you, sometimes you help me. Right now it's my turn. OK?'

'OK,' she agreed, feeling bombarded.

Seth paid the bill, and they returned to the car.

'Still hooked on Jean-Michel Jarre?' he asked, when they were back on the road.

'I bought another of his long-players last week.'

'Say no more, just open the glove compartment.' He grinned when she found the identical rhythms on cassette. 'See, we have the same impeccable taste. Want to give it a play?' Karis switched on the stereo and inserted the tape. 'Great, isn't it?' he enthused, when the throb of synthesisers filled the car.

'Great,' she agreed, but as she listened to the familiar opening strains she found herself wondering exactly *why* she had bought the record. Unlike Seth's purchase, which had resulted from a straightforward appreciation of the young Frenchman's talent, her acquisition was more complicated. Although she enjoyed the music, it had been the face on the album sleeve which first attracted her. With olive skin, glossy dark hair and sultry Gallic glower, Monsieur Jarre was drop-dead gorgeous—he also looked a lot like Seth. Had the album been bought as a substitute pin-up? Karis shifted uncomfortably in her seat. She hadn't thought so, but . . .

Thai drivers can be erratic, to put it mildly, and though the traffic was spasmodic, Seth needed to concentrate. Silence fell between them, and as the music soared and fell and soared again, her thoughts drifted further. She delved back into the past, reliving their affair and the role her aerobics studio had played in it.

On emerging from training college armed with a qualification in physical education, Karis's next step had seemed predictable. She would help keep the nation fit by teaching gymnastics to schoolchildren. That was until she read an advertisement. 'Aerobics instructor required for exclusive health farm in Kent countryside. Enthusiasm essential.' Karis had enthusiasm. Days later, she also had the job. The luxuriously converted manor house was just five miles from her home, so every morning she pedalled there on her bike, and every evening pedalled back. Consortium financed, and

catering for both residential guests and well-heeled local
people, the health farm never lacked clients. It seemed
the world and his wife were desperate to become slim
Jims and firm Janes. She encouraged them in their aims
and her success rate was high. Soon Karis's were the
classes everyone wanted to join.

'If you ever feel like opening up on your own, we'll
support you,' declared a group of her most ardent
admirers.

She had laughed, running wistful eyes over the
mirrored exercise areas, the sleek rowing-machines and
bicycles, the changing rooms with their endless supplies
of thick white towels and robes. That she would ever
aspire to such heights seemed improbable, edging on the
impossible.

That year her annual holiday had been taken in
Thailand, courtesy of her mother's old and dear friend,
Constance. Back in the sixties Aunt Connie had married
a diplomat and become an up-market gipsy, moving
constantly from one country to another. For the past two
years the base had been Bangkok. Ruth Buchanan was
always invited to visit wherever her friend touched
down, and during an earlier stay had been introduced to
Leon. A mutual admiration society had been formed.
Now her mother was anxious Karis should pass approval
on the man due to take the place of the father who had
died while she was in her teens.

With Ruth Buchanan so besotted and Aunt Connie
rah-rahing like a middle-aged cheerleader, responding
with anything less than an affirmative would have been
difficult. Karis knew that even if Leon suffered severe
halitosis, had a hunchback and spikes growing out of his
head, she was expected to murmur acceptance. One
minute in his company banished all fears. Indeed, when
she realised someone so outgoing, so goodhumoured, so

breezy was replacing the man who had seemed only to smile by appointment, and then not always, her acceptance was rapid and automatic.

But the man in Thailand who had made her want to shout a rousing, 'Yes, yes, yes!' was Seth Mauroy. They had met on a balcony at some embassy or other. Bored by the cocktail-party gossip, the meaningless chitchat with people she didn't know and didn't want to know, Karis had escaped the crowds. Out in the night, with a warm, tropical breeze caressing her skin, she had been hanging over the balcony rail when a man had spoken from behind.

'That bad, eh? This far I've resisted the urge to throw myself from a great height, but I know how you feel. These rhubarb-rhubarb evenings would drive a saint to distraction.' He came and stood alongside, peering over. 'Why not aim to end up spreadeagled in that clump of bougainvillaea, with a blossom tucked behind one ear? If you're going to be emblazoned over the front page of tomorrow's *Bangkok Post* you might as well be emblazoned in style.'

His voice was low and smoky, Karis liked it. When she turned and saw who was smiling at her, she decided she liked him, too. Dressed in a formal white dinner jacket, black tie and trousers he might be, yet he seemed as comfortable in them as if they were an old shirt and favourite jeans. He seemed comfortable with himself. Comfortable with life. The quality was immensely appealing.

'Aren't bougainvillaea prickly?' Karis enquired, blue eyes dancing.

Seth forgot that when he had sneaked on to the balcony two minutes ago, he would have sold his soul for one drag on a cigar. 'Suppose we go down and find out?' he suggested, and held out a tanned hand. She took it.

From that first moment everything had been easy. An instant rapport meant there was no need for introductions, no need to feel a cautious way into the relationship. It was as though they had met in a previous life, and were simply renewing acquaintance. The night before Karis flew home they became lovers. Neither of them had meant it to be that way. She had previously scorned couples who rushed headlong into intimacy, believing them to be inspired by lust, not love. As for Seth—aware of making an important commitment, he would have preferred more time. There was no time. That was the problem. Instead the knowledge of fast-approaching separation accelerated their courtship, sent it spinning out of control.

Both had rationalised that last evening when they had entwined nakedly in his bed, kissing ravenously, stroking feverishly, and needing to be close, closer, closest. Karis, while acknowledging that there was a degree of lust involved, regarded it as insignificant when compared to the love. Besides, although it was too soon to speak of marriage, she *knew* eventually they would be man and wife. For Seth's part, he had decided he must, there was an overriding need, his body left him no choice but to make love to this girl, this smooth-skinned, high-breasted, wonderful girl, and *then* he would be able to concentrate on wooing her in the conventional fashion.

From the highs to the lows. By the end of the following day thousands of miles separated them. Seth, who had exhausted his leave attending a family wedding in France, struggled to engineer a visit west, nominally for business. It was not to be. Work nailed him down to Bangkok. The phone bills began to grow. For weeks, months, the postman delivered lovelorn letters. They were desperate to be together, but how?

In the end Leon provided an excuse. He swept into the

small Kent town, married Ruth Buchanan and took her with him to live in Thailand. The new Mrs Thorburn felt homesick, Karis told the management at the health farm a while later. In order to give succour—she felt rotten about lying—please could she take a month's unpaid leave? There was disbelief, much humming and hawing. Only her popularity made them agree.

Those four weeks in Thailand were magical. The days she spent with her mother, anticipating the nights which belonged to Seth. At weekends the two of them disappeared into the depths of the countryside. It was a time of happiness and laughter, of holding hands and gazing into each other's eyes. Of saying 'I love you, I want you, I need you' and demonstrating that love, that want, that need in endless ecstatic ways. They had lived for the moment.

Two months after their despondent farewell across the barrier at Don Muang Airport, her mother had died. As Leon arranged for the Bangkok funeral to be swiftly followed by a memorial service in Kent, Karis stayed at home. Her stepfather came to share her grief. So did Aunt Connie. Seth could not. Involved in crucial company matters, he was required in Bangkok.

Shortly afterwards, Karis and Leon had visited the solicitors to learn the contents of her mother's will. To her surprise, she discovered that not only did she inherit the house she and her mother had shared, but the entire estate. Leon did not receive a single penny.

'That's how it should be, pet,' he insisted, when she had hesitatingly broached the subject. 'I never expected anything. The money's rightfully yours—all of it.'

'Thanks for understanding.'

'Nothing to understand.' He rubbed his hands together. 'Now, you won't have any ideas about what to do with your inheritance, so would you mind if I offer advice? In my line of business I sometimes come across opportunities which cry out for an influx of cash, and funnily enough——'

'I *do* have an idea,' Karis interrupted.

'You do?'

'Yes. I intend to use the money to open my own fitness and activities studio. Mum and I discussed it in the past, so I know she'd agree. More money will be needed, but I'm friendly with the bank manager and if I can find premises locally I'm sure he'd give me a loan.'

'Sounds a splendid idea,' Leon enthused, shaking off his shock. 'I do so admire a girl with spirit. Off you go, pet, full steam ahead.'

Stimulated by his encouragement, Karis continued to elaborate her plans. 'Frances would join up with me. Frances is a friend who teaches ballet. She can handle that, plus tap, jazz dance, whatever,' she explained, gathering steam, 'while I concentrate on the body-conditioning side. We can have classes for kids, flexi-time sessions for office workers, young in heart exercises for retired people.' Suddenly she frowned. 'But if I tie myself down with a studio, that'll complicate things between me and Seth. Getting together's difficult enough already, and—and then there's the future.'

'By future you mean marriage?' Leon queried.

'Well—yes.'

Seth had not proposed. After only weeks spent together, a proposal would be premature. They needed more time to get to know each other, greater opportunities to consolidate, and then . . .

'If you do marry the chap I take it you'll be content to abandon your aims, your ambitions, and live life through him—like Sukanya?'

Karis stared at her stepfather.

'No!'

The question had been like a red rag to a bull. Whatever the state of Seth's first marriage, if she joined him in his second it would only be as an equal. Karis had not the least intention of being an adoring wife, whose whole existence revolved around her lord and master. Putting the aerobics studio on ice for fear of hypothetical problems was a namby-pamby attitude, she decided. Before they met again there were seven months to be lived through. Did she settle for seven lonely, marking-time months, or were they to be used to make a dream come true? She recalled Seth's fleeting mention of a possible future move to his company's headquarters south of London. If that happened, then her owning a studio would cause no problems because surely they could find a house from where they could both commute? Alternatively, should his future, and eventually hers, be in Thailand—couldn't she sell her share to Frances?

She grinned at Leon. Full steam ahead it was.

'I'll phone Seth tonight and tell him what I intend to do.'

'Why? Why not keep everything secret instead, and give him a wonderful surprise when he comes over? He has a reputation for being a hot shot in business,' said Leon, when she looked dubious. 'Wouldn't you like to show him someone else has hairs on their chest?'

It was a challenge Karis could not resist. Over the ensuing months a disused Jesuit chapel was found, a bank loan secured, the chapel bought. Workmen were employed for the major alterations, but Karis—and occasionally Frances—painted walls, sanded floors, cut, machined and hung curtains. Equipped on a shoestring, her studio could not compete with the health farm for style and classy machines; which doubtless explained why her ardent admirers reneged on their promises to enrol. However, the neighbourhood people responded. Her advertisements did not exactly have them pounding on the door demanding to be let in. They came more in fits and starts. But as regular as fits and starts can be.

When Karis met Seth at Heathrow, she was bubbling over with excitement. It took every last grain of self-control to hold back the news until they were in the taxi.

'Guess what I've been doing since you last saw me,' she demanded, as they drew away from the terminal building.

He put his arm around her.

'Perfecting the Lotus position?'

'Wrong!'

'Driving pot-bellied men stark, staring mad with your knees-bend, arms-stretch routine?'

'Wrong!'

Seth smiled, his gaze moving lovingly over her. 'You've spent your time growing even more beautiful, and don't you dare contradict, because I can see it with my own eyes. God! but I've missed you.'

'I've missed you, too,' Karis assured him. 'And OK, I'm beautiful. But I'm also a beautiful entrepreneur!' She said the word with relish. 'I've opened an aerobics studio. My mother left enough money for me to buy premises and have them converted. I did need a loan from the bank, but——' Everything was tumbling out of her. 'It's meant months of hard work, and eating nothing but rushed sandwiches, and late nights and—and at one stage we never thought we'd be ready in time, but Frances and I welcomed our first customer four weeks ago.'

Seth pulled back. 'You've spent six months setting up a business, one month running it, and yet you never said a goddamn word?'

'I—I wanted to surprise you,' Karis faltered, hearing

his hurt. Maybe she should have told him? Maybe the venture was something which needed to be shared? 'I wanted to show how you're not the only one with hairs on their chest.'

Distracted, he grinned; becoming one hundred per cent the sensual male. Hazel eyes slid down, measuring her breasts with a leisurely macho delight.

'These hairs—are they ash blonde and curly? Mmm, I can hardly wait!' Tanned fingers eased the white satin blouse from her skirt, and moved under and up to spread across her ribcage. 'I'd better have a quick reconnoitre.'

'You'd better not,' she demurred, pushing his hand away and hoping the taxi driver had not noticed. 'We could go round to see the studio on our way home,' she suggested eagerly. 'It'd only take an extra ten minutes.'

'Chick, those ten minutes might well poleaxe me. I was working flat out until the moment I boarded the plane,' Seth explained. 'I staggered on, desperate for some shut-eye, but,' he sighed, 'next to me sat a woman with one abiding passion in life—her grandchildren. After sixteen hours of being regaled non-stop if I don't lie down, and quick, I'm liable to fall down.' The arm around her shoulders tightened. 'I thought I might be able to lie down with you?'

Karis kissed his cheek and smiled. 'That could be arranged.'

'Good. I promise I'll come and check out your studio early evening, before we go out on the town. I intend tonight to be memorable.' Seth's eyes were shining. 'Between us I reckon we can make the next six weeks pretty spectacular, too. Don't you?'

'Yes, but——' Karis bit into her lip. 'I'm sorry, I won't be free until around ten tonight. My exercise class doesn't end until nine-thirty. By then I'll be hot and sweaty—it's an energetic work-out—so I'll need to come home, shower and change.'

'In other words, this evening isn't good timing?'

'No. And I work until nine-thirty two other evenings, too.'

Seth gave a rueful shrug. 'OK. We'll save the wining and dining until the weekend. I thought on Friday we could drive up to Stratford, find a nice quiet hotel, and devote ourselves to being gloriously anti-social?' He saw her face. 'Friday's one of your late evenings. So we'll go first thing Saturday.'

'I can't.'

'You have another damn class?' he asked, with ill-concealed impatience.

'Yes. It's dance exercise and normally Frances takes it, but she wants the morning off and——'

'Tell her no.'

Karis squirmed. 'If I do that, she might still not turn up. She isn't as committed as me, and she can be a bit—vague.'

'For crissakes!' Seth's impatience was out in the open, glaring at her. 'I fly from the other side of the world after not seeing you for God knows how long, and find I'm expected to stand around like a lemon while you——'

'It's just this Saturday which has been loused up. All the rest'll be free, and Sundays, and four evenings each week.'

'Big deal!' Seth blasted.

Karis removed herself from his hold. 'I'm sorry I'm not at your beck and call, but I thought you'd understand. After all, *your* devotion to *your* business has helped keep us apart these past months. How come when I devote myself to mine it's wrong?'

He sighed, suddenly contrite. 'I'm sorry. I'm jet-lagged. That's why I'm seeing only problems.'

But jet-lag was not the culprit. A fortnight later Seth

continued to see problems; not with the restrictions placed on them by her working hours, he had stoically accepted those, but with the studio itself.

'Aerobics is rated as a fading flower,' he remarked one evening, as he helped with the washing-up. 'People are supposed to be moving on to tap dancing.'

Karis snatched a plate from the drainer, dried it with a few short, sharp strokes, and thrust it into the cupboard. She felt peeved. The man she remembered from Thailand had been a different species from the man beside her now. Then he had been easy-going, undemanding, fun. Now he was . . . picky. She had taken it for granted he would echo nothing less than Leon's out-and-out encouragement where her business venture was concerned, instead he irritated her by being restrained, thoughtful and—yes! pessimistic. Whenever he had been at the studio, his attitude had been one of an auditor silently working out the pluses and minuses—and invariably finding her in the red.

'How would you know?' she demanded. 'It's not that long ago since you walked in fresh from the jungle.'

'I read a lot,' he replied, impervious to her sarcasm. 'Cast an eye over the commercial sections of the newspapers, and you'll see where I get my facts. Aerobics is a fad. Fads are risky.'

'You've just said people are moving on to tap.' Karis gave him a smile which was all mouth, no eyes. 'Frances teaches tap.'

'And how long is that craze likely to last? Besides, how often has she been late for lessons this week? How many kids and mothers were left feeling short-changed? Frances is so disorganised she'd mess up a one-car parade. That girl has no aptitude for business and you can't afford to carry her. When you do something cut-price, it's essential that everyone involved pulls their weight.'

She glared. Another plate was thrust clattering into the cupboard. 'Cut-price?' she demanded. 'You make the studio sound shoddy. It isn't, it's neat and clean and——'

'I know all that,' he said quietly. 'You've done wonders. But to make any business work there needs to be a solid financial investment, and frankly I doubt you've been able to invest enough. From what I've read it's the survival of the fittest in the exercise business—no pun intended—and with a competitor like the health farm your studio needs to be full of beans. In this situation beanz meanz more machines, plus a crèche service for folk with children, plus somewhere to get a cup of tea, plus——'

'You want me to sell this house to raise more capital?' Karis asked, mainly belligerent but with a hint of enquiry.

'No. For heaven's sake, don't put any more money in. The business may not be viable whatever you do.'

'Thanks for your carefully worded reassurance!'

Seth sighed. 'Chick, why didn't you speak to me before going ahead and committing yourself?'

'Because I didn't consider it was necessary,' she flared. 'And now I'm glad I kept quiet. You're just like my father, d'you know that? If an idea didn't originate with him, he killed it stone dead. He could never bear it if anyone, and especially a woman, did something on their own initiative.' She grabbed hold of a cup and smothered it with the tea towel. 'Leon thinks the studio is an excellent idea.'

His head twisted round. 'Leon's in on this? You never said.'

'He isn't *in* on anything. But he does approve of me

going it alone. He blows kisses, not raspberries!'

'I'm not blowing raspberries. I'm just suggesting you forget the rosy dreams for a minute, and look at this venture in the cold light of day.'

'We're breaking even,' Karis defended hotly.

'But is that because the studio's new? Because people want to come in and take a look around? What happens when the novelty's worn off?'

'Don't complain.'

'I'm not complaining. I'm asking a question. One you should be asking yourself.'

'Before any novelty wears off we'll have built up a regular clientèle.'

'This is a small town. Are there enough interested people to do that?'

Her chin jutted. 'Yes, there are,' she insisted.

The Jean-Michel Jarre tape needed to be changed to the second side, and Karis surfaced. For miles the road had cut monotonously through acres of tapioca trees and more recently rubber plantations, but a long gradual incline brought them out into the open again. Hillocks appeared, growing into hills. Down a glorious, winding valley the Porsche sped, wooded slopes rolling upwards on either side.

'Another ten minutes and we'll be there,' said Seth, as he swung off the road on to a rutted track. He stretched out a hand, reducing the stereo's volume to a background accompaniment. 'I presume bringing in Cliff helped with the studio?' he said.

Karis shot him a look of surprise. Cliff was Frances's brother, and the sudden mention had her wondering if Seth had also spent the last half-hour dwelling on her aerobics venture. No, she was being foolish. He had washed his hands of her, and matters relating to her, many months ago. What rolled around his head were thoughts of big-company deals, how to increase his share of the explosives market—and beautiful Thai maidens.

'Leon buttonholed me a long time ago, must have been around three or four weeks after I returned from seeing you. He was full of some character called Cliff, an exponent of the martial arts.' Seth frowned at the track ahead. 'The guy appears to have leapt in with fists flying. I imagine adding his skills to yours and Frances's built the business up to an acceptable level, and that's how you came to sell so profitably?'

'Cliff was very helpful,' Karis agreed.

'You allowed him to help?'

Karis was not sure about the point he was making. 'Yes,' she agreed cautiously.

'Amazing.' He gave a dry laugh. 'What happened to your mantra—it's *my* problem and I'll deal with it *my* way? Are you still seeing him?'

'Seeing him?' She needed to think fast. 'Oh, *seeing* him. Oh yes.'

Karis wasn't. She wasn't *seeing* anyone, but as Seth appeared to be out on the town on a regular basis, she was not about to divulge she stayed at home nights. What had her stepfather said? she wondered. As usual he must have glossed the facts with fiction, with no other excuse than to improve his story. Seth seemed to be under the impression that Cliff was a six-foot-six black belt with bronzed rippling muscles who, in addition to rescuing the aerobics studio, had also won her heart. Admittedly Cliff was tall and did have muscles, but ...

'Could you let me know whether or not you intend to be in on this meeting with the mine manager?' her companion demanded gruffly.

'Yes, I suppose so.' His irritated tone confused her. 'Why not?'

'One, because the conversation will be entirely in Thai, which means you won't understand a word. Two, because having a woman there's bound to impede things.'

'Sexist!'

'Replace that with realist. You sitting around in your open-necked shirt treating everyone to a flash of cleavage every so often may well raise the blood pressure, but it won't be conducive to uninhibited chat. It's up to you.' He shrugged and added, 'Partner.'

The hands in Karis's lap tightened. Some partner, she thought. Up to her—phooey! He might maintain the choice was hers, but only because there was no choice. Once again Seth Mauroy was effectively calling the shots. Damn him. And damn him for the reference to her cleavage. He had made her disturbingly aware of being full-breasted and feminine, and now she itched to fasten every single button, all the way up to her neck.

'You deal with the mine manager,' she told him, in a voice as crackly as cellophane. 'But I'd like a full report afterwards.'

'Verbatim, ma'am,' he assured her.

The track, which was showing increasing signs of heavy vehicle use, passed through a narrow ravine and dipped downwards. Tall trees cut out the sunlight, reducing the tangled undergrowth to a dark, shadowy mass. Karis's eyes had barely adjusted when a bend was rounded and she needed to raise a hand against the glare. In the midst of what had seemed virgin jungle a vast acreage had been cleared. To one side stood high conical piles of stony waste, while on the other stretched a series of rectangular reservoirs. Central to these, a conglomer-

ate of buildings made large hazy shapes behind clouds of
grey-white dust.

'Tin's produced by means of a wet process, and to our
left are the settling ponds,' Seth explained, as they drew
nearer. He pointed to a hillside. 'Where you see the
conveyor coming out is the mine entrance. And
that——' he indicated a corrugated iron structure '——is
where the ore's crushed. Hear the noise?' Karis nodded.
Even with the car windows closed, there was no
mistaking the whump-whump of a heavy machine and a
clatter of falling stone. 'The ore's ground and put
through a flotation process,' he continued. 'The heavy
part sinks and is retained, the light stuff flows over. That
goes into the ponds as a black sludge and later, when it's
settled, more tin's reclaimed.' He drew the car to a halt
beside a cabin. 'I've no idea how long this talk'll take, so
why don't you stretch your legs?' He pointed beyond
the ponds to a rise where palms grew in profusion. 'If
you follow the path through the trees for about quarter
of a mile, there's a ruined temple. It's worth a look.'

'No snakes?'

'Stick to the path, keep your eyes open, and you'll be
fine,' he assured her.

Although her query had come from common sense,
not an aversion, at first Karis walked warily. Each year
many people in Thailand die from bites, and she had no
wish to join their number. However, snakes, as silent
slitherers, did not worry her over-much. What would
have sent her hurtling up the nearest palm-tree
jabbering like an idiot was the sight of anything which
crawled. Time passed, and when she saw nothing with a
multitude of legs, and nothing with none, Karis began
to enjoy herself. It was pleasant strolling along. Palm
fronds made a fretted canopy to shade her from the sun,
the flashes of sky were deep China blue, and when she

reached the old temple she found it fascinating. She climbed around the ivy-decorated tumble of stone, examining a portion of a carved elephant's head here, the corner of a painted frieze there. Curiosity satisfied, Karis sat for a while, inhaling air sweetened by the almond fragrance of frangipani shrubs, and idly thinking. Every Thai male becomes a monk at some stage in his life, if only for a week, and she peopled the temple with shaven-headed men in saffron robes. Why had they built a shrine out here? she wondered. The area was pleasant, but appeared to hold no particular attraction.

Standing up and stretching, she decided to explore further. A spur of the path led beyond the ruins, and Karis set off. A hundred yards on, the undergrowth ran riot. Branches heavy with scarlet hibiscus blocked her way. She pushed them aside, waded through ferns, burrowed through another barricade of bushes, then stopped dead. She was standing on the edge of a high cliff which provided a natural viewing platform for a panorama of exquisite tropical beauty. Miles of verdant hills rolled out before her, emerging from the heat haze, and among them were lakes, waterfalls, a winding river. She saw villages, people working in fields, a tiny bullock pulling a tiny cart up the brown thread of a road. Beyond the green of the hills, the horizon glimmered blue—the Gulf of Thailand, she reasoned. She narrowed her eyes. There were white beaches, islands. She could even pick out fishing boats. Her mouth split into a grin. The reason why the monks had chosen this site for their temple was clear.

'Karis?' Seth was calling. 'Karis, where are you?'

'Here,' she yelled. 'Come quickly! It's——' She spread out her arms to encircle the view, and sighed. 'It's fantastic!'

There was the thud of running footsteps, a crashing,

the sound of undergrowth being torn aside, then Seth broke through the bushes.

'Are you OK?' he was demanding breathlessly.

She turned to smile. He looked like a rampaging bear answering a dire emergency.

'I'm fine, thanks.'

'Thank God! When you said come quickly I thought——' He skidded to a halt and gaped. 'For crissakes,' he muttered.

'It does grab you by the throat, doesn't it?' Entranced by the view, Karis forgot about keeping her distance, forgot they were not friends. She clutched at his arm. 'If you stand closer to the edge and look down, you can see——'

'No.'

She attempted to draw him forward. 'Seth, there's a patch of mist and rising out of it is a temple with pinnacles and domes. It's beautiful.'

'No!' He switched into a rapid reverse, taking her with him. 'No!' he said again.

'What's the matter?'

His jaw was tight, his face ashen, and he was backing away like someone who had opened a cupboard door and come face to face with an eight-foot-tall gorilla.

'I—I——' he stuttered. A few more rapid steps of retreat and a raised tree-root caught at his heel. Like a claw, it held him. Blindly Seth shook his foot, stumbled, began to fall. In reflex, Karis's grip tightened. He grabbed at her arms, but both of them were off balance. A sway, a topple, and together they collapsed on to a bed of ferns. '—I don't like heights,' he completed, as she lay flat out on top of him.

She gasped for breath. 'I never knew that.'

'Had difficulty coping with them when I worked in tech service, and the older I get the worse it seems.

These days it takes very little to make me feel dizzy.'

Karis swallowed down a giggle. Seth had always seemed the last word in unflappability, but the solid man-in-charge had jumped to panicky child!

'Maybe you should have a word with your doctor?' she suggested, sliding off him on to the ground. 'Ask if he can prescribe something to help combat these dizzy spells.'

He pushed himself up on to one elbow and glared. 'It's no laughing matter.'

'I'm not laughing,' she vowed, but regrettably the words and the tweak of her mouth did not tally. 'Poor Seth, poor old Seth,' she chanted. He muttered something vicious in French, but she took no notice. 'May I offer my deepest sympathy?' Her grin was unstoppable now. 'Are you afflicted if you climb a ladder? Stand on kitchen steps? How about if——'

She got no further. Seth did not allow her to get any further. He thrust a large hand behind her head, pinioned her with his body, and kissed her. The child was all man.

CHAPTER FIVE

USED as a weapon to stun her into submission, Seth's kiss hit her broadside. At the first touch of his mouth, something in Karis's brain short-circuited. The past six months fell away and she was enraptured. That anger, not love, had generated his kiss seemed irrelevant. All she could focus on was the delight of once more being held in his arms, the familiar pressure of his body, the knowledge that he found her desirable. And he did. She felt the need rise in him, need which changed everything. As swiftly as his mouth had bruised, so it became seductive. Seth's second kiss was slow and easy. He drew back, just enough to trace her top lip with the tip of his tongue and coax a response. Boom, went her heart. Mouth opened on mouth. Boom. Tongue grazed tongue. A clamour streaked through her body, to be echoed in his. Boom. Boom. Boom.

'Brings back memories,' murmured Seth, smiling crookedly. 'Doesn't it, chick?'

Karis gazed at him.

'Yes,' she said weakly, too shaken to deny the truth.

He kissed her again. 'Remember that day in the mountains near Chiang Mai?' he whispered, close to her mouth. 'You were teaching me pelvic tilts, and every time I tried you said, 'Push harder, Seth. Put all your effort into the push.' His lips moved into a second smile. 'I rose to the occasion magnificently. We ended up making love, and when——'

Karis broke free. 'Do you mind if we don't hark back to the past?' she demanded. 'It holds as much interest as an out-of-date newspaper.'

He grinned. 'You don't mean that.'

'Yes, I do!'

Trembly with desire, she scrambled to her feet. She was furious with herself, furious and confused. Why had she succumbed to his kisses? What foolishness had had her responding? Their affair was over, yet with breathtaking speed Seth had plumbed a deep hidden pocket of passion; a passion which had been an integral part of their relationship from beginning to end. Karis dragged slapdash fingers through her tumbled drift of ashen hair. All the time in Kent when things had gone so horribly wrong, their passion had been constant. If by day they had been at odds, at night the lovemaking flowed. Even on the last evening before he left, an evening replete with stale conversation and bulging silences, their bodies had been hungry. Hers felt hungry now.

Feverishly she brushed down her trousers, tugged at her shirt, all the time conscious of him watching her, yet unable to meet his eyes. There was a time when she had believed that passion would help surmount their problems—how wrong could anyone be! When Seth had returned to Thailand she had received a brief note saying he had arrived alive, and would write later. He never had. In time she had discovered why and realised that although her passion had been inextricably wound up in him, his was transferable.

'Could the mine manager identify the man with the birthmark?' she demanded.

He yawned, stretched and lazily rose to his feet. Maybe he was scared of heights, but away from the cliff edge and standing in the ferns, Seth seemed completely in charge of himself. Very much at ease. She was the one whose nerve-ends were jangling. How she wished they weren't!

'No,' he said.

Karis waited for more. When nothing came she turned and marched resolutely ahead of him back through the bushes and on to the path. 'No' was not much of an answer, she thought as she plodded along. Not when all hopes of locating her stepfather depended on the mine manager providing a lead. She cast a glance over her shoulder. Seth was ambling behind, hands in his pockets, an infuriating grin playing around his mouth. That his queries had come to nought did not perturb him.

'He couldn't remember him?' she persisted.

''Fraid not.' He strolled after her. 'Do you know, you have the tastiest backside I've ever seen. How you've escaped being arrested for the way it glides in those pants of yours—mmm!' He let out an agonised groan. 'As backsides go, I have to award it ten out of ten for sex appeal.'

Karis's blue eyes blazed. Only Seth would come out with a remark like that, at a time like this! The difference in their blood-lines meant that she, as an Anglo-Saxon, was shockable, whereas he, thanks to his Gallic forebears, exhibited an urbane acceptance of matters sensual, sexual, physical. In the past he had taken great delight in unsettling her with a choice remark, and tardily she recognised that his reference to her breasts, her birthmark and, on this occasion, her backside had been deliberate provocations.

She swivelled to face him.

'Allow me to award you ten out of ten for being callous, uncaring and off-target! We're together for one reason, Seth, and one reason only—to find my stepfather. How you can talk about *backsides*——' the word exploded out of her, '—when we're searching for a man who may well have been shackled to a wall for the past three days amazes me.'

'We're hardly searching,' Seth corrected with benign good humour. 'All I've done is what I said I'd do, ask a question or two.' Broad shoulders moved. 'I did mention a wild goose chase.'

If she had been twenty years younger, Karis would have bawled out loud in frustration. Instead she frowned. With the careless dismissal confirming her belief that in no way had the man with the birthmark been the sole reason for this trip, once again she was set to wondering about his motivation. Whatever he said, Seth would never waste time on a 'wild goose chase', so ... Karis winced as it struck—like a sledgehammer on her head—that maybe *she* was the goose. Could his motivation be a pursuit of her? Considering the kisses, his remembrance of past pleasures, the remarks about her appearance, it seemed a distinct possibility. Had Seth envisaged them joining in a few days of carte-blanche lovemaking? And to think she had begged to come! She glowered, beginning to feel dangerously stage-managed. Then her thoughts stumbled. Suppose lovemaking was not the spur? Suppose, instead, he still cared for her on a deeper level? Suppose he regretted the ending of their affair? Suppose he had wanted time alone with her in order to discuss the past and try to make amends? Suppose——

'Is Leon double-jointed?'

Startled from her reverie, she blinked. 'Not that I know of. Why?'

'Just that he must have had his problems the other night. Wolfing down jumbo prawns while you're shackled to a wall can't be easy.'

If the comment, delivered with a wry smile, was

calculated to make Karis rush to her stepfather's defence, it worked.

'You're full of compassion, aren't you?' she demanded.

'Chick, this kidnapping could well be a case of Leon having built his own plank and being forced to walk it. Unlike you, there are one or two who don't appreciate being bamboozled by the butter-smooth Mr Thorburn.'

'I've not been bamboozled,' she protested, her blood rising.

Seth shrugged. 'To skip back a bit,' he said, in a tone which indicated a total change of subject, 'I ought to make it clear I wasn't talking about backsides, plural. I was talking about yours, singular. And why not? It's rich red, masculine blood which runs in my veins, not ketchup. I also appreciate a good pair of legs. Yours, I'd award a——' taking on a supremely French glint, the hazel eyes toured from her hips to her ankles and back again, '—nine. They lose a point for being a touch too short,' he explained generously.

'They are not short!'

'Just a fraction. Don't worry, Thai girls are often a little stunted of limb, too. Yet it doesn't detract from their considerable appeal.'

Thai girls! Karis thought acidly. That was where his current interest lay. In imagining Seth could be pursuing her, she had been hallucinating. He might admire her backside, but only in the academic style of a judge at the Miss Universe contest.

'You promised a verbatim report on your meeting with the mine manager,' she reminded him. 'Could I have it now?'

'With pleasure, partner. Though I warn you, it's nothing to get excited about.' He gestured down the slope to where the stone slabs of the ruined temple basked in the sunshine. 'Suppose we sit there and I'll bring you up to date?' He led the way this time, and waited until she had found a perch. 'When the man with the birthmark proved a dead end, I discreetly edged Leon's name into the conversation,' he explained, spreading his legs to straddle the block he was sitting on as though it were a horse. 'I needn't have bothered. All I learned was that of late he's become even more buddy-buddy with a guy called Dejo Suksaguan. Dejo's a wheeler-dealer type who, amongst other things, owns a limestone quarry on Phuket.'

'Phuket?' Karis repeated, pronouncing the name 'Poo-ket' as he had done. 'But Phuket's an island.' Her eyes lit up. 'And it's in the south. And a quarry would be an ideal place to keep someone prisoner. And you said Leon might know his captors!'

'I also said Dejo and Leon are friends.'

'They could have fallen out, had a quarrel. And in retaliation——' Her imagination faltered.

'I doubt they'd fall out. They're two of a kind, always looking for the main chance.'

Her hackles rose. 'You're very opinionated!'

'That's not an opinion. That's a fact,' he told her, his gaze unwavering.

'Leon's ... charming,' she said hotly.

'And like all the best con-men he capitalises on that charm.'

'You were never so critical before,' Karis muttered. 'Why decide to victimise the poor man at the exact time he's a victim?'

'I'm not victimising him. I'm telling it you as it is. As for keeping quiet in the past——' Seth batted away an insect which had come near. 'Look, with you and your mother so bloody rhapsodic about Leon, I'd have a tough time selling my views. Yes? And as I intended to be a permanent fixture in your life, naturally I hesitated before casting myself in the role of villain. I was gearing myself up to have a word when he went and married your mother. Then it seemed ... inappropriate. Now everything's changed. I have nothing to lose, so I can tell you the truth. And it is the truth. For Pete's sake, Karis, I've known the guy for years.'

She chafed. 'Cecil Pritchard also knew him for years,' she pointed out. 'Would he have channelled detonators through Leon's agency all that time if he's considered him a con-man?'

Seth sighed. 'Can't you accept Leon may not be the good ole boy?'

'He made——' she began.

'Your mother happy.' He grunted. 'That's basically your entire rationale for liking him.'

'He brought some much needed lightness into her life. He was good for her, to her,' Karis defended.

'He was good in so much as he didn't persuade her to invest her savings in one of his dubious schemes, like he's persuaded so many others.' Seth eased himself backwards until he was stretched flat out on the stone slab. He gazed up into the clear blue sky. 'Where he found the self-control necessary to keep his greasy little paws off her money, I'll never know,' he muttered.

Silence. The breeze ruffled the trees. A brightly coloured bird swooped down into the bushes, hovered, then rose again. Uneasily Karis considered his denunciation. With her stepfather missing, it came as a wanton intrusion. In describing Leon as a con-man, he was going too far. Yet there could be no denying her stepfather's partiality to making the fast buck. And hadn't he attempted to interest her in a money-making venture? She found herself remembering the secrecy which surrounded the contents of his study. Did that imply something—shady?

Suddenly Seth raised himself on one elbow and looked across at her.

'He's got his greasy little paws on your mother's money now,' he said.

'No, he hasn't!'

'OK, but you can't dispute that it's being used for his benefit.'

'Which is not the same, at all,' Karis insisted.

He frowned. 'I wonder why the bandits or whoever it is who've got him decided to demand a million and a half *baht*? Accepted it's a decent amount, but as ransoms go it's relatively small scale. Why not ask for more?'

'Perhaps Leon quoted that as the limit which could be raised?'

'But if they were so amateurish they allowed him to call the tune financially, then why didn't he set a lower limit? Say, half a million *baht*? An amount like that would represent a fortune to a group of Thai peasants.' Seth sat upright. 'During that first phone call, did Leon make any suggestions about how you were to go about raising the ransom? Like referring you to *his* bankers?'

'No.'

'Don't you think that's strange? Don't you think it's even stranger that when he spoke to you the second time he thanked you for paying up, exactly as though he knew the ransom had come from you?'

Karis went tight inside. She didn't like what she was hearing. Did not like it at all. Yet she could not help admitting that maybe Leon *had* taken her production of the ransom too much for granted. She felt a twinge of disloyalty. Seth seemed to be transferring doubts to her like a bad cold—a sniffle here, a fretful cough there.

'You have totally the wrong slant,' she said, fending off these doubts by reminding herself how wonderful to her mother her stepfather had been. 'Leon's under a great strain. He has other things to worry about than where I raised the cash. When he's back and realises it was mine, the first thing he'll do is reimburse me.'

'Suppose he can't?' Seth was quiet for a moment, then gave a terse laugh. 'At least he didn't use up every cent you have.'

'Then you admit he isn't all bad!'

'I never said he was.' He raised his arms above his head and stretched, all languorous muscles and fluid grace. 'What do we do now, chick?'

Karis shot him a look of surprise. Since leaving Bangkok she had suspected him of merely paying lip service to her expressed wish to do things *her* way, but his question had sounded genuine. He was even waiting as though he expected her to supply a constructive answer.

'I'd like to go down to Phuket,' she announced. 'If he and Leon are so close, then there's always a chance the quarry owner might know something.'

'It's a long shot, but I suppose it's the only one we have,' Seth agreed. 'And Phuket does have some great beaches.'

Karis gave a strained smile. Beaches meant swimming and sunbathing which, in turn, meant Seth stripped to the minimum. But if simply being in close proximity with him wearing his clothes was making her behave oddly—melting in his arms one minute, fighting for escape the next—how would she cope if he was bronzed and bare, and lying beside her on the sand?

'Does this Dejo speak English?' she asked,

'Yes. So?'

'So if I can question him there's no need for you to waste any more of your time on detective work. There must be good beaches closer at hand where you can recharge your batteries, and——'

'I understood you and I were partners?' he demanded. 'You can't dissolve a partnership without the agreement of both parties concerned.'

'But it'll be better for you if we go our separate ways. And I'm perfectly happy to be dumped at the nearest railway station,' Karis informed him airily.

His look reeked of acute exasperation. 'There are times when you take this independence kick of yours a bit too far,' he growled. 'Dump you at a railway station? Where the hell do you think this is, the Home Counties? It isn't, it's Thailand. There are dangers, especially where a shapely blonde who doesn't speak a word of the language is concerned. Sukanya, who—may I remind you?—was born and bred in this country, would have thought twice about being dropped off in the middle of nowhere. You are not Sukanya.'

'No, I'm not,' she flared, annoyed by his patronising air. 'I'm not your puppet. I never was, and I never will be.'

The moment the words were out, Karis could have bitten off her tongue. Why had she been so . . . feisty? She had no right to speak about his wife in those terms. No right at all. Everything she had heard about Sukanya indicated that the girl had been gentle, serene, and if she had treated her husband as a god from on high, that was the way she had wanted it to be. A shy and conservative girl who, until her marriage, had been closely supervised by her parents, Sukanya had been a product of her upbringing—just as Karis's upbringing contributed to why she fought tooth and nail against being dominated. Yet, she admitted, Seth hadn't wanted to dominate. All he had been doing was using his common sense. Heart in mouth, she waited for his reaction. If he rounded on her, she would understand. But Seth kept his feelings on ice.

'If you go to Phuket, you will go in my car with me,' he said, in a steely monotone. 'Alternatively, I'll take you back to Bangkok. Which is it to be?'

'Phuket—please.' Karis was properly subdued.

'That's roughly five hours on, which means we can't make it today. I suggest we look around locally for overnight accommodation. That suit?'

'Sounds fine,' she replied, hating his harsh exactitude.

He rose to his feet. 'Then let's go.'

Although the area which lay immediately to the south of the tin mine offered sweeping green hills, clusters of quaint wooden houses and coconut groves, it lacked a shoreline. Thus tourists were frugally catered for. When Seth enquired at the few hotels they saw from the road, he was unable to find any accommodation.

'I guess we'd better cut across to the coast. There's a resort about fifty miles south,' he explained.

Karis heard his sigh, saw his weariness. Another fifty miles meant at least another hour's drive. And already Seth had been sitting behind the steering wheel far too long.

'There's nothing at all around here?' she asked.

'The woman at the last hotel did mention a rest-house, but she said it's run down.' He grimaced. 'Run down can translate as bloody basic.'

'I'm game if you are,' she said pertly.

He studied her for a moment. 'You'll take whatever they throw at you?'

'Yes.'

What they chose to throw was a single-storey ramble of assorted buildings set on a hillside overlooking a lake. Touched pink-gold by the setting sun, the hillside and lake were as enchanting as the scenes depicted in Seth's collection of watercolours. The rest-house was not. It had been originally rough-cast in white, but time had taken its toll. The white had deteriorated into a dingy yellow, splodged with inexplicable stains. Patches of worn brick were exposed. Add a potholed drive, a garden which was maundering back into native jungle, and the establishment could only be described as forlorn.

'Still want to try here?' Seth enquired, as they walked under the shade of the porch.

Karis nodded brightly and, stepping around a sleeping mongrel, went with him into the entrance hall. The bare stone floor, plain beige walls and insect-eaten rattan furniture gave authority to his suggestion of 'basic'. Everything in sight was old, scratched, shabby. The hall was empty, and when Seth pounded on a brass bell only the dog responded. It stirred, raised its head, looked at them through bloodshot eyes, and promptly sank back into sleep. Everyone else appeared to be asleep, too. Seth strode to where a corridor led off the hall. He called. Nothing happened. He crossed to open a door on to the kitchen. Another call. This time a distant voice answered, and eventually the slow scuffle of rubber flip-flop sandals heralded an approach. A nugget-brown old man in string vest and frayed trousers appeared.

'Any luck?' asked Karis, after a rapid conversation in Thai resulted in her receiving a flash of gold teeth.

'As far as luck goes, yes. Though I wouldn't necessarily say it's good,' Seth said drily. 'There are two spare rooms, one twin, the other single. And a woman's due in any minute to begin preparing meals. The kitchen looked clean, so let's hope our digestive tracts will survive.'

The old man produced large iron keys and, with a dig at the slumbering dog as he passed, led the way outside. Skirting a block of ramshackle garages, he took them across an overgrown square of grass to a long low building. With two doors and no windows on the wall which faced them, it reminded Karis of an army barracks. Their guide inserted a key in each door, nodded and shambled off.

An inspection of the rooms, both as big and bare as conference halls, showed that the smaller of the two was equipped with an air-conditioning unit, whereas the larger had only a ceiling fan.

'Suppose you take the single, while I occupy the double?' Seth suggested. 'You have more need of air-con than me.'

Karis gladly accepted his offer. He was unfazed by the heat, but sometimes she found it a chore. It was true that this evening the temperature was not excessive, but she would still sleep better in a cooled-down room.

'I'd like a shower before we eat,' she said, walking with him to the car to collect their luggage.

'Me, too.' He inspected his watch. 'First I'll phone Kovit. I should catch him before he leaves the office.'

Karis gave an impudent smile. 'The big boss is ringing in? What's the matter, do your underlings find it impossible to survive without you?'

'I want to check on the progress of a portable mixer we're having built, that's all. Though "that's all" gives the wrong impression. The mixer's our white hope for the future. For years our research guys have been working on a practical way to formulate explosives on site under tropical conditions,' he explained, 'and at last they seem to have cracked it. As soon as the mixer's ready, we begin trials.' He lifted her case from the car, and reached for his. 'With reference to my underlings, they can survive fine. Kovit, in particular, is shaping up well. He's top management material.'

'Despite his knack of losing company documents?'

she teased. 'I presume he was the culprit on Monday night?'

'He was, but losing things isn't his style. And the documents were only lost for a short time.' Seth pulled a face. 'Mind you, I've yet to be convinced "lost" is the right word.'

'What happened?' asked Karis, as they headed back to their rooms.

'There'd been a minor crisis with the assembly of the mixer I've just mentioned, which involved Kovit driving out to the manufacturers' factory and conferring. The matter dragged on all day. He'd arranged to have a drink with his brother, so when he arrived back in the city he went straight to the hotel. With him he had his briefcase which contained the drawings for the mixer, plus various explosives formulae developed by our laboratories. Because Kovit didn't feel happy about leaving the information in the car—our competitors would give their eye-teeth to get their hands on it—when he went inside, he took the briefcase with him. He reckons he was guarding it with his life, but——'

'The briefcase went missing?' she asked, when he shrugged.

Seth nodded. 'He says he was sitting in a booth with his brother, and one minute it was down by his feet, the next it had gone. The bar's a popular watering hole and people were everywhere, drinking and chatting. Kovit's first thought when he missed the briefcase was that it must have been kicked under the seat. So there the poor bastard was, on all fours among a sea of legs. Then he decided someone must have picked it up by mistake. One brown leather briefcase is much like any other. He rushed around from group to group of drinkers, but got no joy.'

'So he came round to see you?'

'Yes. He arrived white-faced on the doorstep asking what should he do? I suggested he go back to the bar and get the staff to frisk the place over. Questioning whoever was still there, in the hopes they might just have seen something, was also worth a try. Kovit went off, promising to ring back the minute he had results.'

'Which he did,' she said, recalling Seth's relief.

'Yes.' He smiled at the memory. 'When he returned to the bar, a waiter had discovered the briefcase under the seat where he'd been sitting.'

'But you don't think it was there all the time?'

They had reached her room. Karis opened the door, and he entered ahead to deposit her case on a rickety bamboo frame beside the bed.

'The bar tends to be gloomy and the gap beneath the seat does go back a long way.' Seth let out a breath of air. 'But how the hell wouldn't Kovit see something as bulky as a briefcase? He told me that minutes before it went missing he'd been talking to his brother about the mixer, explaining what an innovation it was. How as a company we stood to make good money out of it. For all I know, he may even have said the details were in his briefcase. That being so, I just wonder if someone could've overheard.'

'You think they might have stolen the briefcase, looked at the documents, then returned everything later?'

'It could have happened like that. But there haven't been any repercussions, no rumours about any other company embarking on a similar scheme, so——' he shrugged as he turned to leave '——all's well that ends well. Enjoy your shower.'

If the bedroom was a conference hall, the bathroom was a white-tiled mausoleum which appeared to date back to the beginning of the century. Karis had never seen such huge brass taps fitted to a wash bowl, such splendid lions' feet on a bath. Pity they were mottled with verdigris. A rusty water rose was set in the ceiling in the middle of the room, a grated outlet beneath, so she stripped off, turned the appropriate dial and stood there. She heard a distant gurgle, a liquid cough, and in time tepid water trickled over her. Nevertheless, the shower was refreshing. She enjoyed it.

She also enjoyed the drinks and dinner which came later. Together with a German couple and family of Thais, they dined on a patio overlooking the lake. Lit by candles which had the shabbiness disappearing into mellow shadows, the patio was a romantic place. From it you could marvel at the two moons: one a silver crescent high in the night sky, the other a mirror image lying on blue-black water. The song of cicadas accompanied their meal, and every time they breathed it was to inhale a heady fragrance, reminiscent of orange blossom. The relaxed holiday feel of lunchtime seeped back, and this time Karis could not fight it. After their dawn start, she didn't have the strength.

'Sleepy?' asked Seth, as they wandered back to their rooms.

'It'll be head down, eyes closed, and snooooores!'

'I've never heard you snore.'

One remark said casually, yet it transformed the entire evening. She looked at him. He looked at her. He was clinging on to his grin, but his mouth and eyes seemed to have acquired a serious softness, a tinge of yearning. Was Seth remembering the nights when they had lain together? Was he wishing this could be one of those nights? Karis's thoughts spiralled. The physical chemistry had been good, blissfully good. And could be again. But the physical side was not enough.

'Goodnight,' she said, searching frantically in her bag for her key.

He folded his arms and shifted his weight on to one leg. 'Why is it I make you so nervous?' he enquired, his mouth nudging into amusement.

'You don't!' Karis located the key, but needed two tries before she could locate the keyhole. Seth, and the moonlight, had conspired to trick her, she thought furiously. His look hadn't been nostalgic, instead he had been toying, teasing, playing with her. Again. She almost broke the door open. 'Goodnight.' She threw the word at him like an iron ball.

'Wait,' he ordered, and Karis froze. There was a terrifying, wonderful, crazy moment when she thought he was going to kiss her. 'See you tomorrow, partner,' he murmured, and reached out and gently tweaked her nose.

She accomplished undressing, washing, and cleaning of teeth with maniacal speed. Climbing into bed, she thumped a fist in the pillow. For no reason other than amusement, Seth had embarked on a campaign of being actively disruptive. He could go and take a running jump! Next time she would not react. Next time she would ignore him. Yanking at the cord above her head, she switched off the light. Now was not the time to be thinking about Seth, now was time for a good night's rest. The sheet pulled over her, Karis lay on her back. Then on her side. Then on her stomach. Five minutes later she sat upright. The air-conditioner, a museum piece of similar vintage to the bathroom, was grinding away like a tank on manoeuvres over difficult terrain. She padded over and reduced the fan speed. The noise remained constant. In bed again, Karis curled the pillow up around her head. She was wondering whether to switch off the air-con and take her chance with the night-time heat, when she became aware of a minuscule brushing against her knee.

All her senses snapped to the alert. She went rigid. The brushing had stopped. She waited. Seconds ticked by. Nothing happened. On the point of attributing her alarm to nothing more than the sheet, Karis felt the movement again. Whatever it was touching her leg, it was alive! Hand flying for the light cord, she ripped off the cover. A moment of dazzle, and her eyes were searching the bed. She gulped, and her skin crawled. A cockroach with more legs than a line of chorus girls was attempting to scale the side of her knee. With a shriek, she half fell, half hurled herself out of bed. Blue eyes wide, she looked for the high-heeled sandals she had worn at dinner. It would be one quick thud and— goodbye. She was halfway across the room when a movement caught her eye. There was a second cock- roach! The place was infested. She could not stay here, in this room,' with them.

'Seth, Seth!' She pounded on his door. 'Can you spare a minute?'

She had dashed out in her bare feet, but bare feet are vulnerable. Karis looked down, eyes searching like beacons. Shadows made it difficult to see, but had something crawled out of the grass a mere yard away? She was squinting desperately when the opening of the door diverted her. Bare-chested, Seth was fastening a button at the waist of pyjama trousers which she realised had been pulled on seconds earlier.

'There're two enormous cockroaches in my room, she gabbled, and swung a denunciating finger. 'There's another one.'

The object she had indicated received a bleary inspection.

'That's a dead leaf.'

'Is it?' Karis deflated. 'Oh.' She made a recovery. 'Well, there really are two cockroaches in my room. Do you have any repellent?'

He yawned. 'You think I come prepared for each and every emergency? Sorry, I left the Boy Scouts behind long ago.'

'Perhaps we could get a can from the management? Or you could kill them? Something'll have to be done,' she appealed. 'There's just no way I and cockroaches can peacefully co-exist.'

Without a word, Seth strode into her room.

'Where are they?' he demanded.

Karis looked at her bed, at her sandals. The insects had vanished.

'They must be somewhere around,' she said, and began to search. Sheets were ripped off the bed, pillows shaken, a square of sisal matting peeped under. No cockroaches. 'They *were* here,' she insisted.

Seth yawned a second time, and ambled over to open the bathroom door. '*Voilà!*'

Karis's blood ran cold. On the tiled floor were not just two cockroaches, but six, all marching around like miniature shiny brown armoured vehicles. Seth collected her sandal and swiftly despatched the entire half-dozen.

'Thanks,' she said, but her gratitude turned into a wail as a further couple wandered out from a corner. 'Oh no!'

'They come up through the drains.'

She shivered. 'I can't stay here tonight.' She clutched at his arm. 'I can't, I can't!'

Hazel eyes regarded her. 'I understood you were supposed to be the modern independent woman?'

'I am.'

'Yet you retain the right to become hysterical if the

situation warrants it?'

She snatched her hand from his arm.

'I'm not hysterical! It's just that——'

'At times if feels good having a male around to protect you?'

Mouth open to insist she did not require protection, Karis thought better and closed it again.

'We could swap rooms,' Seth suggested, 'but as mine has the same decrepit plumbing there's no guarantee you won't hear the patter of another dozen tiny feet later in the night.' He laughed at the look of horror on her face, then grew thoughtful. 'I know what we can do,' he said suddenly. 'The spare bed in my room has a frame with a mosquito net rolled up on top of it. Suppose I take it down and see if it's in a reasonable condition? If so, you can sleep there, under cover.' He tugged at the waist of his pyjamas. 'Which means I can stay where I am. I was very comfortable there until you woke me.'

'We sleep in the same room?'

'Why not? That way I'll be on hand in case you have another visitor.' He must have read her mind, for he added, 'And don't think the visitor'll be me. It won't. I've had a long day and I want some sleep. Which means you'll be in your bed, and I'll be in mine—separate.'

Karis surveyed him, surveyed the promenading cockroaches. How could she insist on turfing Seth out of his bed? She couldn't. Neither could she sleep in this room. But with gauze draped over her, she would be able to sleep.

'Let's inspect the mosquito net,' she said.

Half an hour later she was lying wide awake beneath a filmy white cover, listening to the steady rhythm of breathing. Seth was fast asleep. He had fallen asleep with unflattering speed. That her young, female, wonderfully toned body was stretched out just a few yards away had not bothered him in the slightest. Irrationally, that it did not bother him bothered her. She closed her eyes. Counted sheep. Opened her eyes. By peering through the net she made out the position of the luminous hands on his travelling clock; it was midnight. One o'clock came. And two. And three.

Karis awoke to a room golden with sunshine, and she awoke alone. The other bed was empty. A lack of sounds from the bathroom told her Seth was nowhere around. Had he gone for breakfast? Rubbing her eyes, she fought her way through the mosquito net and stumbled out of bed. She felt hot and sticky, and badly in need of a shower. When she remembered the cockroaches which had route-marched across *her* white-tiled floor, she shuddered. No, thank you. She inspected Seth's bathroom and, after a meticulous search, passed it as insect-free. He continued to be absent, so why not use it? An ear cocked for noise of his return, she turned on the water. Speedily she soaped, rinsed and dried herself. Knotting a towel beneath her armpits, she collected up the scraps of nightwear, and took a deep breath. Cockroaches or not, the time had come when she must return to her own room. Adopting an air of determination, she strode to the door, but needed to jump back to avoid a collision. Seth had arrived, almost cannoning into her. Face glistening with sweat and breath coming jerky and fast, he looked like a man in a hurry.

'What have you been doing?' she asked, intrigued to see he was wearing a soggy tee-shirt and shorts.

'Jogging,' he panted.

'You? Jogging?'

'Yes,' he gulped. 'Why not?'

Karis shook her head in elaborate amazement. 'Wonders will never cease!'

'Only doing what you said I should do,' he got out

between breaths. 'You were right. Someone like me—in a sedentary job—who smokes—ought to take care of his body. Otherwise in middle age—who knows?'

She grinned. 'And, of course, you're knocking on the door of middle age now.'

'Like hell I am!'

'Then why all the heavy breathing?'

He lunged, grabbing hold of her shoulders. 'Because I've been running for fifty minutes. Because it's hot out there, and hilly.'

'So?'

'So I demand a retraction. Say after me—young Seth Mauroy is one of the fittest men I have ever seen.'

Karis smiled. 'You expect me to perjure myself?'

'I expect you to tell the truth.' He gave her a shake. 'Say it!'

'I need more proof. One fifty-minute jog doesn't make a—whoops!'

His shaking had loosened her makeshift sarong, and without warning the knot gave way. As the towel slid to the floor, she grabbed. Seth grabbed. Hands collided, fumbled, became confused. Somehow she ended up with her top half naked and his hands around her waist.

He looked down on her breasts. 'Karis,' he breathed.

His voice sounded thick, choked, and reminded her of times in the past. She went hot, she went cold, felt her body blossom and respond. But it mustn't. This was Seth's fault. He had no right to sound so enamoured, had no right to look at her like that. She yanked up the towel, blanketing herself with flushed-face haste.

'I presume you haven't had breakfast?' she demanded.

He gazed at her for what seemed like for ever, then blinked and seemed to flick a switch inside himself. Normal operations had been resumed.

'No, not yet. Give me ten minutes to shower and change, and I'll be with you. Do you think as well as jogging I ought to pick up a few dumb-bells?' he enquired, as she opened the door.

'Wouldn't hurt. How long have you been on this jogging kick?'

'I started the day after my return from seeing you, six months ago.' Seth placed a foot on to the bed and began to unlace his jogging shoe. 'It seemed the ideal time to break with the past, and start anew.' He threw her a sharp look. 'I changed my habits—and in more ways than one.'

CHAPTER SIX

THEY reached Phuket mid-afternoon. Seth had explained how a causeway linked the island to the mainland, but they were three-quarters of the way across the Sarasin Bridge before his sigh of satisfaction alerted Karis to their arrival. Shaking off sloth gathered over what had begun to seem like a never-ending journey, Karis sat up and took notice.

'We're here?' she enquired, surprised because the channel spanned by the bridge was no wider than a river.

'At last, thank God,' he said, as the Porsche hit solid ground. 'Though there's another forty odd miles to do. This is the largest island in the kingdom,' he explained. 'Five hundred square miles of mountain forest, palms and rubber plantations. The interior's lush, but the coastline's the reason why the travel posters promote Phuket as the Pearl of the South. It's magnificent.' Seth made a kissing sound. 'The sand's soft and white, lapped by a crystal-clear sea. And whether you hanker after surfing or scuba diving or just floating around in gentle waves, there's a beach tailor-made. No elbowing your way through the madding crowd, either. The island's relatively unspoiled. A great place for getting away from it all.'

'Or for being held hostage?'

He exhaled in a soft whoosh of exasperation. 'For goodness' sake, Karis, wherever Leon's being detained, it won't be here.'

'I know there's supposed to be honour among thieves,

but suppose in this case there isn't?' she rattled off. 'Suppose——'

'Are you saying your stepfather's a thief?'

She scowled. Seth's jaundiced eye was making him altogether too tricky.

'All I'm saying is that if the Dejo character is as devious as you imply, then anything could have happened.'

'To the point of him kidnapping a confederate? You have a fertile imagination. Like I told you before lunch, at lunch, and after lunch, over the years the two of them have perfected a 'you scratch my back and I'll scratch yours' kind of relationship. The likelihood of Dejo being prepared to wreck anything so beneficial is remote, but if he was he'd never do it for the sake of a million and a half *baht*. He'd go for much higher stakes. The name 'Phuket' comes from a Malay word meaning 'hill', he continued robustly. 'Some of the hills here are rich in tin deposits, others yield the limestone which Dejo Suksaguan quarries.'

Karis sighed. He was right to dismiss the idea of her stepfather being detained on this island. It was no more than a straw wildly clutched at. Seth didn't clutch at straws. He had more sense.

'Where is the quarry?' she enquired.

'In the south of the island. Nearby there's a small bay where a Frenchman's in the throes of developing a cabana-style resort, and if you're agreeable, partner, I suggest we make that our destination. It's a back-to-nature kind of place, nothing so sophisticated as jet skis or windsurfers for hire, but I think you'll like it.'

'You've stayed there before?'

'Once, with Sukanya. She didn't enjoy the seaside much. Nevertheless I pulled a few strings and——' Seth frowned at the instrument panel. 'We need petrol. How about taking a break when we reach the town? I could also do with some shaving-cream.' He switched his attention from the road for a moment, and grinned. 'The prospect of joining forces with you again made me so excited, I forgot to pack any.'

The words were delivered with a light and teasing touch, yet his look seemed to convey a contrary sentiment. As he concentrated again on his driving, Karis began to brood. The previous evening she had thought she deciphered a potent message in those hazel eyes, but she had been wrong. Was she wrong now? Possibly, or should it be probably? It had to be admitted that of late her character assessments had been a disaster. Frances, a girl she had believed to be a steadfast friend, had let her down, and wasn't she currently needing to readjust her opinion of her stepfather? She was, it seemed, gullible.

'Seth?' she said tentatively, wary of being beguiled now.

'Yes, chick?'

His eyes met hers, and he smiled. What a smile! It was warm and wide and ... loving? Her heart sang. Karis was sure—as sure as it was possible to be without demanding he produce a signed affidavit—that the only reason he had embarked on this journey was *her*.

'When we stop perhaps I could have a wander round and buy some postcards?' she suggested gaily.

A minor shopping expedition was agreed and twenty minutes later, the Porsche filled, they drove into the island capital and parked. At first glance Phuket Town had little to commend it. A drab, sun-bleached collection of low-rise shophouses, it was neither old enough to be quaint nor modern enough to be smart. Mediocrity abounded. Then they turned a corner and discovered the saving grace—a single street of traditional Sino-Portuguese mansions. With carved stone arches and bulbous stone balustrades gleaming white in the sunshine, the architecture was an elegant reminder of bygone days. Several of the mansions had been converted into shops, and Karis spent time selecting postcards. A silversmith's caught her interest next.

'Why not have a look inside while I track down shaving-cream?' Seth suggested, when she stopped to admire the brooches, belt buckles and tankards displayed in the window. He gestured towards a pavement café on the other side of the road. 'Let's meet up there in ten minutes.'

The silversmith's was an Eldorado. Karis required a Thai memento for her Aunt Connie, and she moved from glass case to glass case, spoilt for choice. Jewellery of all kinds was considered, but finally she settled on an oval mother-of-pearl pendant, delicately bound in silver. The gift wrapped and paid for, she went outside. Across the road, Seth was sitting at a table. He grinned when he saw her and raised a hand, wiggling his fingers. She wiggled hers in return. Mouthing apologies for being late, she waited for a gap in the traffic. She had to wait a long time. If the madding crowds left the coastline alone, this afternoon they had congregated in Phuket Town. Vehicles were passing in a steady stream. When, at last, her side of the road came empty, she hurdled a storm drain and made it halfway. Here, she needed to wait again. Minibuses zapped past inches in front of her, and inches behind. There were trucks. There were taxis. Deciding to make the final dash between a blue family saloon which came next and a motorbike, Karis poised herself for action. A swift checking glance, right and left, and . . .

She never moved. She couldn't move. Fifteen to twenty yards away, the blue car had swung into the kerb and was stopping to pick up a passenger. Her eyes grew round. Her mouth formed a silent oval. The passenger was Leon! He had walked from a travel agent's and was negotiating a path through the people on the pavement. Of their own accord, her feet executed a half-turn. She had to go to him, rescue him. In a daze, she took a step in his direction.

'Oi! Come here!'

Seth's call switched her eyes. He had thrust back his chair to stand straight and tall. A muscled arm was raised, and he was glaring in a way which warned there would be big trouble, if she did not go to his side—immediately. She looked from him to the car. Her stepfather was stooping to climb inside. He needed her help—also immediately. Torn, she returned her gaze to Seth.

'Come *here*!'

His voice acted like a lasso. It coiled itself around, and yanked her across the street.

'That's—that's Leon,' she stammered, arriving at his side breathless and slightly belligerent.

'I know.'

Karis watched in dismay as the door slammed shut, and the car edged back into the traffic. 'You're not going to do anything?' she asked incredulously.

'If you mean am I going to act first and ask questions later, the answer's no.'

'But shouldn't we follow him?' she appealed, in a voice which said it was their *duty* to follow. 'Even if you don't like Leon, you can't leave him to—to suffer! Let's get the Porsche. If we hurry we'll be able to pick up his trail.'

Seth pulled out a chair. 'Do sit down. Please,' he requested, courteous as a head waiter.

'Now?'

'Now.'

She hesitated. The car was moving off along the street, rapidly dissolving into no more than a blue blur. Karis maintained eye contact until it reached a T-junction, then, as it disappeared, plonked herself down with bad grace.

Across the table Seth was scanning a menu. 'There's coconut ice-cream sundae,' he said. 'Want one?'

'No.'

'I thought you liked them?'

'We can't sit here and eat!' she protested. 'Not now when we've just seen Leon. Leon, who's been kidnapped. We could have tried to rescue him,' she muttered. 'We *should* have tried to rescue him.'

'I doubt he'd have been too pleased if we had. I'm ordering a sundae. Do you fancy one or not?'

Annoyed at being pestered by this irrelevance, she shot him a torpedo of a look, but he showed not the least sign of sinking.

'Yes, I'll have one,' Karis replied grumpily. With him being so irritatingly laid back about her stepfather, there seemed nothing else to do.

'Why wouldn't he have been pleased if we'd attempted to free him?' she questioned, after a woman had noted their requirements. 'Do you think a rescue could have been dangerous? That his kidnappers might have been armed and Leon would rather stay in custody rather than risk someone getting hurt?'

'I'm not thinking along those lines at all.' Elbows on the table, Seth interlocked his hands and rested his chin on top of them. 'You see, I'm very much afraid there aren't any kidnappers.'

Startled blue eyes met steady brown.

'But—but I spoke to them!'

'Karis, the man at the wheel of the car was Dejo. And

before you resurrect the idea of him being kidnapper-in-chief, just ask yourself if you were holding someone to ransom, would you allow them to walk the streets in broad daylight? No way. Remember how Leon approached the car? Did he look as though he was under guard, harassed?' This time he waited for an answer.

'Well . . . no,' she admitted. 'But it's possible someone was pointing a gun at him which we couldn't see.'

'You've been watching too much television,' Seth chastised gently, and sighed. 'This abduction has been irregular from the start. To be honest, I can't say I'm surprised to discover Leon seems to have fabricated the whole thing.'

Head congested, thoughts hopelessly tangled, Karis stared. 'You mean he faked the kidnapping in order to—to rob me? I don't believe it,' she said indignantly. 'You're too quick to think only the worst.'

'Aren't you too quick to think only the best?' Seth responded. He waited as two cream-topped and nut-sprinkled sundaes in tall glasses were set before them. 'In the past Leon's got away with murder, but not this time. This time I'll make sure he——'

'So that's the reason you rushed down here? You thought he was up to no good and you wanted to get revenge?' she inserted, with energetic venom.

'I had no idea what Leon was up to, or even if he was up to anything. I still don't,' he said firmly. 'But set in the context of his background, the kind of guy he is, a kidnapping never seemed strictly legit.'

'Which is why you decided to trail him, like a damn bloodhound!'

'I thought the matter might benefit from being looked into further, that's all,' he said, sounding so calm and in control she could have screamed. 'But what puzzles me is, why isn't he returning to Bangkok until Wednesday?'

'How should I know? You're the one with all the theories.'

Karis was brittle. She needed to be. Brittleness was her way of fighting against a world which had smacked her in the mouth, not once but twice. The first blow—her stepfather's apparent deceit—bruised. Yet it was the second—learning Seth's true motivation for heading south—which had drawn blood. All the time she had been nursing hopes he might still care, Leon had been his sole interest. Leon, not her. How was that for monumental self-deception!

'Who are you angry with, your stepfather or me?' Seth stretched across the table to capture her hand. 'I understand how you must be feeling and I'm sorry, very sorry,' he said, resisting her efforts to break free. 'I'd give anything for this not to have happened. However, it has, and all I can say is give me time to work things through and I swear somehow I'll get your money back.'

'I don't care about the damn money!'

'Once you have this thing in focus, you will. And I do.' He released her. 'I'll make sure justice is done.'

He started to eat the ice cream, and after a minute or two Karis grudgingly did the same. In the past the coconut flavour had been a delight, now she tasted nothing. If she had been duped by her stepfather, then ... She frowned as a whole blizzard of implications swept through her head.

'There's no proof Leon's a cheat,' she said, after a while.

'Maybe he isn't. Maybe his appearance today can be explained.'

'But you don't think so?'

'Do you?'

She sighed. Rather than baying angrily over anything and everything Seth said about her stepfather, wouldn't it be more sensible to take note?

'Tell me about Leon,' she requested. 'About the kind of person he really is.'

'Karis, if I start nailing him to the wall you'll come at me like a one-girl assault force. Quite frankly, I can do without that kind of hassle.'

'No hassle,' she assured him. 'Let's be rational about this.'

'You, rational?'

She refused to rise to the bait. 'As Leon does seem to be involved in something—unorthodox, isn't it time I took off the blinkers and faced facts? I realise you'd never criticise anyone without good reason,' she added, when he frowned.

'That's progress.'

'So tell me.'

'You don't lack determination, do you?' Seth sucked ice-cream off his spoon, and pondered for a while. 'OK, you know how Leon maintains he's a businessman? Well, he should be prosecuted under the Trades Descriptions Act. The guy's nothing more than a manipulator. He'd pull any kind of stunt, so long as it brings him in some cash. Take his ''schemes'', for example. He persuades folk to invest money in all sorts of ventures—snack bars, cheap silk, the export of mangoes. You name it, Leon's touting. Some provide a return, I admit, but whether they succeed or fail, you can bet *Le Grand Fromage* never walks away empty-handed. But the prime example of his expertise at manipulation is the way he made money out of the company, courtesy of Cecil Pritchard.'

'And how did he?' she asked, when Seth paused to take another mouthful.

'By charging customers far more than he should have done for our detonators, paying the company the correct, lower amount and pocketing the difference.'

Karis frowned. 'Cecil was aware of this?'

'For twenty-five years,' Seth said heavily.

She was perplexed. 'But he did nothing to stop it?'

'I understand that way back at the beginning, when the information about Leon's misconduct first trickled through, Cecil asked if he would please be content with a smaller profit margin, and Leon acquiesced. Things were fine for a while, then greed began to get the better of him again. There was another meeting when they went through the same old rigmarole. Six months later, they were back to square one again. Over the years there was a series of appeals, but the situation never changed.'

'Why?'

'Because, in essence, Cecil had admitted defeat from day one and decided to go along with his sharp practice.'

'Why?' she asked again.

'God knows! Because Cecil Pritchard was jelloid, I suppose. Jelloid and not much of a businessman, either. The company used to be private, as you know, and I suspect he only landed the job in the first place because his cousin was a major shareholder. It was the "who you know, not what you know" routine. Same thing applied between him and Leon. They'd first met in the classroom at public school, and were long-time friends.'

'Friends? But——' Karis hesitated. 'I only saw them together once, but Cecil Pritchard struck me as being slightly in awe of Leon.'

'Slightly? Very. Your stepfather was the dominant character.' Seth swallowed his final mouthful of ice cream. 'Cecil's principal aim was a quiet life. Which, no doubt, explains why he never put it on the line that Leon must either shape up or his agency would be terminated. Cecil didn't relish a battle royal.'

'And was it?' she enquired.

He gave a terse laugh. 'Cutting ties with Leon didn't rate as one of the pleasantest tasks I inherited. For a good part of Cecil's reign the company had a virtual monopoly in supplying detonators, but now the Japanese, the Norwegians, the Americans plug their products like crazy. Allowing an indulgence like Leon is uneconomic in today's world.'

'So you stood him on the carpet and told him it was be good, or else?'

'No. I talked the matter over with headquarters and they agreed he had to be ousted, but insisted it must be without any adverse publicity. Company image is important,' he explained. 'We didn't want Leon dishing the dirt, spreading rumours to the effect he'd been ill-treated. The break had to be an easing out, yet incisive. To do that I needed to confront him with proof of his misconduct in black and white, and leave no loopholes. Gathering the information took time. And once I had it, I had to approach with care. As on a tightrope,' he said wryly. 'At one stage Leon did turn a bit nasty, but when I threatened to blow the thing wide open, he backed off. Good job, too. I don't know what I'd have done if he'd called my bluff.'

'He's made only a passing reference to you ending his agency, but he doesn't seem particularly aggrieved.'

'I don't think he is. In the end the parting was more or less amicable. He had had a good run for his money, you know !' Seth rubbed long fingers across his jaw. 'It's odd. There's no doubt Cecil was overshadowed by Leon and yet I always suspected he was somehow sorry for him. But you were sorry for him, too,' he reflected. 'That's what brought you to Thailand.'

Karis nodded disconsolately. Assimilating what she had learnt in the past five minutes was proving painful. 'You know how you reckoned Leon had invited me for no apparent reason?' she began. 'Well——'

'I know what I said, but I find it difficult to believe he arranged a kidnapping and specifically imported you to provide the ransom. Leon might be a chancer, but planning something so cold-bloodedly in advance seems out of character. He's more a day-to-day merchant.'

'You think he did it on the spur of the moment? Thanks, that's a great comfort!' Aware of heading for the doldrums, Karis had swerved and become brisk. 'So, what do we do?'

'As far as Leon's concerned, nothing right now. My guess is he's installed either at Dejo's house or at the quarry.' Seth consulted his watch. 'It's half past four, which means he's hardly likely to up sticks and disappear today. However, it's high time we disappeared to fix our resting place,' he added, and scribbled a message in the air to notify the woman of his wish to pay the bill. 'Whether he's guilty of misconduct or not, it wouldn't be wise to underestimate Leon,' he continued, as they walked back to the car. 'We must plan a strategy. He can be cute as a cartload of monkeys, and——' He stopped mid-stride. 'Ha! Monkey business, that's one of Leon's pet phrases. And didn't the so-called kidnapper say something about monkey business on the telephone? Ten to one he rehearsed him.'

Karis felt beleaguered. Inexorably the evidence seemed to be building up against her stepfather. In the car, Seth alternated between busy silences when she could virtually hear his brain ticking over, and queries about Leon's attitude before he disappeared. She recognised that he was responding to the situation in a logical way, but that didn't stop her from wishing he wouldn't be so single-minded. Immersed in his thoughts, he barely noticed the curving beaches with their swaying palms and huge granite boulders. It was only when a swathe of cut lawn on either side of a driveway signalled a private development that he came back to life. He swung the Porsche off the main road, delving down through pine trees. As they curled around a grove of lacy casuarinas, ahead came a view of the impossible turquoise of the Andaman Sea. They had arrived.

The bay, nestling between wooded headlands, was a tropical haven of sea and sun and vivid blossoms. And among the blossoms were glimpses of guest cabanas. Built in the local rustic style of wood and rattan weave walls, topped with palm-thatch roofs, the cabanas were in sympathy with the surroundings. At the foot of the hillside and close to the shore stood a similar, but much larger, building where, Seth explained, restaurant, offices and reception area were housed.

'That's where you check into paradise?' Karis asked, her spirits reviving.

He laughed, and she saw the bay had worked its magic on him, too. For the moment Leon *et al* had been forgotten.

'Just pray Saint Peter will allow us to stay.'

When Saint Peter, dressed in cut-off shorts and disguised as a stocky, prematurely bald Frenchman, responded to Seth's query, he was smiling.

'*Mais oui,*' he said and, issuing keys, went on to list mealtimes and other pertinent information.

A boy collected their luggage and led the way. Up the hillside they went, plunging into what at first seemed a random profusion of purple and white bougainvillaea. Not so random, Karis recognised as they walked. The bay had been cleverly landscaped; the bushes screening each of the dozen or so guest cabanas from its neighbours and providing complete privacy. Smart, she thought. Her cabana, its own plant-filled patio stretching to one side, also looked smart. Yet as the boy swung wide the door, she was wary. Memories of the rest-house nibbled. To discover the pretty beige and white bedroom being cooled by a faintly murmuring air conditioner removed one fear. A keen-eyed inspection of the bathroom removed the second. Modern and gleaming with chrome fitments, there were no cockroach-contaminated drain outlets here.

'Satisfied?' enquired Seth, with a grin.

'Completely.'

'Then how about joining me for a jog along the shore in, say, twenty minutes?'

Karis had unpacked and showered in less than ten. After pulling on short cherry-red shorts and a brief top, she devoted attention to her hair. The long, straight fall received a vigorous brushing, then, to keep it off her neck while she was jogging, was twisted into a knot and skewered on the top of her head. A cherry-coloured sweatband was fixed across her brow. A look in the mirror, a nod of satisfaction, and she emerged. Trails of amber vapour in the sky gave notice of the approach of evening. The fierce heat had gone, leaving the air pleasantly warm, yet fresh. When she walked down the four or five stone steps to the beach, there was no one else around. Paradise belonged to her alone. Karis stood, scuffing her toes in the sand and admiring the outline of rocky islets against the pinky glow on the horizon. Then her pent-up energy insisted on action.

After so long in the car, she needed exercise. Feet apart, legs straight, arms stretched wide, she bent at the waist and bounced. Bounce. Bounce. Bounce. Ten waist swings, hands on shoulders, came next. She ran on the spot, knees high, and laughed. Her blood was beginning to pound. Another waist-whittling exercise. Karis felt much better, in trim, zingy. A series of star kicks, arms and legs thrown out, increased her exhilaration the way physical exertion does. Now for touching her toes. Legs spread and ramrod-stiff, she started off with arms stretched high above her head. Up and down she powered, as precise as an automaton. This was no rest cure. She pushed herself to the limit. Her well-being increased. Leon and what he had, or appeared to have done, faded from her thoughts.

In the midst of the sixth downward swing, she noticed Seth, and her mechanism jarred, spluttered, cut out. Upside down she hung, gazing at him from between her legs. Sitting on a rock, he was in running shorts and had his arms folded across a tanned, bare chest. There were dark hairs on that chest. Hairs she remembered kissing. Hairs which had once tickled the palms of her hands. Hairs which had rubbed enticingly against her breasts.

Grinning, he bent to meet her eyes. 'There aren't many people who have the gift of turning each day into a twenty-four-hour cabaret,' he said, 'but you do.'

Topsy-turvy, Karis glowered. He was being provocative again.

'I'm exercising,' she said sharply, and straightened. 'Not acting the showgirl for your benefit.'

'I know.' His grin had disappeared. 'That wasn't a macho expression of appreciation. Maybe I didn't phrase it too well, but what I meant was that whenever I'm with you I feel——' His hand flicked with the speed of a lizard's tongue. 'Hell, I'm making a mess of this, I must be out of practice. Come on, let's jog.'

Out of synch with such a rapid change of mood, Karis took a moment before she found the impetus to jump forward and join him. She was intrigued. What had he been going to say? She wanted to know. Could he have been going to reveal that when he was with her he felt— good? Alive? Sexy? Something inside her crimped. It was bound to be sexy. How she wished it could have been good or alive. Good and alive each had a pleasingly solid quality about them. A notion of something to build on. Karis cast a glance at the man jogging alongside. He wasn't interested in building anything with her. But was she interested in building anything with him? For the past six months she would have said no, but now . . .

At the end of the beach, Seth stopped.

'Tired?' she challenged, with a shiny-bright impudence.

'No way. I'd just like to say something.' He scoured his chest with the heel of his hand. 'We set off from Bangkok on the understanding it was as partners, and I want you to know that stands. There could be difficult times ahead with Leon, but don't think you're facing them on your own. You're not. I'm here.' He reached forward to put a finger, just one finger, on her shoulder. 'I'll give whatever support I can.'

Karis looked at him. How she wished that finger could be a hand to stroke and comfort. An arm enfolding her shoulders. A body wrapped around hers. On impulse, she reached up and kissed his cheek.

'Thanks,' she said.

His cheek was freshly shaved and smooth. His skin smelt faintly of lemons. She kissed him again.

'Thank *you*, partner,' he smiled.

Bemused by what she had done, Karis blushed and charged off along the beach. In two strides, Seth had joined her. Bare feet padded on sand. A rhythm was forged. As they ran, thoughts swirled in her head. Seth was right, for the past couple of days they had had a partnership—a good partnership. Maybe it could have been the same in England, she thought wistfully, if her private demons hadn't taken charge and ensured that she had blown it! At the time she had been convinced

Seth was to blame—he had been superior, too dominant, too much the natural-born leader—but he didn't seem like that now, did he?

'Tell me about this martial-arts expert of yours,' he demanded suddenly. 'Have you taught him pelvic tilts?'

'Good grief, no!' She had replied without thinking, but then recalled his involvement with the Thai girl. 'Maybe I will when I get back,' she said, in an effort to salvage something.

'You and Cliff are—just good friends?' he questioned.

'*Very* good friends.'

Seth's pace quickened, forcing her to lengthen her strides to keep up. In silence they ran to the end of the bay, turned, and began running back. Karis grew wary. Her companion looked pensive. Could he be lining up more questions about her love-life? That was a laugh. For the past six months her love-life had been non-existent. In the hope of diverting him, she pointed ahead to where the palm-covered headland rose up at the end of the bay.

'You said the quarry was close. Would we be able to see it from the top of the hill?'

'I imagine so.'

'Why don't we go and take a look? All we need to do is keep on jogging. See, there's a path through the trees.' Karis saw his hesitation. 'Give me one good reason why not.'

Seth caught hold of her arm and drew them both to a halt.

'I can give you not just one reason,' he panted, 'but an entire basketful. Like the path might be a dead end. Like soon it'll be dark. Like how I thought we'd agreed we mustn't rush into anything.'

The diversion had worked, leaving her free to tease. 'Like on the other side of the hill there might be a steep drop which'll give you vertigo?' she suggested.

'That, too,' he grinned. 'Chick, let's sleep on this business with Leon. What I suggest is that tomorrow we have an early swim, say around seven? Then breakfast. Then we'll have a council of war and decide what to do. OK with you?'

Karis gave a shrug of *laissez-faire*. 'OK with me.'

CHAPTER SEVEN

KARIS snapped instantly awake. She looked at her watch and grimaced. It was barely six a.m. Six was far too early for swimming. Far too early for breakfast. Far too early for that discussion with Seth. With a sigh, she lay back on the pillow. By talking about a 'council of war' he had effectively slotted her stepfather into the role of enemy. It was a role she accepted with reluctance, and yet with her own eyes she had seen Leon walking freely on the streets of Phuket. How did she correlate that with the belief that he had genuinely been kidnapped? It was a tricky equation, an impossible equation. Distressing as it might be, there seemed no alternative to admitting her stepfather had lied to her, tricked her, defrauded her of a sizeable amount of cash. Yet the money angle was set to naught by the realisation that if Leon had used her, it followed that he had probably been using her mother.

A lump caught in her throat as she recalled how overwhelmingly *grateful* her mother had been when the middle-aged bachelor had entered her life. Gratitude now seemed, at best, inappropriate; at worst, cruelly ironical. Karis sighed again. Analyse the pairing of the jaunty life and soul of any party, with a fragile, timid woman like Ruth Buchanan, and didn't it seem odd? Could he have married her for her money, or rather for the money he might have imagined she possessed? Aunt Connie and her husband were noticeably wealthy. They lived in great style. Had Leon believed her mother occupied a similarly well heeled bracket? It was possible. Right now anything seemed possible. Karis wrapped a strand of hair around her finger. When the will had been read, his lack of inheritance had not seemed to bother Leon but, as Seth had said, he was something of an actor. Had he been performing then? Perhaps, in reality, he had not received the rake-off he had expected? Perhaps his discontent had festered? And perhaps this kidnapping had been staged to collect cash aimed for right from the start? Perhaps. Perhaps. Perhaps. A nightmare maze of possibilities was growing up around her, obscuring the view.

And where did Monika fit into all this? If she and Leon were close now, perhaps they had also been close before he had met her mother? Or even during their marriage? The strand of hair was twisted into a knot. Why had the German woman exited in line with her arrival? Karis wondered. Had Leon been removing his lover on purpose, distancing her in case something went wrong? What happened when Monika returned? Did the two of them intend to live in style on money essentially provided by her sweet-natured, wouldn't-say-boo-to-a-goose mother?

She swung back the sheet and leapt out of bed. Lying flat on her back, staring at the ceiling and supposing was achieving nothing but a billowy feeling of distress. At breakfast she would discuss these fears with Seth, until then the sensible thing was to be active.

Clad in a white bikini, an outsized navy tee-shirt over the top, Karis marched down to the shore. A couple with two small children were kicking a ball around, but they were the only early birds. She waved a greeting, then strolled off along the water's edge to the end of the bay. Here she hestitated. A U-turn had been intended, but somehow she kept moving forward. Taking the path she had identified the previous evening, Karis went up the hill. At first she walked, then her love of exercise prompted her to jog. By the time she reached the top, she was pink-faced and marinated in sweat.

She rested, hands on knees, then straightened to find her bearings. Her talk of a steep drop had been all wrong. The headland sloped gently down to the sea on one side, while inland it rolled off into another hill. Inland was the area of interest. Frowning against the sun, she picked out a wall of whitish stone among the tropical green. It was a high quarry face which, a swift calculation said, could be no more than a mile away as the crow flew, or as a person walked. Should she walk? Karis wondered. Why not? With another three-quarters of an hour to go before the swimming rendezvous, there was time to kill. Besides, despite Seth's pinpointing her stepfather's location to either the quarry or Dejo's house, sooner or later they would need to know which one.

She set off energetically, going over the crest of the hill and down between shaggy-topped palms, but as she neared her destination, her step slowed. She must take care not to be seen. The slope of the hill levelled off halfway into a wooded ridge, and here Karis halted. The ridge, opposite the working face and with the quarry floor below and between, provided an excellent vantage point, and she saw that the day's work had already begun. Bright yellow dump trucks, excavators and rubber-tyred shovels were moving around like giant toys, ponderously shifting stone. Men in hard hats wandered to and fro. There was activity at a fuel pump, a weighbridge, stock piles. As at the tin mine there were clanking conveyor belts, and crusher sheds, all blanketed in voluminous clouds of dust.

Karis's gaze swung to the far side of the quarry floor. Here, behind an outcrop, stood a wooden hut. The building looked shabby, almost derelict, yet three cars were parked outside. With narrowed eyes, she made an inspection. It seemed unlikely that her stepfather, with his predilection for life's luxuries, should inhabit such unprepossessing surroundings. Also none of the cars was blue. On the point of leaving, she changed her mind and decided the hut deserved a closer look.

To her left a trail disappeared into undergrowth, and cautiously she set off down. Within yards the incline steepened, and she found herself clutching at a branch here, grabbing a clump of grass there, in a desperate attempt to keep upright. Half walking, half slithering, in her espadrilles, she came to rest on a narrow ledge amid bushes, some six or eight feet above the quarry floor. In the midst of congratulating herself on some clever mountaineering, her foot slipped. 'Eek!' she yelped. For a moment she hovered, wavering back and forth. Then, arms flailing, she hurtled down the remaining distance like a human avalanche.

The gods must have been smiling, for she landed on her feet. Jarred and winded, Karis needed a moment to recover. Then she brushed earth from her backside and looked around. Ahead was the wooden hut, while to her left the cars were parked at angles. What did she do? Having arrived so precipitately, maybe she should take the opportunity to tiptoe nearer? On the other hand, did hightailing it back up the slope make more sense? The opening of the hut door solved her dilemma. The sound acted like a gunshot, and had her diving for cover against the nearest of the three cars. Crouched in its lee, Karis heard the noise of approaching footsteps. Ears pricked, hardly daring to breathe, she listened. The footsteps stopped, and after a moment came a tuneless whistle and the swish of water. She sagged, weak with relief.

When the whistling and water noises continued, she cautiously knelt and peeped through the side window. A roly-poly Thai in crumpled shirt and shorts had begun washing a dark green car, next but one away. Karis looked, and looked again. A frisson of recognition shot through her—he was the man with the birthmark! Sinking back down again, she realised her relief had been premature. She was trapped. If a stranger had been washing the car, then it might have been possible to brazen an exit—something on the lines of her being a holidaymaker who had missed her way—but such a withdrawal had become impossible. If she recognised him, he would certainly recognise her. So, did she remain where she was, feverishly praying he would not move on to clean the car she was pressed up against, or make a dash for it?

Karis frowned at the slope she had slithered down. To obtain a foothold she would need to approach at a run, and if she bodged the first attempt, the man was not going to stand by obligingly twiddling his thumbs while she made a second. Dare she chance it? After some tortured thought, she decided—no. Maybe Seth would have come up with a better idea, but to her it seemed the best thing must be to sit tight and wait.

How long she waited she had no idea. It seemed like for ever—then some. The man might be an amateur where collecting ransoms was concerned, but he possessed professional status when it came to car cleaning. He soaped. He rinsed. He wiped dry—all with leisurely, loving care. Karis's legs cramped. Her knee joints stiffened. She sneaked a look at her watch. The time for the swim had been and gone. Next came waxing, clearly the little man's forte. He polished, and polished and polished. Hurry up! she implored silently, and was startled to hear her own impatience echoed.

'Not finished yet, old fruit?' someone was calling in a familiar Big Ben voice.

Unfolding rigid limbs, Karis struggled to her knees.

Leon was crossing from hut to car, a dapper, bespectacled Thai walking beside him. The Thai had over-long greasy black hair and wore a pale blue suit. If he was Dejo, she disliked him on sight. His swaggering gait, a beadiness about his eyes, told of a street-smart mentality.

'Sorry, but I need the Toyota now,' her stepfather apologised, smiling at the cleaner. 'If I don't leave for the airport straight away, I'll miss my plane.'

There was a snatch of Thai, obviously a joky repartee, before the little man collected up his bucket and cloths and ambled away. As Leon climbed into the car, winding down the window to listen to his companion, so his bushy silver brows come low. At ease with the birthmarked man, now his attitude had changed. The Thai spoke, but though Karis strained to hear all she could pick up was a murmur. Leon's reply, however, would have carried to the back stalls.

'What I'd like to know, Dejo, is what do we do if the trial doesn't go according to plan? The machine's been built in a frightful rush. I admit it looks fantastic, but suppose there are teething troubles? And are you sure your chaps have been properly briefed? They must be on the ball. If something goes wrong, Ang won't give us a second chance.'

His identity confirmed, the quarry owner appeared to murmur a platitude, but Leon remained disgruntled. 'I objected to this at the beginning and I object to it now,' he declared. Again Dejo tried to pacify him and this time was successful, for when he next spoke Leon had become the busy organiser. 'I'll ring from Singapore to confirm that Ang and I will be on that first flight tomorrow as planned. Now, don't you forget to telephone the hotel and re-check the luncheon booking. We want the private room, the flowers, the champagne. And do make sure the management realise exactly how important Ang is. Insist they provide nothing but the best.'

Dejo smiled, making a comment which drew a stormy look.

'I understood I had no choice,' Leon proclaimed. 'That being the case, I see no reason why matters shouldn't be done properly. I want tomorrow to be a success. I *need* it to be a success. Everything depends on pleasing Ang. When he leaves Phuket there has to be a smile on his face, and a contract in our pockets.'

Dejo said something else.

'That's not the point!' her stepfather bellowed, starting the engine. 'Not the point at all.'

The Thai watched until the dark green car had disappeared, then shrugged and headed back into the hut. He closed the door behind him. Karis waited. She allowed one minute to pass. Two. When the door remained closed, she rose to her feet. She faced the slope, adopted an athlete's stance, and ran.

Whipped by necessity and fear, she galloped all the way up the hill without stopping. At the top her momentum cut out, and she clung on to a palm tree, gasping in breaths. Slowly she recovered, and slowly she began to walk back across the headland. Although the one-sided conversation she had overheard raised as many questions as it answered, the crucial factor was that Leon's treachery had been confirmed. Karis winced. Yesterday she had felt threatened, now she was—crippled.

'Oh, Mum,' she muttered. 'How could he?'

Her pace increased. This double-dealing was too much to cope with alone. Help was required. She needed to talk to Seth, needed his broad shoulders to cry on, needed to be cuddled. She knew he couldn't change anything, but at least he could evaluate the situation, decide what to do next. From walking, she began to jog. Seth would make her feel better. It was imperative she hurry to him—her partner. She needed to be with him— she must! On high-velocity legs, she powered across the headland, down to the beach, along the sand, up the steps and towards the cabanas.

'Karis!'

Her head whipped round, and the sight of him calling from outside the reception area sent a stupid grin spreading across her face. As she swerved in his direction, so Seth began to move towards her. Her relief at seeing him was matched, for he, too, wore a broad grin. They met in the middle of a lawn. He opened his arms wide and Karis ran straight into them.

'I'm so glad to see you,' she blubbered.

'Not half as glad as I am to see you,' he said, holding her so close against his chest she could feel his heart beating. He pushed his face into her hair. 'Mmm, you still use that apple shampoo. You still smell gorgeous.'

Her grin became a fixture. In the context of endearments a hug was not much, even less a public one, yet to be enfolded in his embrace had released a kind of suppressed lightning.

'Where on earth have you been?' Seth questioned. 'You've had me worried stiff! When I went to collect you for our swim, you weren't in your cabana, you weren't on the beach. I spent a good half-hour searching the grounds, then went into the restaurant. No joy there, either.'

Karis nestled closer. 'They seek her here, they seek her there,' she quoted.

'And you were damned elusive, Miss Scarlet Pimpernel!' He gave a rueful laugh. 'At that stage I confess I began to get a bit uptight. I questioned the staff, visitors, and learned you *had* been on the beach. Only one minute you'd been seen walking at the edge of the ocean, the next you'd vanished into thin air. I guess then I panicked.'

'I'm sorry.'

'Oh, it's all right, *now*.' He gave her a quick hug before returning to his original question. 'Where have you been?'

'To the quarry. I only meant to have a quick look from a distance, but I slipped and——' The words began bubbling out of her. 'Leon is there—I saw him. I also saw Dejo whatever his name is, and the man with the birthmark. They didn't see me. I hid behind a car, and——' Her voice dwindled away. Seth was gazing at her with glittering dark eyes, but it was his immobility which principally alarmed. Although he continued to hold her in his arms, it was as if he had suddenly realised he was holding Medusa! 'I realise going to the quarry was maybe a little hasty,' Karis gabbled, 'but—well, we did want to discover Leon's location.'

'*We* wanted to discover?' He took a swift backwards step, breaking all connection. 'You mean there are actually two people involved in this?'

Her colour rose. 'You know there are.'

'I know nothing of the sort,' he snapped. 'Not now. There was a time, not too long ago, when I believed you felt passionately about us being partners and I thought—great. However, this morning's escapade proves what I should have known all along, that you're constitutionally incapable of being such a thing.'

'That's not true!'

'Then how do you explain this unilateral action?'

'I acted on impulse. I woke early, went down to the beach and——'

'Ah, the beach,' Seth cut in acidly. 'Do you realise how I felt when I was told you'd been down there? Amusing as it may now seem, I had visions of you climbing amongst the rocks, falling and hitting your head. Or wading into the water, only to be stricken with cramp. First I paced up and down the shoreline, covering it inch by inch!' he stormed, his voice getting louder. 'Then I borrowed some binoculars and did the same with the sea. I even imagined sharks might have attacked you, for God's sake!'

Karis cast a wary look around. Seth's fury had begun to attract attention. A gardener was watching from beneath the shade of a tree, while a room-service waiter, crossing the lawn, had paused to rearrange his tray.

'Don't shout,' she appealed.

'I'll shout if I bloody well want to!'

She flashed an all-encompassing smile and forced herself to look casual. 'I thought it was a social offence to lose your temper in public?' she muttered.

'Have you any inkling of what I've been through?' he raged, not caring one iota. 'Have you?'

'But—but you must have realised I might simply have gone for a walk? Karis suggested. How she wished he would calm down. How she wished the gardener and the waiter would move.

'A walk as in setting off on a solo mission to the quarry?' His lip curled in contempt. 'Yes, the idea did cross my mind but, because I thought better of you, like a fool I dismissed it. What I should have known was that the chances of you *co-operating* were remote to the point of impossibility!'

Karis squirmed. She tried hard to summon up an argument, but found self-defence impossible beneath the weight of their audience's interest. 'Can't we discuss this indoors?' she requested, speaking to her feet.

'No, we damn well can't!' he bellowed.

'Seth, *please.*'

He flicked disdainful hazel eyes over the gardener and the waiter, then relented in so much as he shouted something gritty in Thai. Whatever he had said, it served to remind both men of matters which needed their immediate attention, and they hurried off.

Staring at Karis in a cold, objective kind of way, he resumed his attack.

'A woman who's as self-willed and self-sufficient as you needs no help from outsiders. Why I ever imagined we might operate in tandem is a mystery!'

She summoned up the courage to lock into his gaze. 'I do need help,' she told him in a low, firm voice. 'And you're not an outsider.' Realising she might be opening up an awkward question as to his exact position in her life, she hurried on. 'I went to the quarry on the spur of the moment. I apologise. I didn't mean to worry you. I didn't mean to jump the gun. It—it just happened.'

Seth folded his arms. 'I seem to recall you were long on impulse, short on thinking things through in the past,' he grumbled. 'What would you have done if someone had caught you loitering and decided to lock you up? Or there'd been guard dogs on patrol? Or——' He broke off to sigh. 'Anything could have happened, Karis.'

'But it didn't.' The levelling of his tone seemed to

indicate a cessation of hostilities, and she grabbed for peace. 'I won't break our agreement again,' she assured him. 'In future I'll stick with you. Solo excursions are out, I promise.'

'Cross your heart and hope to die?' he demanded, and she dutifully obliged. Seth awarded her a begrudging grin. Equilibrium had been restored. 'Suppose we go and have breakfast?' he suggested. 'And you can explain all about the dastardly Monsieur Leon.'

Roofed in pine, but open to the garden on three sides, the restuarant was a relaxed, airy place. Seth and Karis joined the twenty or so guests already enjoying their meal. They sat at a round table covered with a pale green cloth, and chose tropical fruits from the menu. Croissants, toast and coffee followed.

'So Leon doesn't seem very happy about what he's doing?' commented Seth, when Karis had repeated the one-sided conversation. 'Well, that's something.' He refilled her cup, then dealt with his own. 'You're sure it was Ang he mentioned?'

'That's what it sounded like from a distance.'

'And he's a V.I.P.?'

'Leon thought so.' Karis saw his frown. 'You have an idea who Ang could be?'

'Yes, and I have one or two other ideas as well.' He drummed strong fingers on the table. 'Chick, I'm afraid this is even more of a can of maggots than we realised. There seems a strong possibility Leon was robbing you in order to rob me. Or rather, to rob the company I work for.' Seth paused. 'Let's consider Ang first. Chances are he's Ang Eng Kiap, a Chinese multi-millionaire who's based in Singapore. The guy has business interests in oil, shipping, property, but the bulk of his wealth comes from the extractive industry. Ang owns mines and quarries through south-east Asia. My company supplies explosives and accessories to many of them.'

'So you know him personally?'

He nodded. 'He's a self-made man who's got to the top through sheer hard work and guts, and because at times he's walked on the wild side.'

'You mean he's dishonest?' Karis queried.

'Not so much now as in the past, but he makes up a cosy triumvirate with Leon and Dejo. He's canny, constantly on the lookout for ways of cutting costs, saving the odd dollar. Which is why he's prepared to fly up tomorrow, on a Sunday. I'd say the original plan was to stage the trial early next week, hence Leon's stated return to Bangkok on Wednesday, but Ang's business commitments got in the way. Probably Sunday's his only free day.' Seth drank a mouthful of coffee. 'Ang's also partial to red-carpet treatment. Leon flying to meet him in Singapore and escorting him to Phuket is the kind of touch he'd expect. No doubt they'll travel first class, with Leon providing the tickets. And you can bet Ang'll be wined and dined in style this evening, as well as tomorrow.' He looked at her over the rim of his cup. 'Sad to say, you're financing all this.'

'I hope they both go down with food poisoning!'

'Ditto,' he said wryly. 'But let's move on to the reason for Ang's visit. A trial with a machine.'

Karis had already leapfrogged ahead. 'The machine could be your mixer, couldn't it?'

'All the signs point that way. Agreed there's the chance we're adding up two and two and making five, but the mixer would seem to slot in perfectly. If Leon and Dejo managed to outflank the company by tying

Ang down to an agreement, they'd be sitting pretty.'

'Then I suppose we must place Leon in the bar when Kovit's briefcase went missing,' she said slowly. 'He could have removed it, taken photocopies of the contents, and pushed the briefcase back under the seat later.'

'Yes, except that Kovit knows Leon and there's no way he'd miss his dulcet tones if he'd also been there that night.' Seth frowned. 'He never mentioned him.'

In silence they assessed the situation. There had been a grave shift, Karis thought with alarm. No longer a matter of just her money going missing, this had become a case of big-business exploitation. Seth's company had invested much time and money in developing the on-site mixer. Time and money which could not be wasted. She braced herself. A question needed to be asked.

'Do—do you think we should bring in the police?' she stammered.

His smile showed he understood how much the question had cost. 'Not unless we're forced to,' he said gently.

'But won't your superiors consider that the correct procedure, the only procedure?'

'Probably, but my superiors can go jump in a lake. I don't always put business first, you know. If you don't want to involve anyone official, then for the moment we won't.'

Karis felt a slither of relief. Whatever Leon had done, he was still a member of the family. She knew her need to protect him didn't make much sense, but it was the way she felt.

'Then what do we do?' she asked. 'The trial mustn't go ahead.'

'You and me appearing on the scene at the appropriate time should be enough to halt matters. I reckon Leon'll give up gracefully when he sees us. He might be a rogue, but he lacks the killer instinct. Remember, he didn't misappropriate *all* your funds,' Seth said cryptically. 'Just enough to finance this little caper. Ergo, when he comes face to face with the enormity of what he's done, he'll capitulate.'

'I hope so.'

'He will.' Seth sounded certain.

Karis fidgeted with the spoon which sat in the sugar bowl. 'Will the cost of this trial amount to the full one million and a half *baht*?' she enquired.

'I reckon so. The mixer's constructed from special steel. It's also had to be built at speed, which means there'll have been incentive bonuses, backhanders, bribes, call it what you will. Add in the explosive mix, air fares, meals and the rest, and I'd say your stepfather's got his sums right.'

'He won't have syphoned any money off for his own use?' she asked hesitantly.

'Doubt it.' Seth saw her unease. 'You're thinking he might be short of cash, and an injection would enable him to renew his membership of the golf club, or employ servants?'

'Not the golf club. Not servants. I just——' She writhed. 'I don't like the idea of him spending money on Monika.'

'Good lord, is that what's troubling you?' Well, take my word, he won't be.'

'But you did say they were close . . . and I wondered if they'd been lovers before he met my mother . . . and maybe even while they were married . . . and if he'd cheated on my mother that way then I'd hate it if her money, and basically it is hers, went on him and Monika having a good time.'

'Karis, calm down!' He stretched a hand over the table and touched her fingers. 'It's true Leon and Monika were friends before he met your mother, but I'd stake my life on them being platonic friends. It's only since her death they're supposed to have become lovers.'

She looked wan. 'They couldn't have been having an affair behind her back?'

'No. Throughout their marriage, I never saw him with Monika. Neither did I hear the least whisper to suggest he might be seeing her on the sly. Which means he wasn't, because in the expatriate community it's impossible to keep anything a secret. You blow your nose and someone knows about it. As for pelvic tilts——' Seth rolled his eyes, coaxing out a grin. 'Look,' he continued, 'there's nothing we can do about Leon for the time being, so why don't we forget the bastard and enjoy ourselves? Ever been to a Muslim fishing village on stilts?'

His enthusiasm was infectious, and Karis grinned again. 'Not until to-day,' she said.

The village, it transpired, was off the coast of Phangnga, a province to the north of Phuket, and here they boarded a long-tailed boat which skimmed them across mangrove into the heart of Phangnga Bay. Surrounded by mountains and glittering diamond-bright in the sun, the blue waters were scattered with exotic pinnacles which rose up from the deep for no apparent reason at all. Everything seemed unreal; the limestone rocks sheering upwards like giant stalagmites, the rugged little islands, the gaping caves. Karis gaped as well, and found herself enjoying the sights.

The stilt village, like everything else, had her reaching for her camera. A dangerously fragile construction, looking like a jetty which had lost sight of its limitations, the village included shops, houses, even a school. Wooden walkways served as streets, and although one end of the salt-sprayed timbers was connected to a small, rocky island, the entire community lived over the sea.

'That Panyi,' their boatman said, gesturing towards the island. 'No one live there. Just goats.' When Seth spoke in Thai, he looked startled for a moment, then laughed. 'And the dead,' he translated for Karis's benefit, and went on to explain how there was also a cemetery.

Delighted to find his European client was not just another tourist, the boatman exerted himself to please. Skilfully skipping between Thai and broken English, he introduced them to inhabitants, swapped jokes, showed them how the shrimps which comprised the village's staple economy were dried.

'Before we leave I get you shrimp paste. Very good price,' he insisted, as he proudly led the way into what he assured them was the best of the seafood restaurants. After giving a waiter long and involved instructions on how he must look after them, the boatman departed.

'You speak the language and the result's all this!' Karis exclaimed, as the table was loaded with plates of lobster and prawns and fish and rice and salads.

Seth laughed. 'It's not me who's made an impression. It's you. The Thai male is very much like the French. He's turned the admiration of beautiful women into a national pastime, and after a diet of dusky maidens a

cool, blonde English rose tends to make him delirious.'
His lower lip moved enticingly. 'You must have
noticed?'

'Er, no,' she said, not feeling cool at all. How could
she, when he was smiling at her like that? And who was
he referring to, the boatman or himself? Had Seth's
palate become jaded by dusky maidens? she wondered.
If so, was it a temporary state or a permanent one?

The arrival of tankards of Singha beer left no chance
for her to take the thought further. Obeying the waiter
who exhorted them to eat well, they began their meal.
Fragrant with herbs, each dish was tastier than the
previous one. The conversation drifted, beer was drunk,
and when the boatman returned, both of them were
drowsy. Regardless, he marched them off to purchase a
smelly jar of shrimp paste. Next he insisted they must
not leave without a piece of coral, shells and a sea-
urchin, and so they were laden when he finally allowed
them back into his boat.

The afternoon was spent speeding from one island to
another. One had been featured in a James Bond film,
their guide explained with glee. On another he showed
them a cave, its walls covered in prehistoric-type
paintings. Wind-whipped and glowing, they returned to
the mainland as the sun was setting. When Seth paid he
added a generous tip, thus ensuring they climbed into
the Porsche to the accompaniment of smiling thanks. It
had been a good day.

When they reached the hotel, it was dark. Walking
across a lawn patterned with silver shadows, they were
in the midst of fixing a time to meet for dinner, when
Karis remembered something. That morning they had
telephoned the airport to discover the time of the first

flight in from Singapore, but the line had been engaged. Seth had tried the number a second time, and a third, but in the end had had to arrange for the receptionist to obtain the information for them. The girl had promised to have a note pushed under his door.

'Mind if I see when Leon's plane's due?' Karis asked. 'If we're in for a crack-of-dawn start tomorrow, I'd like to know now.' A moment of insecurity struck and her face clouded. 'The more time I have to prepare myself mentally, the better.'

'Chick, you're bound to feel jumpy about the confrontation, but——' Seth took a key from his hip pocket, and unlocked the door, 'I realise it's pointless telling you not to worry, but remember you won't be alone.'

'Then—then we're partners again?'

He grinned. 'Yes. Ignore this morning. I was just so damned wound up about you going missing that I said things I didn't mean. But I mean what I'm saying now— we're in this together.'

His assurance softened her. She smiled. Seth smiled. Time stood still. The night air began to throb. There were no words, for words would have been superfluous. Karis saw all she wanted to know in his eyes. His yearning was unmistakable. But there was also hesitation. He was waiting for her to take the lead. But if she led, where would the path take them? To lovemaking, and to her losing her heart to him again. But what would he do with her heart? The swiftness of his involvement with another woman six months ago rose up like a spectre.

Karis scanned the floor of the tiny vestibule. 'Don't see any flight information,' she said brightly.

A shadow crossed his face, then taking a cue from her, he became mundane.

'I'll ring Reception and find out what's happened.' An enquiry on the bedside phone revealed that the airport had not been contacted. Full of apologies, the girl promised to make amends and come straight back to him. Seth relayed the message, then dumped himself down on the bed. 'Sit down while we wait,' he said, patting the cover.

It was a simple suggestion, yet Karis hesitated. Maybe she was becoming paranoid, but the prospect of joining him on the bed seemed altogether too dangerous.

'No, no, I'll go.' Rapidly she shook her blonde head. 'You can tell me about the flight later, at dinner.'

'Sit down. Please,' he insisted. 'I want to apologise for losing my temper this morning.'

Against her better judgement, Karis sat—carefully. Seth's weight had caused a dipping in the mattress which meant she needed to perch stiff and deliberate in order to avoid falling against him.

'Apology not needed,' she declared, using that shiny bright tone. 'I was wrong to act as I did.'

'Wrong or not, it's a good thing you went to the quarry. If we'd done things my way and left the visit until later we'd have missed Leon and——' The spread of his hands indicated futility. 'I'm sorry I exploded.'

'It was my fault.'

He cast her an amused glance. 'Yes, it was. You have the most amazing effect on me. But then you know that, don't you?'

'Um,' she said breathlessly. *She* had an effect on him, this tall, dark, and undeniably desirable man? He had it the wrong way round. Karis pressed her knees together and sat a little tighter. 'Um . . . no.'

'You do know,' he contradicted. 'No matter what other people throw at me, I invariably keep my cool. But you make me so . . . hot, do you know! And not just hot under the collar.' The air had begun to throb again. His eyes were sending those sensual messages. 'Have you noticed that when you and I touch, we set up an electric current?' He placed an arm around her shoulders. 'Here, I'll show you.'

Caught off balance, even if Karis had wanted to break free it would have been difficult. But did she want to? As Seth's mouth came down and his lips parted hers, her body provided the answer. Within seconds the flames of the passion they had once shared were re-ignited. Karis felt them streak along her limbs like a forest fire. His kiss was brutally deep, erotically bewitching, and when at last his mouth left hers, she was weak.

'I rate that at least a thousand kilowatts,' he murmured, rubbing his index finger on her lips as if to massage in his desire. 'How about you?'

'Maybe,' she managed to say.

'Only maybe?'

If his second kiss, and the ones which followed, were intended to eliminate her doubts they were successful. The electric buzz reduced her to a state of dewy adoration, and when he whispered, 'A thousand kilowatts, yes?' she told him it felt more like a million. Yet somewhere along the way, the mood changed. Seth's mouth roughened on hers. There was a searching, a growing hunger. He eased her down on the bed and his kisses, his caresses, became the sexual onslaught of a man who needs a woman. Lying half beneath him, she felt his urgency and responded. Her desire joined his.

It spiralled. Twisting her fingers into the mane of raven-dark hair, Karis arched against him.

Seth's hands began to move. With his fingertips he caressed her face, her throat, explored the silken swell revealed in the frilled neckline of her blouse. It was not enough.

'You're wearing too many clothes,' he complained.

There was a moment as the lilac cotton fell away and her breasts were exposed, when Karis wondered whether to call a halt, but the touch of his hands worked a wild magic. Wantonly she pressed her full curves into his palms. His head lowered and there was an intoxicating thrill as his tongue coaxed her nipples into eager rigidity.

'Why did we part?' he whispered, pressing his hot mouth between her breasts. 'From the start there was something special between us, something we were fools to deny. I want to make love to you. Darling, we must. These past few days you've been driving me crazy. I've hardly been able to keep my hands off you. All I can think of is how wonderful it felt when I was inside you. I need to be inside you again, Karis. Now.' He eased himself up. 'Take off my shirt. I want to feel you naked against me.'

With trembling hands, she unfastened the buttons. Seth pulled the shirt from his shoulders and moved, rubbing his chest against her. The mat of dark hair scoured the tips of her breasts.

'I remember all the things you like,' he whispered, as she gasped. He moved again. 'This and ... this.'

The caress of his hand on her inner thigh made her gasp again.

'And I remember what you like,' said Karis, needing

to talk in order to gain a smidgin of control. She thought of how he had once teased her. 'Or what you would like.'

'My toes being sucked by a lovely woman? But you were never in agreement.' Seth gave a low, delicious chuckle. 'Are you now?'

'No!'

'Spoilsport.' He heaved a huge sigh. 'Here I am, thirty-four years old, and never had my toes sucked!'

Karis drew away. 'Never?' she asked, remembering the achingly beautiful Thai girl.

'Never.'

The assurance was not enough. 'Leon told me,' she began, falteringly, 'that he met you one evening soon after you came back from seeing me. You were with—someone.'

'Yes, I was.' Seth gave a curious laugh. 'Boy, was that some night!'

Karis stared. She had not expected him to lie, but she had not expected this air of amazement at what a spectacular night it had been. Struggling to rationalise the admission with his current and so obvious desire, she barely heard the knock at the door. It was Seth, murmuring an oath and pushing himself upright, who notified her of an arrival.

'You'd better disappear for a moment, chick,' he suggested. 'Me stripped to the waist isn't going to cause ripples.' Hazel eyes stroked her breasts. 'You might.'

In a daze, Karis grabbed up her clothes and scuttled away into the bathroom.

'I've brought the flight time you required, sir,' she heard a voice say.

It was the receptionist, spouting renewed apologies and reporting that the Singapore plane landed at ten.

While the girl chatted, Karis hastily dressed. She must go—leave. She and Seth could not make love—now.

'The girl was hanging on to his arm,' her stepfather had reported. 'And she wasn't one of your demure types like Sukanya, she was a real ring-a-dinger.'

Karis knew what that meant. Seth had been out with a good-time girl, and had a good time. Fine, that was his prerogative. And if there had been a succession of good-time girls since then, that was his prerogative, too. But she was not about to join their number!

Head held high, she swept out of the bathroom and across the room. Flashing an excuse-me smile at the receptionist, she spoke to Seth.

'I'm going now. I'm tired, so I won't bother with dinner. I'll see you at breakfast.'

'But, Karis——' he began in bewilderment.

'Tomorrow, eight a.m. OK?'

'No, it's not OK!'

He was too late, she had gone.

CHAPTER EIGHT

ANTICIPATING protests about her hot-and-cold behaviour, Karis arrived in the restuarant the next morning armed with a series of short, peppery retaliations. *She* had no interest in repeating what had been, as could be seen from its end result, an ill-conceived affair. *She* had learned lessons. *She* was not interested in seduction. Thinking over this last point, she frowned. Better not say that. Last night Seth had not seduced her. Instead it had been a synchronised desire.

To her relief, which felt suspiciously like irritation, Seth made no mention of her grand exit. Instead he was the courteous companion, pouring coffee, passing the butter, making amiable small-talk. When she realised he had no intention of chastising her for her change of mind, Karis's irritation grew. His sunny equanimity became an affront. Talk of electricity he might, yet switch off the current and he didn't give a damn!

'Jitters about seeing Leon troubling you?' he enquired, when her responses became briefer and curter.

No, you are! she was tempted to snarl. Instead she gave a plastic smile and assured him she was fine.

'We need to follow the road until just before the works entrance, then cut off up the hill. That'll bring us to the quarry top,' he explained, jollying her along as though she were an invalid. 'The trial will be taking place there. We'll keep out of sight until the ungodly trio make their appearance, and then——'

'Beard the lion in his den?' Karis demanded impatiently.

After caring so much, feeling so hurt, about Leon's

treachery, this morning she could barely focus on it at all. What was done, was done. Now her sole aim was to have the issue settled, one way or another, and to leave Thailand—and Seth—for good.

After breakfast they checked with the airport and, on receiving confirmation that the flight was on time, set off. Forest grew up on either side of the narrow metalled road, and they walked a few yards in, taking care to keep hidden. Above the sun shone high in a deep blue sky, and although the trees provided shade the humidity was stifling. Damp plastered Seth's shirt to his back. Wisps of Karis's hair escaped from her topknot and hung limply around her face. On the alert for passing vehicles, they crouched low when an empty lorry rumbled by. Tramping on, it was only minutes before the sound of a second vehicle had them seeking cover again.

'That's Leon,' Karis hissed, as a dark green Toyota whizzed past.

With a renewed sense of purpose, they continued their trek. A painted board marked the quarry boundary, and here they altered course to clamber up a hillside thick with vegetation. Progress was slow. Thickets needed to be skirted, or sometimes waded through. Creepers lay in wait. Vines threatened to strangle. When they reached the top, they were bedraggled and panting. Moving stealthily, they made their way through the undergrowth, until a nod from Seth indicated a halt. Karis had never been on the top of a quarry before, and as they waited, catching their breath, she took note of their surroundings. A few yards ahead the tangled greenery came to an abrupt end. Trees had been razed, the hilltop levelled, topsoil removed, to expose a barren wasteland. This stretched forward to a jagged edge, where the limestone fell vertically down to the quarry floor.

They had only been there a minute or two, when a

low-pitched rumble warned of the approach of a heavy vehicle. At the far end of the quarry top a yellow truck was labouring up from the work site below.

'Perfect timing,' whispered Seth, as the vehicle came on to the level. He nodded his head towards a machine carried on the back. 'That's the star performer,' he said, sounding impressed, but all Karis saw was something similar in appearance to a common or garden concrete mixer. With eager eyes, Seth inspected the small hopper fixed to the machine, and an electric pump. Both gained his approval. 'Enter the bad guys,' he muttered, as the Toyota appeared.

The truck lumbered to a standstill half way along the top of the quarry and the car followed, drawing up alongside. When her stepfather and Dejo climbed out, Karis needed to swallow hard. Bloody-mindedness over Seth meant she had spared few thoughts for Leon, but seeing him again brought everything back. Despondency swept over her. This was the man she and her mother had trusted. This was the man who had cheated on one of them, and maybe on both.

'Here we are, chaps,' her stepfather declared, in his microphone voice.

He smartened the line of his black linen safari jacket, and smilingly inclined. His manner, as he opened the Toyota's rear door, reminded her of a deferential chauffeur.

'Ang Eng Kiap,' Seth identified, when a portly Chinese in his fifties emerged, blinking against the sunshine. 'I was right.'

Karis cringed. If only he hadn't been! If only Leon had played things straight. If only he, Dejo, Ang, mixer and all would disappear in a puff of smoke. Karis felt the urge to turn on her heel and run. And run. And run. Where, it didn't matter. Any place had to be preferable to here.

Roles appeared to have been assigned, for while Leon chatted with the millionaire, Dejo gave instructions. Three workmen had climbed down from the cab of the truck, and with what seemed to be a Thai equivalent of an 'aye, aye, sir', they leapt aboard the platform and began attending to the mixer. As wires were attached and hydraulics organised, Seth gave a hushed, explanatory commentary. Sacks of chemicals were opened and measured quantities placed inside the mixer. A liquid solution was added.

'See where the blast holes have been drilled?' he said, pointing to a line of small dust pyramids spaced several yards apart along the quarry edge. 'When the mixture's ready it'll be tipped into the hopper and pumped to the holes through a hosepipe.' He frowned. 'We ought to make our entrance in a second or two, before things get too involved.'

Karis's head throbbed. The notion of confronting her stepfather seemed appalling. 'Must we?' she quaked. 'Couldn't we wait a little while longer?'

'Chick, it's now or never.'

She took a deep breath. 'Then it's now.'

'Good girl!'

No time was allowed to change her mind, for Seth grabbed hold of her hand and walked her quickly out of the jungle. Both of them were wearing soft-soled shoes, which made their approach silent; yet it seemed they had also become invisible. Leon was telling a joke, clearly a good one, and he and Mr Ang were engrossed in anticipating the punch line. Dejo and his employees were busy with the truck. But surely one of the group would turn and see them? The constant expectation of discovery had Karis gripping Seth's hand hard. They kept walking and walking, and had covered a good fifty paces before their presence drew attention.

It was Dejo who saw them first. He lifted his head and gazed with startled eyes. His mute cry of surprise was a cinematic action. A whiplash of his hand alerted her stepfather, whose astonishment looked no less theatrical. He jolted back, and Karis saw his Adam's apple quiver as he gulped. An awareness of something gone wrong passed down the line. It affected the millionaire next. He swivelled to monitor their approach. Finally the workmen stopped their exertions, and stood and stared.

'Good morning, Mr Ang,' said Seth, in a voice geared more to an immaculate three-piece business suit than the soggy tee-shirt and creased moleskin trousers he wore.

The Chinese bobbed his head and answered in equally formal terms. 'Good morning, Mr Mauroy.' He paused. 'Might I enquire what are you doing here?'

'I thought, sir, that as you'd travelled all the way from Singapore to watch a demonstration of technology developed by my company, it was only proper I be on hand.'

'Technology developed by *your* company?' He swung from Seth to the dazed Leon, moved on to Dejo, then returned to Seth. 'Would you explain?'

'Mr Thorburn will be better at that than me.' Seth moved a gracious hand. 'Would you do the honours, Leon?'

Karis's stepfather went puce. He cleared his throat, sending his Adam's apple lurching again. He drew himself to attention, took a breath, and opened his mouth. No sound came out; the actor had left his script at home. Karis's emotions pitched and tossed. Seeing her stepfather lost for words was an odd sensation, a sensation she did not like. Her head might tell her he was a villain, yet her heart was awash with sympathy.

'Seth,' she appealed.

'What Mr Thorburn's trying to say,' he explained, acceding to her request, 'is that the mixer has been built to specifications drawn up by my company, and that the explosives formula also belongs to us. Unfortunately our drawings went missing a few days ago, and were—used.'

The Chinese turned to Leon. He was a good foot shorter, yet at that moment appeared to tower over him. 'Is this true?' he demanded.

Her stepfather strove to recover from his shellshock. He shoved his hands in his jacket pockets and frowned. The truck and its load were cast a swift glance, before he blatantly relinquished ownership. 'Yes, but it wasn't me who took the drawings,' he croaked. He coughed, and spoke to Seth. 'It was Dejo. He'd overheard your chap, Kovit, talking about the mixer. We'd arranged to join up for a drink, and when I arrived at the bar I found Dejo outside carrying Kovit's briefcase. He explained what he'd done and—and——' His vocal chords had been operating with difficulty, now they seized up.

'You saw a chance to make money, and copied the papers?' Seth completed for him.

'I didn't want to. From the start I said the idea wasn't pukka.' Leon speared a look sideways. His partner speared one back, but said nothing. 'Dejo insisted. He left me no option but to go along with——'

'You can try and make Dejo the fall guy,' Seth pointed an impaling finger, 'but *you* are involved in this piece of chicanery right up to your goddam neck. Maybe the original idea was his——'

'It was.'

'—but you've played your part. And how! I can understand you being unable to resist the chance to do the dirty on me and the company. Snaffling the mixer out from under our noses must have seemed very neat.' Seth's grip on Karis's hand tightened, and they strode forward. 'But to fund the operation with Karis's money? For crissakes, man,' he blasted, 'how low can you get! What harm has Karis ever done you?'

Leon's throat needed to be cleared again. 'None.'

'Yet you calculatingly defraud her of a million and a half *baht*?' His nostrils flared. 'You disgust me!'

'Did you feel the money should rightfully have been yours, not mine?' demanded Karis, cutting into the conversation. She accepted that this was neither the time nor the place for discussing family matters, but her need to know proved compulsive. 'Were you expecting my mother would leave it to you when she died?' Her throat stiffened. 'Did—did you marry her under the impression you were getting a rich wife? Did you marry her simply for—for money?'

Leon's colour drained. From being red-faced, he was white. 'Good God, no! I loved Ruth, that's why I married her. Naturally I was aware she had something in the bank, but I didn't want it. Karis, you don't think——? You can't think——?' He gulped, and the gleam of tears shone in his eyes. 'Karis, your mother was the best thing that ever happened to me.'

'I believe you,' she said quietly. Leon might be an actor, but these were no scripted lines. His distress was real. This time he was telling the truth. His words were like balm, healing her pain. She sighed. The worst had been surmounted, yet his treachery against *her* remained. 'It must have been you who set up the kidnapping, Leon,' she rebuked. 'You were the one who knew I had the money available.'

'Dejo knew, too. And the kidnap was his idea.'

'Stop loading the blame elsewhere!' snapped Seth. 'Confess, Leon. You saw a chance to gather your illgotten gains while you might.'

'I *didn't*! I found the idea of a fake kidnapping highly

repulsive,' her stepfather replied, his conversation festooned with italics. 'I didn't want *anything* to do with it, but—but I'd opened my *big* mouth once *too* often.' He turned to Karis. 'I'd told Dejo how your aerobics studio had been failing.'

'Failing?' inserted Seth.

Leon spared a moment to nod, then continued. 'I'd told him how you'd been on the point of admitting defeat and closing shop when the hotel came along with their offer. I'd boasted about how you'd doubled your money. He knew it'd fallen into your lap like pennies from heaven. His argument was that having acquired the cash so easily, it wouldn't matter so much if you lost——'

'Excuse me a moment,' Seth intruded. 'There are one or two things I don't understand. Like why the hotel should have put in an offer if——' he jerked at her hand, as if to claim her full attention '——the studio was in such a sorry state.'

'It doesn't matter now,' Karis said hurriedly.

'Oh, they weren't interested in the studio,' her stepfather explained, failing to decode her 'shut up!' look. 'It was the land they were after. They wanted to extend their car-parking space.'

'So the studio's been demolished?'

Leon nodded. 'Knocked down in jig-time.'

Seth turned, fixing her with accusing brown eyes.

'You never told me that.'

'I didn't give you the complete picture,' she mumbled.

'No, you damn well didn't. In fact, you lied through your back bloody teeth!'

Karis's cheeks burned. Everyone was looking at her. She felt like a witness who had gone to court to give evidence in a murder trial, and been unexpectedly denounced as the person seen firing the gun.

'I'll fill you in,' she said, in a voice which defied him to argue. 'So you'd spread the word about my good luck, Leon? So?'

'Dejo knew you had money going begging. Sort of. I didn't have enough spare cash to finance something as expensive as the mixer, because I've always lived up to my income. As you know, I appreciate good food and wine, quality clothes, decent hotels. Don't own any horses now, but in my thirties I played the odd chukka or two of polo. That meant stabling, which cost a mint, and——'

'We get the message,' Seth advised drily.

Having momentarily bounced back, the older man dropped down. 'I didn't have the wherewithal.' He glanced at the quarry owner. 'Neither did he. He'd overheard Kovit mention forthcoming trials, which meant time was of the essence. The money had to come from somewhere, fast.'

'You decided I'd be an easy touch?' Karis asked.

'Not me, Dejo. He thought up the kidnapping, and I went along with it. I had to.'

'Could we ascertain why?' asked Seth.

Mr Ang joined in. 'Yes, why?'

'Tell them, Leon,' taunted an accented voice. Dejo had forsaken the role of bystander to stand with hands on hips and jaw thrust out. The eyes behind the rimless spectacles shone with malice. 'Tell everybody why, *old fruit.*'

'I intended to return your money, Karis,' her stepfather cried. 'If the trial was a success I stood to make millions of *bahts*, and I was going to give you back your stake, plus interest. I regarded the cash as no more than a loan really. Pet, I'm fond of you—very fond. And you're Ruth's daughter, dammit. You don't think I'd

have gone along with all this unless my arm was being
twisted?'

'But how *was* Dejo twisting your arm?' Seth
demanded impatiently.

Leon took a backward step. 'I—I can't explain. Please
believe I never had designs on your money, Karis.'
There were two more steps of retreat. 'Please believe me
when I say reasons exist which left me no choice.'

His withdrawal had separated him from the group,
and Dejo went in pursuit.

'Reasons!' he derided, stalking forward while Leon
fell back. 'If you have reasons, state them loud and clear.
Otherwise,' he threatened, 'retract everything you've
said about me.'

'I won't,' her stepfather defied, but a menacing
advance from the Thai forced him backwards again.

'Hold it,' ordered Seth. The gap which the two men
had created meant he needed to raise his voice. 'I'd be
obliged if you'd forget this private vendetta and come
back here.'

Involved in a slanging match, Leon and Dejo took no
notice. Karis watched for a moment, then took a step
forward. She tugged at Seth's hand, urging him to
follow. By shouting instructions over a distance of
several yards, he was putting himself at a disadvantage.
Mr Ang had gone a stride or two ahead, and swivelled to
wait for them. What's holding you back? his expression
said. Karis cast Seth a quizzical look. His delaying tactics
had no rhyme nor reason. Instead of being rooted to the
spot, he should be advancing. Again she tugged at his
hand, and when his fingers tightened on hers she
understood.

All movement had been towards the quarry edge and
the subsequent sixty-foot drop. Still yards away from it,
her stepfather and his companion were in no danger.

Neither would Seth be if he followed. But he *couldn't* follow. Karis looked into his face, and read his fear. Having taken it for granted he had been holding on to her hand to give *her* courage, now she wondered if it could have been the other way around.

'Leon, come here this minute!' she barked. 'And you, Dejo, and you, Mr Ang. I have something to say.' For a moment the trio stood and gaped then, like well-trained dogs, came to group themselves around her. 'As I'm the person who has financed this morning's display, then it's my right to have it cancelled.' Karis spoke to the Chinese. 'However, you are invited to a legitimate demonstration of the mixer in, what——' she glanced at Seth. '——a month's time?'

'Two weeks,' he said, with a smile of gratitude. The squaring of his shoulders showed a recovery. 'I'll phone your office and fix a date, sir.'

Mr Ang nodded. 'I look forward to hearing from you.'

Next Karis turned to the quarry owner. 'Did you steal the drawings?' The Thai scowled. In his world women were an inferior breed, and he did not appreciate being questioned in such a scalpel-sharp manner. 'Did you?' she demanded.

There was a split-second consideration of a denial before he gave in. 'Yes,' he said sulkily.

'And concocting the kidnap was your idea, too?'

'Yes, but Leon——'

'You are aware that Mr Mauroy and I possess ample grounds for summoning the police and preferring charges against you?'

'Please, pet, don't call the police,' her stepfather babbled, gasping in air as though he had forgotten how to breathe. 'If you do my whole life will be in ruins. It's in ruins now, but—oh, the shame!'

Dejo surveyed him with sullen black eyes, his distaste

one hundred per cent proof. If the Thai wanted to get himself off the hook, it would never be by resorting to impassioned pleas.

'Suppose we return the copies of the drawings?' he suggested. 'And the mixer?'

'Plus the pump, hopper, chemicals, the lot,' Seth cut in. 'Deliver the entire package to my works within the next four days, and we'll call it quits. Leon, it's your responsibility to drive up with the gear to see nothing goes astray. If it does——' For the first time since they had walked out of the jungle, he let go of Karis. Two strong hands reached out to mime a throttling of her stepfather. 'You suffer the consequences.'

'Everything will be there,' Leon assured him with a shaky smile.

'Good. And I'd like you two gentlemen to know that should you indulge in any shady deals in future, this matter will be brought to the attention of the authorities. Karis and I intend to write full reports and lodge them with our banks. Understand?'

Dejo pouted. 'Yes,' he muttered.

'We're so grateful. So very, very grateful,' Leon declared. 'The whole thing's been a ghastly mistake. The matter escalated so quickly, I had no control.' He pressed a hand to his brow. 'I shall be in your debt for ever.'

Seth knifed him with a look.

'It's not over yet. You still have some explaining to do. Karis deserves to know the truth, the whole truth, and nothing but the truth, about this sordid little escapade of yours.'

'She will. She will.'

'She'd better,' Seth said darkly.

Mr Ang inspected his watch. 'I've wasted enough of my time,' he announced. 'Dejo, I'd like to be taken back to the airport. I've no idea when the next flight takes off to Singapore, but with luck I shouldn't have too long to wait.'

'Mind if the rest of us hitch a lift?' Seth enquired, as an advance was made towards the car. 'Karis and I are staying just along the coast, and you'll understand Leon has——' he frowned at her stepfather '—decided to join us for a *tête-à-tête*. If we could be dropped off there, it'd save us a walk.'

'Please, be my guests,' Mr Ang said magnanimously.

It was noticeable that throughout the journey to the bay, Dejo and Leon, who sat in the front, never said a word. In the back, however, Seth and the millionaire talked non-stop, swapping observations on the explosives scene. Squashed between them, Karis felt very much a spare part.

Mr Ang reached for Seth's hand as they arrived at the bay. 'Nice to have met you again,' he said.

'And nice to have met you, sir. I'm just sorry the circumstances were not more—appropriate.'

The millionaire smiled. 'They will be, in a fortnight's time. That mixer of yours has great potential. I'm sure we'll be able to do business.'

Seth grinned, and climbed out of the car. 'Call in on your way back, and collect Leon,' he instructed Dejo through the open window. 'His true confessions should be over by then.'

Her stepfather gave a pale smile.

'Seems you could have made me a friend for life there, Leon,' Seth remarked, as the Toyota disappeared and the three of them walked across the lawn. 'Joined by adversity and all that.'

'Thanks for not bearing a grudge,' the older man mumbled. 'You could have dropped me in the——'

'Yes, I could. But it's Karis who deserves your

thanks.' Seth ran his fingertips down the back of her bare arm. 'She's the one with the soft heart.'

They sat on the patio amid a bower of bougainvillaea. Seth produced chilled beers and a large bowl of salted peanuts.

'Very civilised,' commented Leon.

'Unlike your behaviour.' Seth's reply was terse. 'Before you start on your confessional, let's deal with the practicalities. Did you dispose of all Karis's money?'

Her stepfather hung his head. 'Every last *baht*. Setting up the trial was expensive. Didn't you think the mixer was rather splendid, though?' he asked, perking up a little.

Seth nodded. 'I hate to admit this, but the damn thing looked superior to the one that's being made for us in Bangkok.'

'A chap with a metalwork shop in the north of Phuket was responsible. I could put you in touch, if you like. After all, if the trial's successful, and there's no reason why it shouldn't be, a fleet of mixers will be required.'

'Supplied through you? Not on your life. You can simply hand over the man's name and leave the rest to me. As far as this mixer goes, I'll arrange for the company to buy it and reimburse Karis the money.'

She smiled. 'Thanks.'

'And I'll make up the shortfall,' her stepfather put in.

'Thanks,' she repeated, somewhat less energetically.

Seth rested back, legs stretched out and hands clasped behind his head. 'Confession's supposed to be good for the soul, Leon. Isn't it time you explained about this hold Dejo has over you?'

'Er, yes.' Her stepfather took a fortifying swig of beer. 'It's—it's to do with my past.' Just a sentence, and already he was making heavy weather. 'How Dejo found out, I've no idea, but—but there was an indiscretion.'

'What kind of indiscretion?' Karis prompted, when he dried up.

At that moment, a gecko, a little lizard, appeared from among the grass. It ran on to the patio and froze, as lizards do. Leon stared at the intruder for a long moment, then lifted his head.

'I have a criminal record. Once, a long time ago, I—I was in prison. Only a month. I worked as a clerk. The pay was a pittance. Some cheques weren't filled in properly, and I——' He was speaking in fits and starts. 'Storm in a teacup really. The sum involved was small. Foolish boy, very young. But the temptation, you know?' His eyes darted between her and Seth. 'I had so little, and the other chaps had so much. Never dreamed there'd be such a ruckus about a few quid.'

'You had so little?' Karis questioned.

'And you were a clerk?' said Seth.

'Yes.'

Seth glanced at her, then spoke for them both. 'You're not making sense. You were the product of an expensive public school, and yet you quote a sob story about being a poorly paid clerk? You'll have to do better than that.'

'I did work as a clerk,' Leon said doggedly.

'Was this before or after your time in the Household Cavalry?'

He studied the gecko again. 'I was never in the Household Cavalry. A long time ago I hinted that way, and because I looked the part everyone appeared to believe me.' He gave an aimless shrug. 'From leaving school to coming to Thailand, I was a clerk in an insurance office. I had a room, not much more than a cupboard really, in Clapham, and when I'd paid the rent there wasn't much left over. I lived on a diet of tinned tomatoes and bread.'

'How come your family didn't help?' Karis asked.

'Yes, your father could have dipped into his pocket,' added Seth.

'He was dead by then, but he never had a shilling to spare in any case. He was a guard on the railways, and my mother worked as a cleaner.' Leon gave a sheepish smile. 'I got to the school by means of a scholarship, you see. Half a dozen were handed out each year for poor boys, and I fell into that category. Even with the fees paid, my parents still needed to sacrifice because the uniform, cricket gear, various in-school club subscriptions needed to be paid for. Naturally, they were thrilled when I won the scholarship, and so was I. But I didn't find it easy, being bottom of the pile.'

Karis frowned. 'The other boys lorded it over you?'

'Some took great sport in taunting me about my background, so I—well, I started to speak like them, act like them, and in time most of them accepted me as one of their own. My father accused me of becoming toffee-nosed. I suppose he was right.' Leon returned to examining the gecko. 'What you have to understand is the frustration I felt, being surrounded by the privileged. What made matters worse was that some of them were dimwits, whereas I had an excellent brain. I was top of the class in just about everything. The masters wanted me to go to university and study law. They said I had a great future. Then, when I was fifteen, my father died. That not only knocked university for six, it meant I had to leave school there and then, without a qualification to my name.'

'And you became a clerk?' asked Seth.

'Yes. My mother received a small pension, but it was only enough to support her, not me. I had to take whatever work was available.' Leon sighed. 'I kept in touch with some of my school chums, but I'm afraid that was my undoing. Being a proud young man, I tried to keep pace, and—and I ended up in prison.'

Seth helped himself to a handful of peanuts from the bowl. 'Did Cecil know?'

Leon nodded. 'He wasn't academic and for years I'd helped him with his homework. This resulted in a bond growing up between us. He was the only one who knew where my mother lived, and when I disappeared, he contacted her. I'd begged her not to tell a living soul what had happened, but she'd always thought what a pleasant chap Cecil was, and she gave the game away. Although he was on the brink of departing to take up a post in Bangkok, he came to see me. He saw my depression, realised how devastated I was at finding myself behind bars. To cut a long story short, I was released one week and found work on a ship the next. I had to get away—staying would have been too demeaning. I spent time in various countries, but eventually wound up in Thailand.'

'Cecil took you on, and over the years you repaid his kindness,' Seth remarked drily.

'He didn't mind me easing out a spot of extra cash. Not too much. He recognised that I'd developed a taste for the high life, and knew I needed all I could get if I was to live like a gentleman. It was only when Ruth came along I began to realise I could be happy with far less.' Leon was thoughtful for a moment, then leant forward and touched Seth's knee. 'Thanks for not forcing my prison record out of me when we were at the quarry. I know you could have done. I also know you feel I'm a get-rich-at-any-price merchant, and I admit in many respects I am. Or was, I should say. But beneath this bold façade lurks——' Leon stopped, as though he had discovered he was blustering and felt ashamed. 'I couldn't bear it if word about my time in prison got out,' he said, taking a simpler path. 'There'd be talk behind my back, maybe I'd be ostracised and—and having a place in society matters very much to me. I need to belong, to be part of a group.' His eyes settled on the gecko again.

'Was my mother aware of all this?' Karis asked.

'I told her before we were married. She understood.' He gave a wistful smile. 'I knew she would. Ruth understood everything about me.'

'Is—is Monika so understanding?' Karis faltered, not wanting to ask the question, but determined the air must be cleared once and for all.

'Monika?' He repeated the name as though he'd never heard it before.

'Your fräulein,' Seth reminded him, reaching forward to take another helping of peanuts.

'Monika used to be a good pal. Before I met Ruth she and I had an arrangement whereby if she received an invitation which stipulated a partner, she'd ask me. And vice versa. It worked well.'

Seth slid Karis a wink. 'There was never any monkey business?' he enquired.

'Not then.' Her stepfather looked pained. 'Monika was always smartly turned out. A credit to a chap, y'know. But she did have a tendency to hog the limelight, and I found that a trifle wearing.'

'I can imagine,' Seth commiserated.

Karis looked away and tried not to smile.

'It was such a relief when I met Ruth. She was so gentle, so comforting.' Leon sighed. 'After she died Monika came to offer condolences, then started dropping by regularly. I'd tell her how wonderful my marriage had been, how lost I felt. In company I could wear a brave face,' he explained, 'but when Monika and I were alone my feelings poured out.'

'She sounds to have been very sympathetic,' Karis commented.

'She was, and yet——' Her stepfather lifted his glass from the low table. 'I regret to say her sympathy had a purpose, because after a while she began dropping hints about *our* relationship developing. She felt that as I'd found such happiness in marriage, I ought to get married again—to her. One evening she became rather amorous.' A tinge of pink suffused his cheeks. 'And I had a moment of weakness and—and we ended up——' He looked pleadingly at Karis. 'I didn't love the woman. I just needed affection. But after that everything changed. Monika said my misery was self-indulgent, told me it was high time I snapped out of it and paid more attention to her. She gave everyone to understand we were lovers. On occasion we were,' Leon said awkwardly, 'but in the main she was a partner at bridge, someone to make up the numbers, a convenience, actually. We'd started pairing up again a couple of months after Ruth died—Monika reckoned it would do me good to get out and about, and I do enjoy meeting people—but as time passed she applied the most tremendous pressure.'

He spoke with such anguish that once again Karis was tempted to smile. 'Oh dear,' she said.

'It was more than "oh, dear", it was damned unpleasant,' her stepfather declared, with a grand air of outrage. 'It reached the stage where if I gave Ruth so much as a passing mention, Monika would round on me. When I invited you to stay, she threw a shocking tantrum. Screamed and stamped, and——' He looked horrified. 'She said if I wanted a morbid trip down memory lane, fine—but count her out. And so she got out.'

'Home on leave?' Seth enquired.

'On leave, but with the intention of looking for a job in Germany. She's a computer programmer, so she shouldn't have any problem getting herself fixed up. She said she'd finished with Thailand. I think maybe I have, too. Here there are so many reminders of Ruth to haunt me, that I think I'd do better to pack everything in and retire to a thatched cottage somewhere.'

Seth popped a peanut in his mouth. 'Thatched cottages don't come cheap.'

'I know, that's the problem. The apartment's mine so I'd get the proceeds from that, but once installed in a cottage there'd be precious little to live on.'

Karis sat up. 'I'll support you,' she said. 'Ever since my mother died I've been thinking about selling the house back home—it's big and old, and not my style. Once I've invested the money from that, and combine it with what I already have, there'll be a sizeable yearly income.'

'You'd do that for me, pet, after—after all that's happened?' stammered Leon.

'Yes, I would,' she replied.

Seth had also sat up. He was on the alert. She could not read his expression but, just to be on the safe side, she thrust him a defensive look. If he thought she was crazy, or too soft for words—let him!

'My mother once told me her life was only half a life until she met you, Leon, and it was true.' Without warning, Karis's eyes filled with tears. 'You're such a contrast to my father. He was hard and sour, a despot through and through. He ruled my mother, and she was never able to stand up to him. He instructed her daily on what to do, what to wear, what to damn well think! And when she did what he wanted to the best of her ability, he paid her back by being critical.' Karis brushed a hand across her eyes. 'My father was a monster. I was *glad* when he died.'

Seth frowned. 'I never knew you felt like that about him.'

'How could you?' she demanded. A primal urge to lash out had taken control, and she lashed out at their relationship. 'In Thailand our time was too precious to waste on talking about him, and in England we did nothing but battle over the aerobics studio.' She turned away to face Leon. 'It'll take me a while to sell the house, but as soon as everything's clear I'll let you know how much of an income will be available.'

'Oh, pet, I don't deserve you!' He took a deep, shuddering breath. 'I tarnished myself early on, but you're solid gold—a diamond, a gem. I never thought that in my old age——'

'Quite so,' said Seth, and earned himself a look of gratitude for cutting off Leon's thespian tendencies before they got out of hand.

Karis spoke to Seth. 'You were right about the aerobics studio. It was suspect from the start. Launching a project like that required serious thought, instead I rushed in. And I should have had more sense than to involve Frances. She might do a very mean skip and shuffle, but otherwise she's hopeless.'

'At least her brother was A-team material,' Leon inserted, showing that although he had forgotten his flowery declarations, there was small chance of his remaining silent. 'Cliff put in a hell of a lot of time, with the idea of making amends for his sister's behaviour,' he explained to Seth. 'The chap worked all day as a butcher, and at night taught martial arts. He never let up. His energy was amazing, especially when you consider he had a house full of——'

'Cliff was great,' Karis said in swift agreement. 'We

don't need chapter and verse.'

'I do.' Seth's voice had acquired a dry edge. 'The fine print sounds fascinating. What does Cliff have in his house?' he asked Leon.

The older man frowned, realising he was guilty of having said too much. 'Children,' he muttered.

'How many?'

'Four. Two girls and two boys,' he could not stop himself from adding.

'Interesting.' Seth gave Karis a look which made her shrivel. 'I would never thought your solid-gold step-daughter the type to have an affair with a married man.'

'She's not! She isn't!'

'Then would you kindly explain why you chose to give me the impression they were lovers?'

'Because I felt sorry for her. I knew the state she was from her letters, and——'

'What state was that?'

Karis leapt to her feet. 'I was upset. Is that so remarkable? Look, I'm hot and sticky, and if you'll both excuse me I'm desperate for a shower.'

Throughout her outburst, Seth's gaze had remained on Leon.

'What state was that?' he repeated, as though she had never spoken.

'Well, upset and—and alone, and still very much in love with you,' Leon elaborated, moving into his usual expansive style. 'I felt it would have been disloyal to Karis to reveal how broken up she was, so I pretended she was coveted.'

Now Seth shifted his hazel eyes to Karis.

'I thought you were desperate to have a shower, my ... coveted chick?' he drawled, his full lower lip quirking.

'I—I am,' she vowed.

For a moment she remained motionless, looking into his eyes. Then, unable to cope with the message she read there, she sped away.

CHAPTER NINE

THE shower lasted a long time. Karis was busy psyching herself up into the right frame of mind to face Seth again. The emotion she had seen in his hazel eyes had been love. Once she would have been delighted, now scepticism ruled. Love! Hadn't someone once said falling in love is like going down with the measles? In Seth's case, the description seemed particularly apt. When he had loved her before, it had taken the form of a fevered bout. Any physician, noting his delirious speech, the rashness of his smiles, would have written him off as beyond recovery. Yet in no time at all he had recouped his good health. Such a turnaround would have demanded a re-think of medical science. It had certainly demanded a re-think from her!

Karis turned off the jet of water and reached for a towel. Yes, his look had said he loved her—in his measly way—but it had also revealed that he knew she continued to love him, six months on. That when she had fallen in love it had not been a temporary illness, but a fatal affliction. This meant Seth was bound to make an approach, an approach which must be resisted. Somehow she had to find a way of exiting from the scene with dignity. Her dignity mattered, and her pride. With his love so shallow, he must never know the depth of hers. The imbalance was degrading.

She stepped into a pair of stone-coloured cropped trousers and topped them with a loose, silky top, cut low at front and back. Catching up her hair with one hand, Karis located a length of narrow black ribbon and fashioned a style which sat a glossy, blonde doughnut on top of her head. Make-up came next. Already tanned by the tropical sun, all she needed was a light fingering of beige/gold eyeshadow, jet mascara brushed on her lashes, a touch of lipgloss. She was ready. A mask which approximated the cool modern woman had been achieved. Yet as she closed the door behind her and walked across to Seth's cabana, she felt woefully unprepared. Suppose he asked questions, made statements centring on her never having stopped loving him—how did she answer? Could she bluff her way out? Karis fussed with her hair, a sure sign of agitation. She suspected none of her repudiations would be believed; which meant her dignity and pride were destined to be trampled to pulp.

She was approaching the bank of bougainvillaea, when—clickety click—a way of escape came to her. She grinned, and increased her pace to round the bushes at a canter. Surprise acted as a brake—the patio was empty. Pushed back chairs and discarded, half-filled glasses gave evidence of a hasty departure. As a precaution, Karis called indoors, but received no reply. Across the patio she pounded, past the hedge of purple blossoms and out again on to the grass. She stopped short when she saw Seth ambling towards her.

'Where's Leon?' she demanded. 'I want to hitch a lift to Bangkok. I assume he's leaving today, and now that everything's been sorted out I'd like to get back there.'

'But everything hasn't been sorted out, chick. Has it?' He stopped in front of her and folded his arms. 'What about you and me?'

'What about us?' Karis became the personification of chutzpah. 'We're ancient history, a past number, obsolescent. Now, if you could kindly direct me towards my stepfather I'll——'

'He's gone.'

'Gone? Already?' Her chutzpah went splat. 'But I didn't think Dejo would be back for ages.'

'Apparently he arrived at the airport just as a Singapore flight was being announced. He waited until Ang had checked in, then turned the car around and came straight back. He collected Leon minutes ago. Your stepfather left burbling profuse apologies. He said he'll see you in Bangkok in a few days.'

'But I want to travel there with him now,' Karis wailed.

'No.'

'I do! Look, if you run me to the quarry——'

'No!'

'Seth, one of the reasons you came down here was to lie on a beach.' She wafted a hand towards the arc of white sand. 'There's a beautiful one. Go and lie on it, while I head back to Bangkok.'

'No.'

'Can't you say anything except no?' she demanded, almost hopping with frustration.

His lower lip moved. 'Ask the right question and there's a strong likelihood I'll say yes.'

'You're impossible!'

'At times. And so are you.' He took hold of her elbow. 'Let's go and talk about it.'

Karis shook him off. 'I don't want to talk.'

'But if you remove that option, all we're left with is

either battling on or making love.' He gave her a wink. 'I know my choice.'

'We'll talk.'

On the patio Seth poured fresh beers, then sprawled back in his chair. With a glass in his hand and feet resting on a low rattan table, he looked the relaxed holiday-maker. Only the gravity of his brown eyes said different.

'Last night——' he began.

'Forget last night, it was a mistake,' said Karis, cutting in and cutting off. 'What I'd like to know is, do you understand why I made the offer to finance Leon?'

'Yes, I do.'

'And you approve?'

'You want my approval?'

'No,' she said, but she did.

Seth lifted his glass and gazed through the amber liquid at the sun. 'In your shoes I guess I'd have done the same,' he said reflectively. 'Leon and I had a long conversation after you left. He was telling me how the need to be one of the boys had been the driving force of his life. He aspired to the glitterati. My God, how he aspired! He made false claims, created wrong impressions, and ended up with a superficial persona. A persona which, over the years, became difficult to separate from the real Leon Thorburn, and one which needed costly support.' He took a drink of beer. 'I've often wondered why it took him so long to get married, now I know. It seems he was engaged twice, but backed off at the last moment, terrified his fiancée might find him out.' Seth sucked in his lower lip. 'I think that's sad.'

'Poor Leon, he wove a tangled web and got caught up in it himself.'

'With a vengeance. At the time of life when his contemporaries were getting married, having families, he soldiered on alone—through fear of discovery. I told him he was making too big a deal out of his spell in prison, that people don't necessarily throw stones, and he accepted I might have a point. But even so, he said he never trusted anyone until he met your mother. He kept both prison and his humble background dark secrets.'

Karis sighed. 'And when he told her, she didn't mind.'

'Ironical, isn't it? And tragic. Leon reckoned that although he always knew it's the kind of person you are inside that matters, it needed your mother to spell it out loud and clear before the message sank home. He told me he's attempting to reorganise his life and shed some of the flim-flam. He quoted the dismissal of his servants and his resignation from the golf club as examples.'

'He's being re-born?' she asked in amused surprise.

Seth laughed. 'That's the general idea.'

'But he still talks like a master of ceremonies! And I can't ever imagine him going around in chain store clothes, can you?'

'No. Old habits die hard. When he gets to that cottage he'll be dressing for dinner and spending hours agonising over the wine. It's funny, though, by exposing himself as a charlatan, he's gained my sympathy. Even admiration in an odd kind of way. He is, at least, a trier. And merry with it. I can see why you prefer him to your father.' Seth pursed his lips. 'I suspect it was thoughts of your father as much as your mother which prompted you to offer Leon your support?'

'What do you mean?' Karis asked, half indignant,

half curious. She had never been comfortable talking about her father, and wasn't sure how she regarded his abrupt entrance into the conversation.

'Remember I said no one does anything for one reason? Well, how's this for a theory? Isn't it possible you might wish, subconsciously, to make your father pay for the pain he caused?'

'Mmm?' she murmured, waiting.

'The money your mother left, plus the house, originated from your father, yes? So to all intents and purpose, won't he be maintaining Leon? To me it has the hallmark of a posthumous smack in the eye.'

'Does it?' Karis thought for a while. 'Maybe.'

'Your father has a lot to answer for. He was certainly no friend to me.'

'You?' she said in surprise. 'But you never knew him.'

'No, and yet when I lived in his house with you, you saw me as playing his role—to a certain degree.' Seth leant forward. 'Didn't you?'

'This is all getting very deep,' she protested.

'But it makes sense.'

'I suppose it does.' Karis gave a little laugh, surprised at something she had never thought about, but which seemed obvious now. 'I'd been conditioned to resenting my father's attitude, so all you had to do was make a suggestion and I bristled.'

'I noticed. You were very assertive.'

'I was very aggressive,' she corrected.

'Whatever, it was fortunate you never had an axe handy.'

'It's a bit late now to apologise, but I do. At the time I felt you were hounding me, but——' She lifted her shoulders and let them fall. 'I suppose being in my father's environment was at the root of why I felt so damned rebellious.'

'Other factors involved.'

'Like what?' she scoffed. 'We—I never argued when we were together in Thailand.'

'I have a theory on that, too.' Seth took his feet down from the table. 'When I came back here six months ago, I tried to work out what had gone wrong between us. Like you say, in this country everything had been sweetness and light. Move us to another continent, and our relationship fell to pieces. There had to be a reason.'

Karis surveyed him from beneath her lashes. For a man who, weeks later, had dusted himself down, brushed himself off and started all over again, he sounded alarmingly concerned. So damned sincere.

'The reason was me,' she said, trying to appear flip but not quite succeeding. 'Battling Bertha.'

'No, it was me, too. I was at fault.' The sweaty tee-shirt had stuck to his chest, and Seth plucked it free. 'I've given this a lot of thought, and you were right. Sukanya was my puppet. She did what I wanted—not that I ever asked her to do anything she didn't want to do—but I was always the decision-maker. Taking charge seemed second nature. When I look back I can see how I'd taken it for granted that relationships with the opposite sex were like dancing, the man leads, the woman follows.' He frowned. 'Perhaps part of that was because I'd spent my formative years in the East.'

'Where women tend to be more subservient?'

He nodded. 'And in my family life, the idea of women being a passive audience for male derring-do was reinforced. My mother didn't work. It never occurred to her to work. She was content for my father to go out and deal with the world, while she stayed home and arranged flowers.'

'But you went to school in the U.K., and university in France,' Karis pointed out. 'You must have realised plenty of women, particularly the younger ones, prefer to control their own destinies?'

'I did, but I returned to the East when I was in my early twenties, so my exposure to such independence wasn't that great. Meeting you was——' Seth grinned. 'I said before you were a twenty-four-hour cabaret, but I'll change that to a glass of champagne. You sparkled, you refreshed, and I loved the way the bubbles got up my nose. All the women I knew, the women I'd ever met, seemed flat and stale in contrast.' His grin faded. 'Even Sukanya.'

His sombre look disturbed her. 'You had a happy marriage,' Karis insisted.

'We did, and yet——' There was a faraway look in his eyes. 'Shortly before she died, it had begun to dawn on me that I was bored. I know you shouldn't speak ill of the dead, and she was a lovely girl, but she didn't *contribute*. She never took the initiative, never put forward ideas, never ever dreamt of arguing. I know she'd been brought up to be a docile wife and I accept I'd married her on those terms, but——' Seth grabbed a handful of tacky tee-shirt and lifted it off his chest. 'I'm a Western male. I was made to respond to a Western female. It's taken me a long time to realise it, but Oriental girls aren't my style.'

Karis arched a brow. 'No?'

'No.'

'I fear you've been in Leon's company too much of late.'

He frowned. 'What's that supposed to mean?'

'That you're talking humbug.'

'Like hell I am!' he responded, looking quite put out.

'OK, so tell me—exactly when did this revelation about Oriental girls not appealing occur?'

'When I met you.'

'Then how come when you left me, you rushed straight back into a pair of dusky arms?'

'I didn't. Ah!' Seth jabbed a long index finger. 'You're referring to the girl Leon saw me with, the same girl who had you rushing out of here yesterday evening. I wanted to explain, but with everything that's been happening today I haven't had time to get around to it.'

'Forget about explanations,' Karis said coolly. 'The girl doesn't bother me.'

'She bothered you yesterday.'

'Yesterday I overreacted.'

'And now you couldn't care less?'

'Got it in one.'

'Good. So if you don't care, you won't mind if I tell you. Which I'm going to do.' Seth moved his hand in a Gallic gesture of laying everything out for inspection. 'First the night when Leon saw me needs to be put into context. It was a few days after he'd regaled me with details of your grand romance with Cliff. According to him, you were walking on Cloud Nine to the accompaniment of angelic choirs. It was cupid shooting arrows, two hearts entwined, and——' he boomed, Leon-like '—the real thing. I knew he was exaggerating, but even so the thought that you could look at another man just three weeks after we'd split was debilitating. I felt dreadful. I'd come back on the plane saddle-sore and broken-hearted. So broken-hearted, it was a toss up when I landed whether or not I went straight to the desk and booked myself a ticket for the next flight back to England.'

Karis was wrenched. 'But if you felt so bad about things, why didn't you?'

'Because flying straight back would have been impulsive, and I try not to act on impulse.' He sighed. 'In retrospect our relationship appeared to be bursts of incoherent passion, broken up by long gaps, and I needed to work things out. That said, you can't imagine the number of times I lifted the phone, how often I started to write. I had a long letter prepared when I met Leon, but what he had to say took the skids from under me. I'd been all set to ask, plead, beg, order, threaten you at the point of a sword, to give us the chance to start over again, but this muscleman had muscled in.' He winced at the pun. 'For the next few days I went to work like a zombie, came home like a zombie. I felt numb. I didn't know what the hell to do. Then one evening Kovit decided I needed cheering up. He inveigled me into going to a bar and joining him for a drink. After an hour or so he went home, but I decided to stay. The alcohol had begun to infiltrate by then,' he remarked drily. 'Up sidles a girl and sits next to me. She was a hooker, and obviously a hooker.'

'Yet she appealed?' Karis asked in amazement.

The excitement of the sleazier portions of Bangkok's nightlife was famous, and had numerous addicts. Yet Seth had always steered clear of what he called 'well used women'.

'That's why she did. I was on my sixth or seventh double gin by that time, and joining forces with a tramp seemed a neat way of getting my revenge on you. It was juvenile, I know, but there you are.'

'So you took her around and about?'

'At the time, being noticed seemed a vital ingredient. I swept her through all the best hotels, and reaped some very strange looks in consequence. We were in the Oriental when we came across Leon. His eyes nearly popped out of his head! But seeing him made it all worth while. I knew he'd never be able to resist telling you. As the night wore on the girl started hinting I should take her home but, drunk as I was, I had the sense not to do that.' He shuddered. 'Instead, I booked a hotel room and—my God!'

'She was pretty spectacular?' Karis demanded tartly.

'She wasn't anything. It was me. I—I was impotent. I couldn't believe it—it was the end of the world. I felt as if I'd been castrated!'

Karis grinned. 'What you mean is, your masculine pride was hurt,' she said, feeling better than she had done in a long time.

'Hurt? It was lacerated. I'd lost my girl, and now I'd lost my ... manhood.'

'You crept home with your tail between your legs?'

'Apt description. Yes. I fell into bed convinced I was blighted for all time.'

'Which, of course, you weren't,' she said crisply.

Now Seth was grinning. 'You've noticed?'

'Once or twice.'

He pushed himself up out of his chair. 'Chick, this tee-shirt's so damned clammy it's driving me mad. Come inside and talk while I have a shower.' He reached down and caught hold of her hand. 'Don't be shy. If the going gets too tough, you can always close those big blue eyes of yours. I haven't finished detailing my theory on why we peacefully co-existed here, yet fell apart in England,' he continued, urging her up. 'You need to come and listen.'

Without delving too deeply into the reasons why, Karis allowed herself to be persuaded. Yet one thing she made sure of; she happened to be gazing out of the bedroom window while he undressed. Things became easier when Seth went into the bathroom. Seen through the opaque glass of the shower cubicle, his outline was blurry. Nevertheless the sight of him standing there, even without the fine detail, had her heart booming. She had seen him naked so many times, yet after a gap of six months it was as though everything was brand new.

'In Thailand,' Seth said, speaking over the noise of the water as she hovered uncertainly just inside the door, 'I was on home ground, you were the foreigner. This gave me the edge. I had the knowledge about which places to visit, what to do, and so on, while you were happy to go along with each and every one of my suggestions.' He tipped shampoo into his hand and began lathering his hair. 'In England it was role-reversal. Which, if I'd had any sense, I should have taken account of. Instead I breezed in and expected you to follow.' He turned his head to look at her. 'Yes?'

She thought how he had had a weekend in Stratford organised, yet had never consulted her.

'Yes,' she agreed.

He rinsed his hair and picked up a tablet of soap. First his torso, then thighs and legs received attention.

'I was acting a bit like Leon, I suppose. You know, blustering in order to create the aura of confidence? I haven't lived in England for sixteen years or more, so when I go back there are occasions when I feel out of my depth.'

'Do you? Did you?' Her initial reaction was surprise because Seth had always seemed so *sure*, no matter which part of the earth he walked. Yet when she thought further, Karis realised it could be no other way. 'And just at the time you were floundering, I began to see what I thought were my father's traits. Hey presto, the start of World War Three!'

'That's right,' Seth agreed ruefully. He leant against the glass wall, raising first one foot to soap it, and then the other. He straightened to move directly under the spray. 'We were a couple of idiots, weren't we?' he asked, rinsing the soap away.

'Crazy.'

'Our own worst enemies.'

Karis grinned. 'Mad as hatters.'

'Lacking in common sense.'

'Needed to be certified.'

He switched off the water and turned, flicking a hank of wet, dark hair from his eyes.

'Speak for yourself. You might have been a lunatic, I consider myself more of a clown.' To illustrate his point, he pressed close to the glass and pulled a face.

Karis's grin grew wider. She stepped forward and raised a hand, deliberately positioning her finger in line with where the end of his nose was squashed against the cubicle wall.

'Funny man,' she said.

'Funny lady.'

He slid his face, nose still squashy, along the panel. Karis followed with her finger. So determined was she not to lose track that his swift wrenching aside of the glass door took her by surprise.

'Oh!' she gasped, when abruptly there was nothing between them but air. Her finger, held high, was two inches from the end of his nose. 'Get dressed,' she ordered, and made as if to dab.

The dab never hit base. Seth jerked back his head to capture the protruding finger between his teeth. 'Gotcha!' he growled, from the back of his throat.

'Fiend!' Karis accused, attempting to get free.

He held on. 'It was touch and go before,' he muttered, the words emerging like those spoken by a ventriloquist's dummy. 'But you're not touching and going again. This time you stay.'

'And who's going to make that happen?' she demanded, wiggling her finger.

'Me. Will you marry me?' he asked, in a 'gottle of geer' voice.

The wiggling finger stopped. 'Could you say that again, please? In an identifiable language?'

Seth opened his mouth, and her finger fell away. She waited, but when he spoke it was to confuse her with a mouthful of Thai.

'Beast,' she said, and he grinned. He spoke a second time—in French. Karis called him something much worse. The suspense was killing her.

'Will you marry me?' he asked, speaking in English at last, and with a gravity completely at odds with his naked and dripping appearance. 'I love you so very much. My life's nothing if it's not spent with you.'

'What happens if I say no?' she prevaricated, dishing out some of his own medicine.

'I shall bite you again.'

'Then I accept.'

'Good, but I'm going to bite you anyway. Grrr!'

Despite his standing inside the shower cubicle and Karis being outside, he wound his arms around her and nibbled furiously at her neck. Then, sobering, he raised his head and kissed her. It was a deep kiss, a long kiss, a knee-weakening kiss.

'Now my clothes are all wet,' Karis murmured, when he finally drew back. 'What shall I do?'

'If you kiss me again, I'll come up with something,' he promised.

'I thought you already had.'

Seth laughed. 'I never malfunction with you, do I?'

'You haven't done yet.'

'And I never will.' He traced a finger down her throat, to where the honeyed swell of her breasts began. 'From the moment I saw you on that balcony, I've never stopped loving you. Every morning when I wake up, you're the first thing I think of. Every night I go to sleep with you on my mind.'

She gave him an old-fashioned look. 'Yet you had to ask, "Karis who?" when I rang.'

'I was playing for time. Hearing you again out of the blue, realising you were only a few miles away, completely threw me.'

'That's why you put the phone down?' Karis asked, grinning.

'I put the phone down because Kovit was due to ring, and—and I hadn't a clue how to handle you. You were so impersonal, so deft, while there was I unable to string two sensible thoughts together. I needed time to take stock, but everything was happening at once that night. Then I spent Tuesday desperately trying to think up an excuse to get in touch.' Seth chuckled. 'Thank God for

Leon going missing! He gave me the perfect opportunity to be with you.'

'But your intention was to come south on your own.' She frowned. 'Wasn't it?'

He chuckled again. 'No, never. Granted the kidnap seemed . . . odd, but I wouldn't have bothered to take a trip unless I'd been sure you would insist on coming with me.'

'You mean the whole thing was a con? Heavens, you're no better than Leon! There was I thinking that——'

He blocked her words with a kiss. Karis sighed and kissed him back, telling him, beyond all doubt, that she had never stopped loving him, either.

'I think,' Seth said, when at last they drew apart, 'I'd better be dried and you'd better take your clothes off. Or maybe I could do that for you? And quickly. After six months when I've lain in bed alone and fantasised about making love to you, there's some doubt about how much longer I can wait.'

Drying six foot one of naked male, while he's undressing you, is no easy task, but Karis succeeded— more or less. If the body which entwined itself around her moments later was damp, who cared? She didn't. All she cared about was kissing and being kissed. Touching and being touched. The heat grew between them. Fingers stroked a stomach. A hand defined the inner curve of a thigh.

Seth groaned. 'I love you. I love you. I love you.'

He bent to kiss her breasts, first tenderly, then, as his need grew more urgent, with a desire which made her gasp.

'Yes. Please, darling. Yes,' she heard herself say.

His body, hard and hot and thrusting, made claim. An intense thrill engulfed her. Heaven was hers again. She moved her hips, enclosing him, nesting him inside her. Karis, with eyes closed and teeth clenched, caught at control. Seth sighed. There was a hungry moment when the sound of ragged breathing filled the room until suddenly, like a runaway car, their passion careened out of control. Down and around it went, then rocketed up and up and up into the heights of exquisite relief.

'You and I together make even sweeter music than I remembered,' Seth murmured, a long time later.

Held close in the crook of his arm, Karis smiled. 'Perhaps six-monthly gaps are what our love-life needs? Would you like me to get my diary and pencil in a reminder for half a year from now?'

'You have the time-scale wrong. From now on it'll be six-*hourly* gaps.'

'Braggart!'

'You don't believe? Then try me.'

'OK, I will.' She raised the large hand which covered her breast and looked at the watch strapped to his wrist. 'That leaves five hours to kill. Any ideas?'

'Six hours was a ballpark figure. It could be reduced. At a pinch.' Seth smoothed his free hand along her hip and round. 'At a delicious pinch,' he murmured.

'Ouch!' Karis exclaimed, when he gently nipped her bottom.

'Suppose I spend time looking for that birthmark of yours?' Seth suggested. 'And if I'm not successful today I could devote tomorrow to it, and the day after, and the day after that, *ad infinitum*.'

'Aren't you supposed to get back to work some time?'

'Work? What's that?'

'Something you were hooked on, once upon a time.'

'But not now. Now I have it in perspective. I told you my habits had changed, and it's all thanks to the teachings of Chairman Karis.' He gnawed playfully at her shoulder. 'In addition to lecturing me in a fabulous line of pelvic tilts, she also taught me there's more to life than being a business executive.' The gnawing changed into a kiss. 'Being a lover, for example.'

'At six-hourly intervals?'

'Sounds like a good idea.' He moved his hand to her waist. 'Right,' he said, 'I'm ready.'

Karis squinted at his watch. 'But there are four hours and fifty-eight minutes to go.'

'Ballpark figure, remember?' His smile was magnanimous. 'Besides, who's counting?'

'Not me,' she said, snuggling closer. 'Not me.'

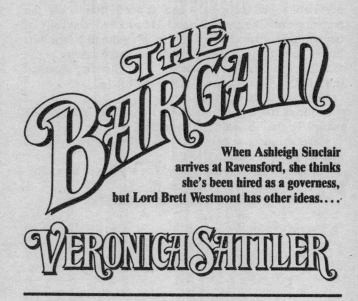

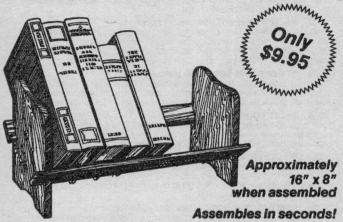

Harlequin Presents

Coming Next Month

Available in December wherever paperback books are sold, or through Harlequin Reader Service:

In the U.S.
901 Fuhrmann Blvd.
P.O. Box 1397
Buffalo, N.Y. 14240-1397

In Canada
P.O. Box 603
Fort Erie, Ontario
L2A 5X3

**For the millions who can't read
Give the Gift of Literacy**

One out of five adults in North America
cannot read or write well enough
to fill out a job application
or understand the directions on a bottle of medicine.

**You can change all this by joining the fight
against illiteracy.**

For more information write to:
Contact, Box 81826, Lincoln, Neb. 68501
In the United States, call toll free: 1-800-228-8813

**The only degree you need
is a degree of caring**

"Sea of Heartbreak is a challenge to all of us of the need to demonstrate the compassion of our Lord."
Pat Robertson, Pres. CBN-700 Club

"The flight of the Vietnamese boat people is one of the epic stories of our time, and no American is better qualified to write about it than Stanley Mooneyham."
Peter Arnett, Associated Press

"The outreach and concern of World Vision International under Dr. Mooneyham's guidance well illustrates what can be done to make this a better universe for our children and their children."
John McCarthy, Director of Migration and Refugee Services, U.S. Catholic Conference

Sea of
Heartbreak

Sea of Heartbreak

by W. Stanley Mooneyham

Jeremy Books

5624 Lincoln Drive, Minneapolis, Minnesota 55436

LOGOS INTERNATIONAL, Plainfield, N.J. 07060

SEA OF HEARTBREAK
Copyright © 1980 by W. Stanley Mooneyham
All rights reserved
Printed in the United States of America
Library of Congress Catalog Card Number: 79-93009
International Standard Book Number: 0-88270-414-1
Logos International, Plainfield, New Jersey 07060
Co-publisher, Jeremy Books, Minneapolis, MN 55436
International Standard Book Number: 0-89877-013-0

To Mrs. Tom Scarborough,
the "Miss Idell" of
my boyhood, who cared.

Acknowledgments

The writing of this book was done on two different sides of the world—Asia and the United States—and the interviews were conducted in such scattered places as Baltimore, Bangkok, Jakarta, Los Angeles, Singapore and Manila. The stories have come out of more than a dozen different refugee camps.

I am deeply in debt to four of my colleagues who shared the interviewing responsibilities— Cheri Goodman, Milt Kohut, Ken Waters and Dr. Kenneth Wilson.

The research and data collecting was done primarily by Burt Singleton and Mary Janss-Clary, also on the World Vision staff. However, much of the background material on the Hmong refugees was supplied by my friend, Dennis Gray, chief of the Associated Press Bureau in Bangkok.

My administrative assistant, Nancy Moyer, coordinated the entire project while I was traveling around the world. She also polished and typed the final manuscript.

My debt includes all these competent people.

Finally, I express appreciation to the British magazine, *Buzz*, for the title, *Sea of Heartbreak*, which they used first in an article about the boat people.

I gladly acknowledge these invaluable contributions.

—Stan Mooneyham

Contents

Introduction

Every generation has its own holocaust. Ours is taking place in Southeast Asia right now, happening in front of our eyes. The death toll runs into millions—as many as four million in Cambodia alone. Perhaps as many as a quarter-of-a-million Vietnamese boat people have drowned in the South China Sea.

But some have survived and every survivor has a story to tell, each equally as terrible as the last. The stories in this book are from actual interviews with many of these refugees. Some are told in simple broken English, exactly as they were recounted. Others have been slightly restructured to make the English more understandable. All the stories are true. To read them is like walking through a torture chamber. These mind-staggering events actually happened—and others like them are still happening!

Anyone who reads the tragic stories of the boat people can no longer disclaim any responsibility for this holocaust. All who read this litany of horrors must understand that knowledge brings responsibility.

What is the powerful motivation that sends people like Tran, Phan Van Tinh, Phan My Thang, Thieu, Quoi, and tens of thousands of others on their perilous voyages to the edge of hell? They simply want the freedom to make a living, to worship as they please, and to live under a fair government. In their quest for these basic human rights, the refugees face corrupt and cynical local officials at home, inhuman sea pirates, wretched and rickety little boats, food and water shortages, sudden and vicious storms, heartless police and officials both within and outside their country.

"You have to develop callouses on your heart; otherwise you will bleed to death," remarked the prime minister of Singapore, Lee Kuan Yew, when speaking of the refugee situation in Southeast Asia.

That statement chills me. Even though I know something of the political problems faced by the long-suffering nations of Southeast Asia by Vietnam's expulsion of tens of thousands of its unwanted citizens, I am troubled by the prime minister's statement.

I believe the world does not bleed enough over the wrongs, the injustices, the sufferings inflicted upon the powerless millions who are victimized everywhere. Already we are too calloused, too comfortable, too indifferent. Too few care too little. For God's sake, we don't need anyone to encourage us to be less compassionate.

The organization of which I am president, World Vision, is dedicated to helping the world's victims and to encouraging the world to be more compassionate.

It is only fair to warn you, I think, that this is a troubling book. You may sleep less well after reading it. I know from experience that it is painful to have your emotions wounded. I walk among the world's suffering people much of the time and sometimes I hurt so much I can hardly stand it.

I cry, too. I'm not ashamed to admit it. I don't ever want to become so coldly professional that I can no longer weep over the agonies of others.

And I bleed.

Now, I don't indulge these emotions to satisfy some masochistic quirk. I don't like to hurt. I'd like to avoid pain, but often my emotions are too raw to permit me to sleep well at night. I don't like that either.

But I'll tell you what I'd like less. And that is to

have callouses on my heart. I want to remain a human being, not become an insensitive brute. So I weep from sheer frustration, from sadness, from white-hot rage. I weep without shame. I hurt. And I bleed. So does our loving Christ, I am convinced, who is touched by the ordeals of these tortured people like Tran—another innocent one who went through her own Calvary.

Sea of
Heartbreak

PART I

THOSE WHO DARED

1

Voyage to the Edge of Hell

Tran's begging eyes frantically swept the faces on the deck of the little boat, searching for help.

"Please!" they silently pled as she scanned each face in turn.

The only movement was a shuffling of feet, a turning of heads, an averting of eyes.

Tran saw tears in the eyes of some. But no one came to help.

It was then that panic seized her.

Where could she run? Where could she hide? Nowhere.

That was the mocking answer. How could she run away when around her was nothing but water—250,000 square miles of it, known in the world's atlases as the South China Sea?

Most of all, Tran wanted to cover her nakedness. But this was no more possible than was escape. The pirates had taken her clothes when they forced the seventeen prettiest women and girls on the refugee boat to strip.

Tran's slim body began to shake even though the tropical sun burned her flesh. Her mind refused to think ahead to what might happen. It must be a horrible nightmare from which she would wake up. Or, if it was really happening, help would come at the last minute and she would be saved. She grasped the straw. Yes! That was it! Help would come. Somehow . . . some way . . . she must be spared what her mind refused to accept.

She prayed.

No deliverer came.

The hellish, awful, unthinkable moment was at hand.

Some of the women resisted. Those who did were beaten and threatened. The sharp point of a knife held against the throat of defenseless women insured submission to the attacker's orders. One young man whose fiancee was among the seventeen selected by the pirates struggled to save his beloved. He was left on the deck, unconscious and bleeding.

There was no more resistance. An eerie quietness settled down on the little boat, broken only by the fiendish squeals of the attackers, the soft sobs of the women and the lap of the waves against the hull.

As the pirates began their brutal attacks, the rest of the refugees turned away. They would spare Tran and the other tragic victims the ultimate indignity of an audience to witness their shame.

"This is not the way it was supposed to be," Tran thought, sobbing with shame and terror.

Before leaving Vietnam she and the others talked about the reports they had heard of attacks on other refugee boats. Their captain had said they would steer clear of Thai waters because of the vicious reputation of pirates in the Gulf of Siam. The freedom-seekers would go to Malaysia instead. At the time, they did not know that the Malaysian destination was equally perilous because of a hard-line government attitude that refused entry to any more Vietnamese refugees.

The only thought then was to get out of Vietnam.

In July, 1979, getting out of Vietnam was not difficult, with the right connections. Local Communist officials were selling exit permits for gold in amounts up to $3,500, depending on what the traffic would bear. Ethnic Chinese, like Tran, easily obtained the permits since the Communist government wanted all Chinese out of the country, even those whose families had been in Vietnam for three or four generations.

Tran, whose husband had left her and their seven-year-old daughter, decided to join the exodus. "We left because we were hungry all the time," she says. "The only food we had was a kind of rice powder. I wanted my child to eat."

A friend made contact for her with a boat captain and a deal was closed for nine taels of gold (one tael is equal to 1.25 ounces). At the prevailing price, that was about $2,700.

So in full daylight on the afternoon of June 30, 1979, the sixteen-by-sixty-foot boat with its cargo of 253 human beings—including Tran and her daughter—sailed out of Bien Hoa, Vietnam. Their destination was freedom, but for Tran, it was a journey to the edge of hell.

Not counting the small cabin which stood above the deck, each passenger had less than four square feet of living space on the boat. The sense of exhilaration at being free more than made up for the crowded conditions, though. Any inconvenience could be tolerated for the five or six days the captain had allowed for sailing to Malaysia.

What the captain hadn't allowed for was getting lost. Steering by the sun and without any charts, the boat with its cargo of refugees was sailing dangerously close to the pirate-infested Gulf of Siam on the third day, when the refugees spotted a boat coming toward them. Because of the distance, it wasn't quite possible to make out the flag, but some thought it was an American vessel.

However, the excitement which swept through the refugees massed on deck was short-lived. When the approaching boat was close enough for the Thai flag to be clearly visible, fear and apprehension took over. The family leaders held a hurried strategy conference and decided to see if they could satisfy the pirate crew with an offer of $1,000 to help them get to Malaysia.

They thought their bait had worked when the captain of the renegade fishing vessel invited the refugee leader onto his boat for negotiations.

Actually, it was a ploy. Once on board, the leader was held captive for about three hours until two other pirate fishing boats appeared. The first one had obviously radioed for help. With the arrival of the other boats, all pretenses of assistance were dropped.

Then began the ordeal which has been repeated hundreds of times with sickening sameness in the treacherous waters off the coasts of Vietnam, Thailand and Malaysia. For those who have left Vietnam with high hopes for a new start in a free land, the cowardly and brutal attacks have turned the South China Sea into a sea of heartbreak. For the pirates, pillaging the slow and unarmed refugee boats has become far more lucrative than the pursuit of their usual vocation of fishing the fruitful waters.

The boat carrying Tran and her 252 companions

was just one more victim. The fishermen/pirates, armed with knives and guns, boarded the defenseless refugee vessel and took virtually everything that wasn't nailed down. Threatening and abusing the terrified people, the pirates methodically stripped them of gold, jewelry, watches, money and all decent clothing.

That was not the end. Next came the violent gratification of the pirates' lust. This was the moment of Tran's shame. She was the second one chosen. Before the rough brown hands grabbed her trembling body and forced her down onto a chair where she would twice be raped by the same man, Tran had a moment to be thankful that her little daughter was lying sick upstairs in the small cabin. The child would be spared the psychological scars which the mother will have to bear the rest of her life.

After the first attack on her, Tran managed to slip away to the cabin which was the only place to hide. She felt dizzy and sick and thought she would vomit. Most of all, she felt dirty. There was no water for washing. She took out the one dress she had managed to hide and put it on, then she lay down beside her sick daughter.

From below she could hear the horrible sounds of the cruelty that continued for four or five hours. Later she learned that fifteen of the women had been raped, most of them repeatedly and one of them by seven different men.

Terror gripped Tran when she heard heavy footsteps on the ladder and realized one of the pirates was coming for her again. She wanted to scream, but her emotions were so spent that she just collapsed into tears. The man jerked her up roughly and ordered her back to the deck. She begged to stay with her sick daughter, but her pleas and her tears had no effect.

At the point of a knife, she was forced back down the steps and once again attacked.

Daylight began to fade before the nightmare finally came to an end. When the evil in the depraved men had finally spent itself, the three pirate boats sailed away. The agony, which lasted through an afternoon, had seemed like a lifetime.

Undoubtedly, the pirates never thought twice about the carnage they had left behind them. Certainly they didn't care. What did shattered innocence, broken dreams and brutalized bodies mean to them? When they sailed away into the setting sun, they took with them more than the possessions of a destitute people. They took the honor of gentle women, the purity of young girls, the manly pride of husbands and fathers unable to fight for their women, and the dignity of a proud people.

They also took all the food, water and fuel on the boat. Having stripped the refugees of everything else, they now intended to take away life itself.

The boat which was supposed to take them to freedom lay powerless in the water.

For a while it looked as if death would claim them all and their boat would become the Flying Dutchman of the South China Sea. The pangs of hunger became unbearable, but the awful, agonizing thirst created by the relentless equatorial sun was even worse. People drank their own urine.

Finally, after nine days of drifting, when all hope was gone, land was sighted. The refugees had no idea where they were, but they were determined not to be put back to sea. As soon as the boat beached itself, the men chopped a large hole in the bow to make it unseaworthy. They were sure this was the only way to prevent being towed back out to sea.

As it turned out, this action resulted in their ultimate rescue. They had beached just two miles from Songkhla, one of the southernmost towns in Thailand and the site of a major refugee camp for Vietnamese boat people. The local authorities thought they had all they could look after and wanted no more, so the new arrivals were told they could stay on the beach only one night and then they must repair their boat and put back to sea again.

Providentially, a French doctor from the refugee camp turned up just as these negotiations were going on and upon hearing the story of the brutality at sea, insisted to the local police that the women who had been raped be placed in the camp hospital for observation.

Under this pressure, the local authorities agreed to a temporary stay of their order and permitted the other refugees to camp on the beach while they waited for the return of the women.

Every day the doctor found new excuses for their continued hospitalization. His delaying tactics worked, for soon the Bangkok office of the United Nations High Commissioner for Refugees learned of their plight and sent a representative to interview the refugees and begin arrangements for their resettlement.

Finally, the local police relented and after forcing the refugees to spend a month on the beach, permitted them to move into the camp.

It had been an incredible forty-two days from the time the boat sailed out of Bien Hoa until the 253 hopeful voyagers were assured of acceptance in a free country!

For Tran it had been a trip to the edge of hell and back. Her greatest fear was that she had become pregnant.

"Every day I asked the doctor at the camp and each time I was afraid to hear his answer," she recalls. "He told me it would not be possible to tell for ten days. The waiting was nearly unbearable. I did not want any part of the one who attacked me. How could I carry the child of such a man?

"Finally, the doctor said I was not pregnant, but I found it hard to believe because I had lived with fear for so long."

At a transit camp in the heart of Bangkok, as she and her daughter were on their way to a new life in Australia, Tran was asked if she thought she could ever forget that terrible day on the South China Sea:

"You see me smiling, but inside it is very hard to forget. I am trying. Everything in my past is gone now. I have a new life, a new future. I am not going to look back."

2

Thang's Terrifying Ordeal

Eighteen-year-old Phan My Thang (pronounced like *fon me tongue)* sits impassively on a makeshift bench in a refugee camp on an island in the South China Sea as she tells her sad story.

She has a small round face, typical of the Chinese. Her skin is unblemished. She has wide-set deep brown eyes. Her arms bear the scars of healed-over wounds. She has no money and is wearing a simple skirt and blouse. It is ill-fitting and mismatched, probably the donation of one of the relief agencies active in the camp.

Thang is alone in the world and homeless. She is intelligent and sensitive. Her speech is softly eloquent.

"I am a young girl, eighteen years old. What I

am going to tell you is exact and true. I am a victim of brutality and barbarism during my voyage across the sea to seek freedom in a civilized country," the girl says without emotion. "I left Vietnam on June 9, 1979. The boat that carried us away, TG 909, was twenty-two meters long [about seventy-nine feet] and carried 500 souls. My family included seven persons—my father, an older sister and brother, two younger sisters, a younger brother and myself.

"As we were sailing to a new life, we were robbed twice by the Thai sea-rovers who were cleverly disguised as fishermen. Since our boat was small and crowded, we all felt like we were suffocating inside. We could hardly breathe. Without wind, we probably would die in great numbers. However, the first unfortunate persons to die were one man and two young children.

"On June 14, our boat ran out of fuel and water, so we had to make a stopover at a Malaysian shore. Unexpectedly we landed at five o'clock in the morning, but the inhabitants attacked us with sticks and knives. They also threw stones at us. To avoid danger or death, we withdrew and stood in the sea. We stayed there a whole night. At seven o'clock we were saved when a Malaysian troop came and interfered with those angry, unbalanced people.

"When we got to the shore, these soldiers told us to hand them money and gold. And if we accepted their proposal, to guarantee truth and certitude, they would give each of us a receipt. For our part, my father gave them five ounces of gold. Still they kept us as prisoners. We sat on the beach, just like small mice before a throng of hungry cats. In the meantime, they began the search. Confronting each victim one by one, they would repeat the same words: 'Dollars, gold or death!' The seek-and-search operation lasted all night long while we were sitting still—sleepy, tired and hungry. Perhaps on account of the cold wind and bleak atmosphere, one person died.

"On June 16, late in the afternoon, we were transported to another place. We spent one night in the open air. Next day we had to walk to a place where we stayed fifteen days. The so-called benefactors did not give us anything. To soothe our hungry stomachs we got our own rice and began to cook. But sadness followed sadness and another man swooned, then died. Was it because of cold or tiredness? We didn't know.

"On July 2, we were told to get down to the sea and they would bring us to an island. However, no boat came and we followed them back to the place we had left. To our surprise, we found that the small huts set up by our own hands had been burned down. Therefore, we had to sleep outdoors.

"On July 3, they led us to six small boats— numbers B1, B2, B3, B4, B5 and B7. Each would contain ninety persons, some overcrowded. At the head of these was P49, which towed us behind in a long formation. At midnight, they called two girls up, leading them to their boat. Later we were told that each of these two unfortunate girls must endure the sexual indecencies of nine men.

"We were still being towed on July 4. In order to reduce suffering and hardship, we collected money and gold to hand them. We passed them five more ounces of gold and on receiving the bribery, they made some rearrangement reducing the number of boats. It was five instead of six. Then they began to tow us again," Phan recalls.

"Now the sea got rough and the wind was strong. We thought they foresaw the bad weather; however, they kept towing us toward the storm center. Evidently, they wanted to kill us in an indirect manner.

"Everybody in the boat was frightened—fear of death was strong as we faced high wind and heavy sea. The speed was so rapid, no one can imagine. We were five boats of unseaworthy size, without food, water, fuel. There was not even a man to steer the fifth one.

"At ten o'clock in the evening, B5 was leaking. We cried for help three times but they pretended not to hear. At eleven o'clock, B5 began to sink. Outside it was very dark. When B5 was almost going down, they cut the rope for all the boats with complete indifference. It was in this unfortunate boat that my family was sitting. My

father, my sisters, my brothers were no more—
one by one, they disappeared into the deep sea.

"During this heartbreaking moment, I was
holding in my hands my little two-year-old
brother. But he had died on account of the strong,
cruel sea waves. I laid him in the water and
without buoy or anything I struggled through the
water to B7 and climbed up." Phan's face reflects
her grief.

"Once inside, I saw water everywhere. The boat
was leaking and had no fuel. We asked for
supplies, but they shook their heads. It was not
until the moment when B7 was about to sink that
Malaysian P49 began to approach us. About sixty
strong young men were able to jump over,
whereas the little children, women and old
people stayed behind in the boat. However, P49
did not save them. It ran away instead. These
poor souls died before their eyes. They witnessed
the tragic scene without a little bit of feeling. I
somehow manged to get to B3.

"In a brief moment the sea swallowed B5 and
B7. Only B1, B3 and B4 remained afloat, but they
did not know where to go. To my thinking,
instead of using guns on us, the Malaysians
managed to manipulate such a tactic. Did they
not fear the reaction or judgment? Or perhaps
they presumed the world would think we died of
shipwreck and not of assassination by Malaysian
hands.

"On July 5, they carried sixty persons to another boat, No. 1501. There these men behaved just like their previous counterparts. They touched our bodies in a beastly manner. This boat sat at anchor one day and one night while the soldiers were watching over their 'trophies.' At noon on July 6, the Malaysian P49 towed two other small boats, numbers 476 and 477, to our side. Those persons on No. 1501 were forced to go to the P49 which started to sail again, pulling the other two boats behind.

"At 2100 hours, it anchored at a deserted island. They ordered boys and men to go to 477, whereas girls and women and children stayed in the P49.

"At about midnight, ten soldiers pushed me down to the hold. They began their immoral acts by turn, two among them raped me four times successively. It was not until next morning I was allowed to leave the dirty place and was released. During that course of time they displayed their sadistic brutality, threatening to stab me to death and boasting before they began to satisfy their sexual desires.

"Although I was tired and fainted, I would remember one rapist. His name was Fozi, stenciled on the flap of his shorts. As far as I knew, he was the chief mate on the P49.

"On July 7, they towed No. 476 to a deserted island in search of B4 which got lost on July 4.

The men and boys who were ordered to spend the night on No. 477 returned to P49. Thus the total rose to 166 persons. These were all people who had left Vietnam on TG 909. In the afternoon, the boys and men were moved to 476 and 477 where they passed the night. Meanwhile, the whole line of boats continued their course. At 7 A.M., following their gestures, the rest of us also stepped down into 476 and 477," Phan says.

"Then they cut the linking ropes and disappeared, running away just like ghosts. We thought we were then in the international sea because we saw big boats and ships shuttling to and fro.

"To have some economy of fuel, No. 476 had to tow her sister, No. 477. Fortunately, we were able to move far enough that we caught sight of the Indonesian lighthouse. It was in the dead of night. We had no more fuel and the engine stopped. The boats drifted to the edge of the isolated island and all the people got off. Next morning when getting up, we found that one boat was sunk.

"On July 10, at 9 A.M., a light of joy appeared, for we saw an Indonesian boat approaching us. First, it carried sixty-three persons to Keramut, but many were afraid because they thought we were once more being taken away. But the next day, the boat returned for the rest and all of us went to Kuku camp.

"My family was so unfortunate. My father, my sisters and brothers are now no more. They died innocently and left me alone—no clothes, no money and no personal I.D. card. I lost everything, and nothing is now within the reach of my hand.

"At present I am a friendless, homeless young girl. Without relatives, I must rely on my boat companions to love and help me. I am one among the most unfortunate survivors and each of my words contains a tear, a sob, a cry which I hope will resound to your ears and the world."

3

Saigon Sets the Stage

Saigon's Tan Son Nhut Airport was a flurry of frantic activity in April of 1975 as foreigners and Vietnamese alike sought for priority space on flights that were leaving around the clock. What was supposed to have been an orderly departure, with priorities predetermined, turned into a panic. Hundreds of thousands who had fought the Viet Cong, served the Nguyen Van Thieu government, worked with Americans, or simply hated Communism wanted out of Vietnam after the Communists took over.

Of the more than one-half million Vietnamese who probably qualified for evacuation in some category, only 135,000 got out in the first wave. Families were split apart. Sometimes it was agreed that one would go and the others would come later when and if they could escape. Decisions affecting a lifetime had to be made in split seconds.

One Vietnamese staff member of an American private organization had to leave his two youngest children behind with relatives because families were limited to six members on U.S. government evacuation flights.

When the last helicopter lifted senior government personnel from the roof of the American Embassy, people were left grasping for the rope ladder which swung beneath the carriage.

An era was ended, and the doors to the country slammed shut.

The Communists could now begin to reshape that part of Asia which they had unified through violence and treachery and over which they now held uncontested control. When the new masters came marching from the jungle and riding in their tanks into Saigon, there was no victory celebration.

A quiet fear gripped the city.

Ng Ngoc Thong was sure something terrible would be done to the people who had, with the help of the Americans and other allies, withstood the Viet Cong for so long. Thong was a thirty-four-year-old bachelor lawyer, but during his country's struggles he had given up law for soldiering. Now with all the other residents of Saigon, he waited for the hammer and sickle to fall.

"But we were surprised. For the first month things went smoothly and we thought these kinsmen from the North might not be as bad as we had been led to believe. At first, things didn't seem that much different from the old days except for the soldiers who walked around town wearing different uniforms. The most noticeable thing was that the boom of the guns had stopped," Thong says.

"We began to feel some nervousness after fifteen days, though, when the first subtle signs began to appear, indicating that things might not remain the same. The new regime announced that all enlisted personnel of ARVN (Army of the Republic of Vietnam, the defeated soldiers of President Thieu) would be required to attend a three-day reeducation camp.

"I signed up to go even though down inside I expected we would not be allowed to return home. I was wrong.

"The three-day course consisted of lectures on socialism and the sayings of Ho Chi Minh, the revered founder and long-time leader of the Vietnamese Communist movement. There was no mistreatment of the ex-ARVN soldiers, not even any threats.

"I began to relax when I got back home. Now I realize that was exactly what the North Vietnamese wanted me to do.

"It was all a ruse," he says, "a part of their strategy

to get us to trust them. And it worked because a few weeks later, when the new masters called all former officers and high government officials to a ten-day reeducation camp, everyone went willingly, thinking they would come home after their political indoctrination.

"This time we were wrong. None came home at the end of ten days. Most didn't return for months and in the meantime their families had no word from them. Some have never come back and it is assumed that they are either dead or viewed by the Communists as politically unreliable. I am sure the whole exercise was meant to determine who was capable of experiencing a political conversion and who would likely always be politically suspect. The former went home after appropriate reeducation; the latter ones disappeared," Thong finishes. "Who could feel safe living under such a government?"

So, having successfully moved against all former military personnel, the Communists turned their attention to what they considered their next most serious threat to reshaping the society—the so-called "rich capitalists." The term was very loosely applied to anyone who was more than just a simple merchant. There were undoubtedly some unscrupulous profiteers among them, but most of those targeted were nothing more than reasonably prosperous businessmen who had managed to acquire some wealth and property through honest business transactions.

Such a man was Phan Van Tinh.

"My family and I were Christians, having been brought up in the Tinh Lanh (Evangelical) Church. My father had taken me into the family jewelry business when I was twenty-three. Like most Vietnamese young men, however, I did my turn in the army for four years, between 1962 and 1966," he says.

"After military service, I returned to the family business in Bien Hoa. I married a Christian girl, Sarah, and we were blessed with six beautiful children. Our business prospered and I bought some houses as investment property. Then I bought a drugstore, and a piece of farm land. I expected I would have enough to get the children started in life and then see my wife and myself through our old age."

He pauses, recalling the events of April, 1975:

"Seven days after the fall of Saigon, the Communists struck the first blow at the despised 'capitalists.' It was announced that as of that moment, all precious stones, all precious metals and all foreign currency were the property of the new government. Nothing in those categories could be bought, sold or traded.

"The Communist officials came to my shop and put me out of business. Oh, it was all done legally enough. The entire stock of jewelry was inventoried and when it was taken away to the bank for safekeeping, I was given a receipt for every item!

"Although I was out of the jewelry business by government expropriation, I still had my drug-store—but only for seven more months. In January of 1976, the government decided it wanted a mon-opoly on medicines, so I had to close my pharmacy as well."

Tinh knows of a number of businessmen who resisted these measures and were shot. And still the Communists were not through with the capi-talists.

In the same manner that the Communists had announced new regulations regarding businesses, houses also came in for some strange edicts. For example, any house with over 200 square meters (about 1850 square feet) of office space would be confiscated by the government. In addition, houses should fit the number of people living in them, not the ability to own or maintain them. Consequently, each person was allowed only seventy-eight square feet of living space.

Tinh lost on both counts. His home at Bien Hoa had over 3,000 square feet so it was immediately confiscated. Next he was notified that his house in Saigon was also due for confiscation. (It was fifty-nine square feet over the "legal" limit.) How-ever, Tinh managed to keep it until his escape because of the number of people living in it.

"Because none of my family members had gov-ernment-approved work positions, they were unable to get rice ration cards," Tinh continues. "Jobs were not handed out on the basis of talent, skill or training, but rather on family relationships with Communist Party members. Even a ration card, however, would not have guaranteed rice to my family. It would have meant only that when rice was available, we could get it at the official rate. For the favored ones who possessed the treasured card, it was no small benefit since rice on the black market cost up to ten times over the official rate.

"But it was from the black market, which we also called the 'running market' because the vendors would set up their stalls on different streets at random times and run away when the Communists learned of it, that I had to support my family from 1976 to 1978. We managed, because I had kept back some of the gold and precious stones from my jewelry store before the Communists took my stock. The poor people who had neither ration card nor resources went hungry," Tinh finishes.

While the new masters in Saigon were incredibly stupid in some things, they were very shrewd in things that mattered. For example, even the officers of the North Vietnamese army who took over all government posts in the South didn't know how to use a flush toilet. They would put towels in the toilet for washing and then blame the Americans for swallowing their towels when they were flushed away. They also tried to clean their fish in the toilets with the same disastrous results, according to the refugees.

When they finally found out what the toilets were for, they still squatted down beside the fixture and then dumped the deposit in the water as they triumphantly flushed it away!

However, these people are not loutish. They are real fighters—they follow orders to the letter and can be relied on to advance toward an objective without second thoughts. They excel in controlling people.

They were very skillful in dividing each village into several smaller and more manageable units with a Party faithful installed at the head. They also had a very effective internal spy system which minimized the possibility of counteraction by anti-Communist groups.

They didn't necessarily know how to drive a car, use a toilet or turn on a hot water tap, but then those things were not necessary to the Revolution. What was necessary was controlling the people and at this they were expert.

The Communists altered family relationships. Children were coerced into joining "Ho Chi Minh youth camps" where they were encouraged to report their parents if the adults were not following the Party line.

Traditional family customs changed drastically. Because the father might no longer be the chief breadwinner, his authority in the family structure was undermined.

Gradually, the Communists' grip was tightening.

Not only was "capitalist" Tinh hit with confiscation of his businesses and homes, but the government kept looking for some way to administer the *coup de grace* to the entire bourgeois class. A simple and ingenious plan was devised, as effective as it was devilish. All tradesmen, merchants and businessmen would be presumed to have cheated on their taxes under the old regime and it would be up to the new government to redress this wrong. New taxes were levied on the income the Communists supposed these businessmen could have made. It didn't matter that the figure was an arbitrary one and had no basis in reality. And there was no appeal from the grotesque assessment on this fictional income which was sometimes as much as 200 times more than the taxes previously paid!

If the person couldn't pay in gold or currency, houses or land or any other marketable commodity would settle the debt. If people were wiped out in the process, well, that was the object of the whole exercise.

Still the pressure came. Sometimes it was subtle. It could take the form of being awakened at night by the security police. Sometimes the questions they asked were simple and meaningless, but Tinh says, "The psychological pressure of the experience was awful. When that knock came in the night, you thought it was the end of the world.

"There were other pressures, too, like having to get a permit from the local officials in the town where we lived before we could stay elsewhere overnight. The permit had to be renewed each month.

"I know of two Montagnard pastors who came to Saigon in 1978 from their home in Dalat, a city in the highlands. They had the appropriate documents for travel and as night approached, their host, who was a local pastor, went to the local government office to register them. A low-ranking officer gave them permission to sleep in the church, but did not tell them the request had to be approved at a higher level. It wouldn't have mattered anyhow, for it was getting late and the other office was closed," Tinh explains.

"Security police came in the night and arrested the pastor, the assistant pastor, the president of the congregation and the two visiting tribesmen. The senior pastor, who was over seventy years old, was released a few days later, but the experience brought on a heart attack.

"The other four were sent to a concentration camp in central Vietnam and I've heard that they are still there."

Tinh says there is a difference between reeducation and concentration camps:

"A reeducation camp is where you are brainwashed with Communist ideology and where you are made to work hard. You are told that the reason for this is that you made others work before, so now you must be made to understand what hard work really is. Even the work is supposed to be part of the reeducation process.

"A concentration camp," he says, "is like a prison. You are not permitted outside your cell and you are not allowed to work. You are sent there as a punishment for some crime.

"These four religious leaders are in a concentration camp for the crime of sleeping in a church without the necessary permission!" Tinh continues. "While the new regime did not forbid worship, they put Ho Chi Minh's picture above all the others in the churches and strictly regulated congregational meetings.

"The Communists hate all religion, but especially Christianity because they say it opened the way for foreigners to enter the country," Tinh adds.

Pastors and priests have been forced to attend political education classes and all church services are closely monitored. Any activities at the church building must be scheduled a month in advance, and all sermon material must be prepared a month in advance and submitted to government authorities for approval. Any deviation from the schedule or the subject will bring difficulties, say Christians who have fled Vietnam.

Even home prayer meetings, if several people are expected, must be reported and approved. The Christians get around this by meeting only in twos and threes for which they never ask permission.

But each time the congregation meets, two people are sitting in the church to take notes of what was preached that day. These are cadres working for the government and they report fully on each service. There is no freedom of worship.

Soon after the Communists came to power in Vietnam, seminaries and Bible schools were closed so that there is no longer any place where a pastor may receive formal training, say Christians who fled the country. Neither is the congregation free to choose a pastor or change pastors. Previously the Tinh Lanh congregations extended calls to pastors every two years. Now every pastor is on permanent assignment by government order.

Evangelization outside the church building itself is not permitted. Youth meetings at the church have been discontinued. Summer camps for children are also on the forbidden list, although some churches have persisted in requesting permission for these. In the rare cases where they have been approved, it has been only after a thorough investigation of the backgrounds of the teachers.

As is true in most Communist countries, the practice of religion is not totally prohibited. The regime just makes it exceedingly difficult, if not impossible, for the church to function normally. For example, the church in Vietnam has lost virtually all its young people. They are not forbidden to attend the services—the government just makes sure other activities are scheduled for them at the same time.

Most of these activities are in the form of work projects. Sunday is street cleaning day or rice planting day or land cultivation day and the young people are formed into work brigades. Sometimes they are sent outside the town for a whole weekend, especially if they have jobs with the government—and there aren't many other kinds of jobs available in Vietnam today.

Tinh says bitterly, "There are no more weekends in Vietnam. Sunday is just another day. My own children were assigned on Sundays to trim the trees in our town of Bien Hoa."

Preoccupation with the border war with China in 1979 led to a relaxation of some restrictions and the churches were once again crowded, indicating that faith among Christians still runs deep.

Tinh recently received a letter from a relative in Vietnam, which read, "A lot of people go to church now and their faith is getting stronger because it is too sad outside. Life is so desperate that we have to go to church to seek hope, calmness and peace."

Easter, 1979, was especially significant for the churches in what was known as Saigon, now called

Ho Chi Minh City. An eyewitness reported that "more people came to church on Resurrection Day than before, and many of them returned to Christ. At the close of the service, the pulpit was surrounded by people coming forward to dedicate themselves to the Lord. And many new believers turned to Christ." It is certain that the government will never allow Christianity to flourish.

Since Buddhism is less formally structured than Catholicism or Protestantism, there seems to be less the authorities can do to control it as rigidly, but they have moved against that religion as well. As with priests and pastors, Buddhist monks were also sent to reeducation camps, and shrines and temples have been closed. One strongly anti-Communist Buddhist sect, the Hoa Hao, has been effectively put out of operation by the arrest of all the leaders.

Apart from the concentration camps, perhaps the next most feared punishment was being sent to the New Economic Zones. These were tracts of virgin jungle which had been targeted for clearing and cultivation. Far away from the cities, the living conditions in these regions were Spartan at best and inhuman at worst.

Hundreds of thousands of unemployed people were rounded up and sent off to these Vietnamese versions of Siberia. Thousands managed to escape, since security was minimal, and among the boat refugees today are many who did a full or partial tour of duty in the NEZs.

Ex-lawyer Thong is among them. Since there was no law to be practiced in the new Vietnam and since he had come from a wealthy family, Thong found himself scheduled for shipment to a New Economic Zone in 1976.

He recalls, "It was like a trip back 200 years in time, to the Moyen Age in my country. The work schedule went seven days a week, 362 days a year. the only holidays were Tet [Chinese New Year], when we were given two days off, and Ho Chi Minh's birthday.

"Our day started at 5:00 A.M. with work in the fields. The noon break lasted fifteen minutes for lunch and rest. Since the meal consisted of only one small bowl of rice with soy sauce, sometimes there actually was five minutes or so to rest. The work day ended at 7:30 P.M., when we were given two bowls of rice.

"But before the day was really over, there was another hour and a half of political work which consisted of group singing of Communist songs, and Party indoctrination lectures.

"Finally," says Thong, "we were allowed to sleep. Our beds were just bamboo slats, but after a sixteen-hour day, they felt like beds in a five-star hotel."

Thong served out his full two years, not returning to Saigon until April, 1978. It was about that time that other radical changes began taking place throughout the country, and especially in the former capital of the South. A decision had apparently been reached in Hanoi to eliminate as many of the ethnic Chinese in the country as possible. As is true in virtually all Asian countries, most of these Chinese families had been in Vietnam for several generations. But that was of no consequence to the new masters.

The Communist regime in Vietnam, which had come to power with the aid of the Soviet Union and was now one of Russia's client states, saw the Chinese as untrustworthy and a potential fifth column, so a plan had to be devised to "encourage" them to leave. To have simply deported several million people who had no place to go would have been bad international public relations.

In Saigon, these Chinese families had created a bustling and thriving section called Cholon. Many of them owned small shops, usually one-door-and-a-window-on-the-street with the family living in two or three rooms over the shop.

Most of them were typical mom-and-pop enterprises—with the omnipresent children helping out as well.

Having moved against the wealthy capitalists earlier, the regime now decided to enforce another tenet of the Communist faith by prohibiting all private enterprise. So in mid-1978, the order went out: All private shops must close and the merchandise will become the property of the government. It was doubly convenient that virtually all of these small, family-owned shops were properties of the Chinese.

Faced with the loss of their livelihood, many Chinese began to look for ways to leave the country. The Communist government had certainly anticipated this, for they had a plan all ready.

The Chinese were given two choices—either go to the New Economic Zones or build a boat and go away.

They could go anywhere.

Prior to this, most of those leaving Vietnam by boat were ethnic Vietnamese who sneaked away in the dead of night in small boats. These escapes along the coastline had been going on for two years, but the numbers had not been overwhelming.

Now the rules were changed. The government would actually help the Chinese arrange boats for their departures and their exit would become a regularized procedure—for a fee, of course! It was an ingenious plan that achieved virtually everything the Communist government wanted: (1) It ended all private enterprise; (2) it got rid of a potential fifth column; and (3) it enriched the Hanoi regime—by as much as an estimated three billion dollars.

So Saigon had set the stage for Asia's exodus, and Ng Ngoc Thong and Phan Van Tinh were two of the thousands who made their separate plans to leave Vietnam.

4

Desperate Dash to Freedom

For Phan Van Tinh, the plan to leave Vietnam was an old story.

"Between 1976 and 1978, I had made one official attempt to leave and nine unofficial ones," he says.

"I began my legal efforts in early 1976 when I received sponsorship papers for my family from relatives living in France. Using these, I pursued every avenue I could find for getting official permission to emigrate. In addition to the bureaucratic red tape which caused endless delays, money was also an important factor. If I was willing to pay, exit visas for my family were available.

"The amount was negotiated and I agreed, only

to discover when I returned to get the documents that the agreed-to price had jumped considerably. This escalation game was played through several rounds before I finally gave it up as a lost cause. It took two years.

"Meanwhile, I was searching for other ways to leave the country. On two previous occasions I tried to make arrangements for my entire family of six. At other times, I negotiated for various members of the family, especially the older children who seemed to have the least hope of a future in Vietnam.

"Each attempt—nine in all—resulted in failure. And each time, I lost money because deposits were never returned and there was no one to whom I could complain.

"The nearest we came to making it—before the tenth and successful dash—was also the most dangerous.

"Even now, I can feel the fear as I tell it." Tinh tenses up as he speaks.

"Careful negotiations had been going on with a fisherman from one of the coastal provinces who had a boat. I agreed to pay the man twenty-five ounces of gold for the boat and to finance the rest of the escape, including payoffs for the local officials. The fisherman agreed to handle this part of the arrangement and I gave him the money.

"As the planning progressed, the fisherman

insisted on sending thirteen members of his own family with us. I agreed to this arrangement, however, it was then discovered the boat was not large enough for the passenger load, so I also agreed to put up the capital for the purchase of a larger vessel.

"This required another twenty-five ounces of gold. Then there were repairs on the larger boat, which took more gold. In all, I paid over sixty ounces." (At 1979 prices, this amounts to over $25,000.)

"But it looked like the plan was going to succeed so I really wasn't counting the cost. To leave was worth anything—even everything, if need be.

"Finally, word came that the escape mission was ready. My wife, Sarah, left a day early for the rendezvous city. On the day of the planned departure, I arose at 2:00 A.M. and took the remaining family members to the bus station. Before we could even start our perilous journey to freedom over the South China Sea, we had to make an equally risky trip 200 miles up the coast. That trip took twelve hours.

"When we arrived, Sarah met us at the bus station to tell us that we must go back to Saigon right away. She was terrified.

"The fisherman said he had been questioned by the local officials who suspected he might be planning an escape. He now refused to go. There was no way to determine if he was telling the truth or if he was cheating us and taking our money.

"But his decision had placed our family in grave danger, for now it was three o'clock in the afternoon and we knew we must be back in Saigon that night. If a house was left empty overnight, the local officials assumed the owners had skipped the country and the house was confiscated.

"We were disappointed and afraid, and we started to retrace our steps. First, we hired a microbus to take us halfway to Saigon. Then we found another bus to take us to the city, from where our journey had begun twenty-two long hours before. We arrived about one o'clock in the morning and had to sleep on the floor of the bus station until four o'clock because of the nightly curfew.

"As soon as it was safe to be on the street, I hired a car to take us home. We arrived about 5:00 A.M. We were exhausted, frustrated, and sad. However, our old servant who answered our knock was delighted to have us back. We were right where we started—and much poorer," Tinh says.

Tinh was determined there would be another day. The last escape attempt came in September, 1978.

Chinese were leaving by the thousands with

42

the encouragement of the government. Tinh tried to get permission for his family to go on one of those boats, but he was rebuffed by the organizers.

He was told: "No Vietnamese. No Christians. No intellectuals. Just Chinese."

"Each person had to pay anywhere from twelve to sixteen ounces of gold just for permission to leave," Tinh recalls. "In addition, the organizers had to collect money to buy the boat and pay for repairs. When this was done, the boat was inspected by government officers who would tell them how many persons it would hold."

If a boat might safely carry fifty people, they would put the number at 200 because they were charging the local organizers about twelve ounces of gold for each person. Since the petty local officials wanted their cut, too, they would certify the boat for even more passengers.

This would up the total take from the departing Chinese, so it usually meant that a boatload of 200 people would leave something like 150 pounds of gold in Vietnam. Since all the boats were horribly overcrowded, many did not make it to land but deposited their victims at the bottom of the South China Sea.

"People would take a look at a boat and know they wouldn't make it, but they went anyway," Tinh says sadly.

"Even when they saw how crowded the boats

43

were, people would not back out—never! They would rather die than stay in Vietnam," Tinh emphatically exclaims.

"I finally found a Chinese organizer of a boat who agreed to list our entire family as Chinese, in spite of the fact that there is only Vietnamese blood in our family line. We were given Chinese names and the local authorities couldn't tell the difference when we were put on a long list with scores of other Chinese. As long as the appropriate amount of gold accompanied the passenger list, the officials never bothered to check whether we were really Chinese," Tinh recalls.

"Although a boat was being organized from Bien Hoa, I was too well known to risk leaving from my home province. I knew I would have been recognized and prevented from leaving, and my family and I would have gone to prison, probably.

"The escape was finally arranged from Rach Gia province. Plans were complete within a week, but the price was higher and it cost eighteen ounces of gold for each family member. I paid a total of more than ten pounds of gold for nine people.

"We had little gold or money left. We had to buy food on the black market, and had paid for nine unsuccessful escape ventures. But this was our last desperate effort. After prayer together, we plunged into the uncertain future with never a backward glance.

"Before boarding the boat, each person had to strip for a clothing and body search; the women were allowed to wear only their bras and panties. Each family was limited to a maximum of $300 and six ounces of gold. Our family wealth was down to $400 and five ounces of gold. We were forced to surrender $100, and my eldest son, Minh Hoang, had to give up his Rolex watch as well.

"But at last, we were on our way to freedom, we thought.

"Our boat set sail on the evening of September 7, 1978, but somehow the signals for clearance had not been passed to all the patrol boats down the long canal to the sea. There were delays, boardings, searches and much fear until the confusion was sorted out at daybreak and the boat was permitted to continue out to the open sea.

"Our boat was forty-five feet long and eleven feet wide. The passenger load was 110 men, women and children. Now made into a double-decker, the boat's lower hold had contained many tons of fish during its lifetime. The fish were gone, but the smell was still there. The upper deck had been prepared to provide some shelter from the sun.

"My family was below where one couldn't vomit over the side. And every man, woman and child became seasick. Each one was given a plastic bag.

"There was no room to lie down. Each person had to assume a squatting position with each body supporting another body. Sarah stayed in the bottom of the boat with her eyes closed and didn't move during the entire trip—two and a half days. She held her stationary position even when a storm struck. She found that the less she moved, the less she became sick.

"The only food we had was oranges. And the only water was dirty river water which had been put on board.

"On the night of September 8, while the boat was still in Vietnamese coastal waters, we were stopped by a patrol boat and ordered to proceed to a nearby island for another inspection and clearance. Once again we felt that deadly fear. But a coast guard security vessel which had been tailing our boat until it was in international waters, intervened on our behalf and once again we were permitted to sail away.

"Now there was nothing between us and Malaysia. We hoped for the best.

"On the morning of September 11, after a vicious storm which we rode out at anchor, we spotted the coast of Malaysia. At about the same time, we were intercepted by a small Malaysian police boat which instructed us to follow the official craft to shore. Other patrol boats were shepherding other refugee boats to land, but the boat in which we were riding couldn't keep up.

"In a short while, the engine stopped and our boat was left behind, apparently unnoticed, wallowing in the swells. I think we were about five miles from land at the time. It was too deep to anchor and although we signaled many fishing boats and commercial ships which came close, no one stopped to give aid.

"Pounded by the waves and without engine power, the boat started to leak and for the next twenty-four hours, I was sure we would perish within sight of land. Fear tormented me. We were the only Christians on board, and we sang and prayed. We also cried and repented because we were sure it was the end. My nine-year-old Bich Son took my hand and smiled weakly. It was too much. I thought, 'What have I done to them? God, forgive me.'

"There was work to be done, though, and little time for self-pity. Every able-bodied person worked bailing out the sea water which kept seeping into the hold. It looked like a losing battle until another Malaysian patrol boat came into sight and tossed a tow line to our disabled boat.

"We were towed into the mouth of a river where the waters were calm and the boat would not be buffeted by the waves. For four days we were permitted to stay there and the men were taken to the market in small boats to buy food and bring back water.

"Although the future was still uncertain, we felt safe, even when on the fourth day we were removed from our damaged boat and placed aboard a Malaysian fishing vessel. We were sure that having come this far, people in the free world would not abandon us. We did not yet know how much trouble was ahead." The Tinh family was taken to a refugee camp on the island of Pulau Bidong, twenty miles off the coast of Malaysia, and one of the most notorious of the camps.

Meanwhile, back in Vietnam, the exodus continued.

Even after Ng Ngoc Thong had finished his two years in one of the New Economic Zones, he still didn't think about leaving Vietnam. "It is not an easy thing to think about leaving the land of your birth," he says.

"Many Vietnamese families were urging their young men to leave. The hope was that the strongest and youngest should leave quickly and establish a new life, become successful, and then send for the others. This is what most Asians who consider moving to the West do.

"My mother kept asking me to go, but I was afraid," Thong now confesses. "What if I would be caught and put in jail? But more than that I was afraid of leaving my home and familiar surroundings even though I hated what my country had become.

"Finally, I became convinced that escape was my only recourse if I ever expected to have a life with promise.

"I had to be extremely careful in shopping around for an escape boat," Thong recounts. "I was afraid of going to a fellow Vietnamese because there were so many cheats around who would promise you anything, but after taking your money they would run away, never to be seen again."

Tinh had learned this the hard way. Now Thong did what Tinh had done. He found some Chinese who had been given permission to leave. They were building their own boat and he got them to agree to take his entire family. For three ounces of gold, he obtained phony papers attesting that he and his family were original ethnic Chinese.

"We were scheduled to depart on Christmas, 1978, but for some reason the police refused to let us leave. Our disappointment was keen, but we kept searching for a way out.

"While I waited, I visited my younger brother in prison. He had been there since his arrest in 1975.

"I had not seen him for a long time and he looked terrible," Thong sadly recalls. "He was haggard and half the size of his former self. It was obvious he had been starved and beaten, yet all we could say to each other in the presence of the Communist guard were dumb remarks like, 'Isn't it wonderful the way Chairman Ho takes such good care of us,' and other stupid things.

"I so much wanted to tell him that the family was going to leave Vietnam, but I couldn't say a word because the guard was with us the whole time. It broke my heart to leave him and it still breaks my heart today. I really don't know whether he is alive or dead.

"In early 1979, I began to search for a good boat and an honest captain. Through a Chinese friend, I met a man who was building a large boat in My Tho, about forty miles south of Saigon. The boat looked good, and I arranged once again for my family to be on board when she sailed.

"The escape cost ten ounces of gold for each family member. The rate was different from province to province and from time to time, because others have told me they paid more or less than I did.

"The list of passengers was given to the police for their review and inspection," Thong recalls. "I held my breath, thinking that at any moment our deception might be discovered and they would burst in on us and arrest my whole family. But the phony papers were not questioned, and we were approved along with all the rest of the Chinese people.

"The departure from Vietnam was set for

May 25, 1979. My family traveled from Saigon to My Tho in three small groups and at different times to avoid detection. We boarded the boat and immediately set out to sea—escorted by a Communist patrol boat. Apparently this protection was included in the price or else the government wanted to be sure no one turned around and came back.

"The boat was terribly crowded. It carried 575 people, but it was so good to be leaving, I didn't mind being crowded," Thong says.

The trip did not go smoothly. There were numerous changes in direction, and although Thong may not have known this, it likely had something to do with information about which countries were being most lenient with refugees. At first, the boat was headed for Australia. Then it turned toward Hong Kong.

"It became a madhouse," Thong grimly remembers. "People were getting sick, complaining about the lack of food and water, the pitching of the boat, the heavy seas. As the days went on and the conditions on the ship worsened, we decided to put in for the closest land—which happened to be Malaysia.

"On the third night out, when the boat was about 100 miles from the Malaysian coast, we spotted two large boats bearing down on us. Searchlights illuminated our unarmed vessel as the two boats came alongside. The crews of the intercepting boats pulled out what appeared to be machine guns. Then a third boat appeared across the bow, forcing us to stop.

"Now our boat was hemmed in and we were terrified. We had not been warned about pirates.

"Our captain shouted for all of us to scramble into the hold and hide. But I was mad as hell! We had planned months for this escape, agonized over leaving our homeland and paid dearly in treasure and heartbreak. I grabbed the captain and shouted, 'No way! We're going to fight! There are only a few of them and we have at least 200 strong young men on our boat!'" Thong recounts.

"Maybe my bravery was partly based on the fact that I was pretty sure their machine guns were phony. I got a good look at one they had thrust out of a porthole and it looked like a cheap toy gun. But it was a risk nonetheless.

"I rallied about 200 of our men, told them to grab anything they could put their hands on and line up shoulder-to-shoulder around the deck of our boat. There we stood—waving sticks, knives, pieces of metal. I shouted at the pirate boat commander and told him, in English, that we were not going to let them take us and I dared him to try.

"One of the pirate boats tried to ram us, but we fired up our engine and banged into him instead.

"Our bluff worked! We ran right through the blockade and sailed free of the pirates. All our men cheered and waved their crude weapons in the air.

"About fifteen minutes later, we saw another refugee boat enter the same area, but these people were not so lucky. We saw the pirates board the boat and I do not know what finally happened to them.

"Our boat continued on course for Malaysia, but was forced to stop about 350 yards from shore because a Malaysian gunboat blocked the way to the beach. A line was hitched to our boat in preparation for towing back to sea. We collected ten ounces of gold and passed it to the captain of the gunboat as a kind of insurance policy.

"It worked, and our boat was safely towed toward Indonesia where, some thirty hours later, it was cut loose within sight of the island of Keramut in the Anambas group," says Thong.

Thong, in August of 1979, had been selected as vice-chairman of the refugee committee at Kuku camp on Jemaja Island in the same Anambas group. His education and leadership qualities are put to good use as he helps direct the activities of a thriving primitive "town" of 16,000 refugees, all awaiting resettlement. Every day he hears stories of terror and grief, many even more heartbreaking than his own.

"We don't know how many people have left our country since the Communists took over," Thong muses, "but we do know that as of

October 1, 1979, 400,000 of the boat people made it to land. Most authorities and rescue organizations say probably only about half who leave the country survive. So many people at the camps cannot locate friends or relatives who left Vietnam that I am sure it is accurate to say that only half make it.

"Although the free world did not set out to murder us, they allowed many of us to die. Whether murdered or allowed to die makes little difference to the victim. It was much easier to look away from the South China Sea from 1976 to 1979, I am sure, and most countries did. Perhaps they were afraid of the responsibility of resettling refugees in Western countries.

"No one seemed to care enough to help us. If we could make it to shore in the leaky, disabled boats, we might be allowed to stay—depending on when and where we landed. But to throw a life preserver out to us while we were on the water was viewed somehow as interfering with fate, and creating problems for the government who would have to feed and clothe and shelter us. Only a few private organizations cared enough to try to help rescue the homeless refugees on the sea. They had to deal with strong disapproval of most governments," Thong says. (World Vision of the United States was one of the organizations which helped the refugees.)

"Since I have been at the camp, I have met

many people who have come here as refugees, or have come to help us. The things I hear are incredible. We know now that shipping companies had trouble unloading any refugees they might have rescued, so orders went out to the ships of many flags to stay away from areas where refugee boats were likely to be, and to ignore any they might encounter," adds Thong sadly.

It is the first time in history that SOS cries on the high seas were so callously ignored. Sea captains were faced with the cruel dilemma of violating the first law of the sea—rescuing persons in peril on the seas is a universal law—or losing their positions with their companies. Humanitarian acts saving refugees took up precious time in trying to unload human cargo, while the ships could have been hauling money-making cargo.

Most chose to follow company policy. The personal consequences of doing otherwise were too great to give a ship's master such free choice. The navies weren't much more help than the merchant fleets. The United States had the largest naval flotilla in the area, the U.S. Seventh Fleet, based in the Philippines. They helped a few refugee boats, but it was not until July of 1979 that President Carter ordered them to actively assist and rescue refugee boats.

The Italian navy sent three vessels from the Mediterranean Sea. They came just as the

Vietnamese government clamped down on the fleeing boats in response to massive international opinion. The Italians sailed around the South China Sea for a while with no success, so the Malaysians cooperatively towed out 700 refugees from their own beaches to be "rescued" by the Italian ships.

The Malaysians must have decided the Italians shouldn't be sent home disappointed and empty-handed. They had previously played this little game with the French hospital ship, *Ile de Lumiere*. That time they got rid of over 800 of their unwanted guests.

But before the South China Sea came in for all that naval attention, the world was unaware of, or ignoring, those little boats with their tragic victims. Still, more and more were leaving the shores of Communist Vietnam with hopes for what another refugee, Nguyen H. Quoi, describes as "freedom, justice, brotherhood and civilization."

5

Through Dangers, Toils and Snares

Quoi was a twenty-year civil service veteran with the government of the Republic of Vietnam when he left his homeland in April, 1979. He knew all the dangers. Because he spoke English and his wife taught French, they listened regularly to foreign news broadcasts. From the Voice of America, Radio Australia and the foreign news service of the British Broadcasting Corporation, they knew about the pirates, and that refugees from Indochina were becoming increasingly unwelcome throughout Southeast Asia. They also knew that if they tried and failed, the inevitable result would be prison and hard labor.

However, they decided to try to escape anyway. "We had come to the conclusion that living in Vietnam was no longer a life," Quoi says at a refugee camp near Jakarta, Indonesia. "My wife and I talked very deeply about our chances of making it. After much profound consideration, we accepted the high risk.

"There were two basic reasons. One had to do with ourselves. If we remained in Vietnam, we would live as agonized people and ultimately die in frustration, in despair, in poverty.

"The other reason was our children. In Vietnam, they would have no future. We have a daughter who is crippled from an early attack of meningitis. We could get no medicine or help for her nor could we get milk and enough food for our other children. Consequently, none of us had a future in Vietnam.

"We believe in God and we believed He would help us. Even if we had only one chance in ten, we knew we had to take it for the sake of our children. We accepted that the odds were heavily against us, so we prepared to die."

The free world allowed people like Quoi—simple and hard-working—to perish. Quoi was not a capitalist or of the bourgeois class, like Tinh. He was not a lawyer, like Thong. He was a simple civil servant who got caught on the losing side of a war he had little to do with and found that under the totalitarian society established by the victors, he couldn't provide either today's necessities or a future hope for his children.

Allowing for the slim chance that they might

somehow survive, the risk of death seemed not too great a chance to take.

"Because I was a poor man, I could not possibly afford the cost of an escape for my entire family," Quoi says. "My wife insisted that I go alone. Once on the outside, I could try to make arrangements for the rest of them. It was only a vague hope, but there was nothing better to hope for.

"Three times I tried to arrange an escape. An old friend who knew I was a poor man arranged to include me in these efforts without having to pay any money. Each time they failed through betrayal or a sellout of the organizers.

"In the meantime, my sister, who lived in the United States, had found a way to get money to my family. We lived on part of it, but saved the rest to invest in a fourth escape attempt.

"Four of my old trusted friends and I were the organizers of this plan. By now we had stopped trusting others. However, among ourselves we did not have enough money for a boat and papers, so I was given the responsibility of finding more investors who would join our escape.

"Gradually, our plan began to come together. Many people wanted to leave, so it became a matter of choosing the most compatible and trustworthy among them. Before long the money was in hand and the organizing committee had made a trip to the southern province bordering Cambodia from which we would attempt our escape. We purchased and repaired an old fishing boat. It was small—only thirty-five feet long and ten feet wide. With a normal capacity of only thirty people, it had to be made ready for sixty-eight, for that was the number included in the escape conspiracy.

"The planning and organizing took months, for it all had to be done secretly. We were Vietnamese, not Chinese, and it was impossible to buy off the local officials even if we had had the gold," Quoi goes on.

"Since all the families were coming from Saigon, this meant that travel to the distant province had to be done in small groups at different times. Safe places had to be arranged where we could stay temporarily. A gathering point had to be determined which would give a legitimate reason for so many people being in the same place at the same time. No detail could be overlooked without disastrous consequences.

"Our departure was scheduled for December, 1978, but had to be postponed several times for technical reasons. Once it was delayed because the man who was staying with the boat noticed military operations going on in nearby waters between the Vietnamese navy and some ships belonging to the Khmer Rouge in Cambodia.

"At last, the coast seemed clear and we set our departure for Sunday, April 15, 1979. Two days earlier, family groups started leaving Saigon. On the morning of departure day, as we made our way to the rendezvous points, we were amazed to discover there was scarcely any possibility of detection. We had gathered right at the Sunday morning provincial farmer's market and the place was teeming with people!" Quoi smiles.

"I believe God helped me select these points, for I had not been to the town on Sunday and did not know the weekly market was held almost exactly where I had designated the three meeting places.

"There was another circumstance when I believe God especially helped us. Since the fishing boat which would take us to freedom was being kept at an island six miles off the coast, I had arranged a river boat to pick up my passengers and transport us on a journey of seven hours through rivers and channels until we could then make our dash across the ocean to the island.

"This was going to be the most difficult part of the whole operation, we knew.

"With joy, I discovered many river boats being used as ferries that day to take people to and from the market in the provincial capital. My boat looked like just another ferry!

"We got an early start and things went smoothly. Only once on the journey through the island waterways were we stopped by a patrol who wanted to see certain papers and documents. All these had been carefully forged in Saigon and we were permitted to pass without difficulty. We arrived at the open sea early in the afternoon—a time when we would never have been suspected of attempting an escape.

"But still we were not out of Vietnam. For the six-mile trip across open water, we couldn't risk being seen with so many people. All but four—two on the bow and two on the stern—lay down in the bottom of the boat and were covered with canvas. Thirty-six of the total were children, and they were literally stacked on top of each other.

"If the trip had lasted longer than expected, I'm afraid some would have suffocated," Quoi says. "The noon heat was awful.

"We now looked like a small supply boat going from the mainland to an isolated island. When we arrived at the fishing boat, careful organization paid off again. The transfer of sixty people and baggage was made in fifteen minutes. Once again, the passengers were told to lie down to avoid detection. But almost immediately it began to rain, lowering visibility and making it difficult for any cruising patrol boat to spot us.

"We had provisions for what we thought would be a three-day run to the Malaysian coast, and our boat got underway during the rainstorm. We managed to evade a Communist patrol boat the first night, but our little vessel was not so lucky on the second day. A pirate fishing boat came bearing down on us. It was larger than our boat, and it flew the flag of Thailand.

"Without gold and with almost no money, our unfortunate group tried friendship. We inquired about the direction to Malaysia and the pirates responded with pretended sympathy. As if offering assistance, they threw a line from the fishing vessel to our craft. As soon as it was secure, two men armed with a gun, a knife and a hammer boarded our boat and the robbery began," recalls Quoi.

"We had decided before we left Vietnam that we would not resist any attackers, rather than risk harm to our wives and children, so we didn't try to fight them.

"I don't think that these were very wealthy pirates, or perhaps they were new at the trade, for they seemed delighted with everything they found—even an old cigarette lighter. They weren't too upset over not finding gold and seemed to understand that our particular group of refugees had spent everything we owned just to get a boat.

"But within an hour after the first attack, a second pirate boat appeared. After boarding our vessel and discovering that everything of value had already been taken, they vented their wrath by taking all our personal papers and documents, including educational diplomas, and throwing them overboard. After this indignity, they left.

"The third attack that day was more bitter.

Finding nothing of value after hours of searching, the pirates took apart the engine compartment, believing gold must be hidden somewhere. They threatened us severely, but finally left when they were convinced we truly had nothing left to steal.

"After taking the last 200 liters of our diesel fuel, the third group also took the boat's compass. Now our boat was totally stripped.

"Our morale hit rock bottom. Quarreling broke out among us and a number of the women began to question their husbands' decisions to make the escape. It was a bad time, but we took counsel together and decided to stay with the original plan as much as possible. We would steer by the sun during the day and by the stars at night, head south and hope to hit the Malaysian coast. We would run the engine intermittently in order to conserve the precious fuel which was left. Rice and water were also carefully rationed since the trip would now likely be longer than originally planned.

"On the fourth day—just one day behind schedule—our little boat arrived off the Malaysian coast at the town of Kuala in Terengganu. We anchored about 300 yards offshore and I and two young men who could speak English volunteered to swim ashore and try to see the local officials. We took water cans with us also, not simply as a disguise since the supply on board was exhausted.

"On reaching shore, we were surrounded by

police and military men who said they would inform the Malaysian authorities and the office of the United Nations High Commissioner for Refugees about our arrival. We were also told we probably would be sent to a nearby refugee camp.

"With our water cans filled and our spirits encouraged, we swam back to the boat.

"Shortly after, a small patrol boat came and stood by the refugee craft most of the day. If we had had gold to give them, I think the patrol boat would have taken us to the camp. Finally, in the late afternoon, we were told we would be directed to the camp after all," recalls Quoi.

"It was a lie. Instead, we were guided to a Malaysian gunboat, the P36. Five of the men, including me, were taken on board the navy ship as hostages and a tow line was attached to the refugee boat. The others were informed that if the rope was cut while they were being towed, we five men would be killed.

"The towing went on all night at very high speeds for about twelve or fourteen hours. It was raining and the seas were rough. We were terrified for our families in the fragile little craft.

"Finally, I found courage enough to speak to the captain. I said, 'Please, sir, remove the tow line. Let our boat follow you or come alongside you. We are afraid it will capsize if you continue like this. I beg you, consider our wives and our children as if they were your own. We ask you for mercy for them.'

"Whatever it was the captain found in my words, it wasn't long until the towing operation stopped. We were placed back in the boat and it was cut loose.

"Without a word, and without supplies, we were left without directions, to drift.

"I think we were about 200 miles from where we started. Our propeller was broken from the towing, so some of the men had to go over the side to repair it.

"Again, depression set in. I wondered if the agony of living on the brink of disaster would ever end. I wondered how much more my nerves could take.

"The next day, we came within sight of land again. Another Malaysian craft—the P34—bore down on us. We signaled that we would not enter Malaysian waters and said that our destination was Singapore.

"Our words were unheeded. The man on the P34 threw a tow rope to us, and when at first we refused to attach it, the Malaysian fired shots over our heads and we were forced to tie the rope.

"The towing continued for another ten hours of terror. When it finally stopped and they detached the rope from the P34 and threw it back to us, the women asked the commander of the vessel for water. The fresh water supply was completely gone. Sea water was being used for mixing milk for babies and for cooking rice. The situation became desperate and the women then turned their asking to tearful pleas.

"The captain shouted back, 'Stop crying! We are not your God! Stop crying! Stop crying!'

"Then the boat sailed away.

"On the sixth day—April 21, 1979—we were on the edge of the busy shipping lanes between Singapore and Hong Kong. We saw huge ships pass not too far away, and we signaled with everything available—flags, clothes, torches. No one stopped.

"The next boats we encountered were two fishing vessels from Singapore.

"From them we experienced the first act of kindness we had seen in six days," Quoi's voice breaks as he recalls this event. "They gave us water, food and some diesel fuel. And even though it was the policy of the Singapore government not to receive refugee boats, the fishermen pointed us toward their home port.

"We headed down the channel, past Horsburgh Lighthouse, toward the small city/state of Singapore. Remarkably, we were not spotted by any patrol craft even though both Singapore and Indonesia patrol these narrow straits watchfully. Perhaps it was because it was raining and we were sailing the straits by night, but I am also certain that God had a hand in it.

"The next morning—the seventh day—we

beached our boat, still undetected, near Changi Airport. With relief and excitement, we tumbled over each other to set foot on land. One of my friends, a graduate from the University of Michigan, was also a civil servant in Vietnam. He and I both had spent two months in Singapore during 1970, and we decided to hitchhike downtown to seek help from a friend we remembered.

"Our friend was not at home. It was Sunday, and a call to the office of the United Nations High Commissioner for Refugees (UNHCR) produced no answer.

"Almost frantically, I put in a call to the French Embassy. They told me to call back on Monday.

"I made one last desperate call to the American Embassy, and was told by the guard who answered the telephone to be there at noon. We arrived at the embassy at 11:59 and were met outside by three Singapore policemen. Our clothes and unkempt appearance gave us away as refugees, but one policeman asked: 'Are you Vietnamese?'

"When we said we were, we were immediately arrested. We wondered if the Americans had betrayed us. They had not. Shortly after we had left our group, scores of local police showed up and surrounded the refugees on the beach. On learning that we had gone downtown, the police assumed that the American Embassy would be the most likely place for us to show up," Quoi comments.

"Although we were questioned at length about how we had managed to get past the naval security blockade, we were not mistreated in any way. It was explained to us that Singapore is a small place with no room for refugees. We were told we would be given a boat and supplies so we could go to Darwin, Australia.

"They made it sound so reasonable and attractive that we agreed to take the offer on condition that we be given a compass and a detailed chart showing the way to Australia," Quoi says.

"Later, we were reunited with our group on the pier and we were given another boat together with a marine map showing the route to Australia. We were told the monsoons were due anytime and so a Singapore navy boat would tow us some distance in order to help us get a good start.

"Not until two days later, when we were running out of food, fuel and water did we realize we had been tricked. By this time we were in Indonesian waters, which was probably what those in Singapore intended. The little country wanted to keep friendly relations with both of its big neighbors. A chart showing a line to Australia, along with only enough fuel to get to Indonesia was their dishonest way of not angering either.

"When our boat pulled into one of the Indonesian islands, we were warmly welcomed by the local people. They gave us food and clothing, together with another map showing the way to the Indonesian capitol of Jakarta. They said it would be a much shorter and safer journey than the one to Darwin," remembers Quoi.

"We will never forget the kindness of the Indonesian people, and we will also remember the generosity of the unknown Singapore fishing boats. When our boat arrived at Jakarta on the evening of April 26, we were once again courteously received, although we were required to wait on our boat at the pier for three weeks before being given permission to enter a refugee camp in the country.

"The journey took twelve days. We had been through many dangers, toils and snares," Quoi concludes, "but by the grace of God, sixty-eight precious human beings had survived. We had not joined those on the bottom of the sea."

6

Deepwater Roulette

Russian roulette is played with a loaded gun. Deepwater roulette is played with a loaded boat.

Where a gun is used, only one chamber out of six contains the bullet. Thus the odds are five to one that the player will draw a blank chamber.

But in the deepwater version which Vietnamese boat people are forced to play, half the "chambers" are loaded. Against them are corrupt officials, rapacious pirates, treacherous weather, leaky boats, vicious police and army, and indifferent governments.

Their chances for survival are only one in two. It is, no figure of speech intended, a deadly game.

We do not know the terrible experiences of those who don't make it, for, as in murder mysteries, dead men tell no tales. But there are thousands of stories from the survivors.

From a collection of interviews with survivors in refugee camps all over Asia, some stories of tragedies and triumphs will give you an idea of what it is like to be a refugee in Southeast Asia today.

Lam's Escape

There was enough money in Lam's family to buy an escape for only one of the children. When her mother asked the eighteen-year-old girl and her older brother which one of them wanted to go, Lam did not hesitate.

"Me!" she said immediately.

Then she was ashamed of her selfishness. But as it turned out, other circumstances actually determined she should indeed be the one, for the boat organizers needed one young girl to fit the passenger roster. They wanted a fifteen-year-old, and Lam's youthful appearance fit the bill perfectly.

"For more than three years, I had been talking with my parents about the possibility of trying to flee. Even at fifteen, I knew there was no future for me in Vietnam.

"My chance came in early 1979 when, with 329 others, I boarded a fifty-foot fishing boat at Song Be, about twenty miles east of Saigon. Like so many other Vietnamese, I was on the boat because my parents had bought forged documents for me, indicating that I was ethnic Chinese.

"I knew there was great danger on the boat," Lam says, "but I decided I must go at any cost. I would rather die trying to find a future than live where there was none.

"On the first day at sea, our boat was stopped by a Vietnamese navy gunboat. They forced our small craft back to land and all 330 passengers were put in jail. My heart pounded all night and there were no family members to comfort me.

"I didn't know what would happen to me," she recalls. "I was afraid they would discover my false papers and send me back.

"Three days later, the authorities released all but twenty-five of us. Those detained were young men—all Vietnamese—who had tried to leave with false documents. The regime wanted them for the war being launched in Cambodia. This was one of the main reasons why so many of the young men were trying to flee the country.

"I felt very sad for them," Lam says. "And I was ashamed I was able to leave while they were still in jail.

"But once again I had been chosen, and I wondered why. As we started out again, I thought about my family. My mother, father, two older sisters and three brothers—now they were all depending on me. How long could they survive in Vietnam? Could I establish a new life somewhere and save enough money to get them out someday?" says Lam in a low, gentle voice.

"Six days the boat sailed the choppy waters of the South China Sea. I became seasick, as did many of the others. There was no room to stand, lie down, or stretch. There were no toilets, no room to bathe. The stench was sickening.

"Finally, we arrived at a small island off the coast of Johore, Malaysia, and gratefully beached our craft. We clustered together for protection and ate food from supplies still on the boat.

"After we were on the beach for a week, the Malaysian authorities gave us additional food and water and we were permitted to go to the village and buy plastic sheeting for protection against the wind and rain.

"We remained on the beach for four weeks before we were gathered back into our boat and towed away by the Malaysian navy," Lam remembers.

She echoes the story heard so many times before, "They were going very fast and we were afraid our boat would capsize. We didn't know where they were taking us.

"The rope was cut after twenty-four hours, when the boat was near the Anambas Islands of Indonesia. We drifted toward the shore and on March 26, 1979, thirty-eight days after beginning our journey, we beached near the town of Letung. The Indonesians didn't turn us away.

"I was put in a refugee camp with thousands of other Vietnamese, yet I felt very much alone. Everyone else had families," she said softly. "I felt very sad to be alone and many times I thought I did not have the courage to continue. I missed my family very much."

Then she brightens: "But when I compare living in the refugee camp to living in Vietnam, the difference is literally like night and day. Vietnam was all the time like living in a heavy jungle with no sunlight coming through the trees. Life was black. Here I am happy to be free, to see sunlight.

"But I am sad to be so far away from my family."

"Where Is My Father?"

For months Nguyen Duc Tho had tried to find some way to get the three members of his family out of Saigon. But in 1976, even making such kinds of inquiries could be highly dangerous for a professional man.

So Tho and his wife, Mai, agreed that he should go first.

"We decided I would try to leave later with our six-year-old daughter," Mai says. "My husband made it, and I received a letter from him as soon as he arrived in Singapore. He was waiting for some country to take him. Then there was no more mail. I am sure it was intercepted or just not delivered.

"My chance did not come for two more years. In

the meantime, I had to make up all kinds of stories for my friends at work to explain my husband's absence. Finally, I told them we had quarreled and he had just left. I said I didn't know where he was. That, at least, was true.

"At last, I made the journey across the South China Sea with my daughter, who was then eight. Now that we are here, I still search for my husband. Two years is a long time, and there are many people looking for lost relatives," Mai whispers, her eyes filling with tears as she waits at the Laem Sing camp on the shores of the Gulf of Thailand.

"I don't know how to answer the question my little girl asks so many times: 'Tell me the truth. Where is my daddy?'"

Family Split, Half in Jail

When Manh found out he was on the arrest list late in 1977, his decision to leave had already been made. As a former air force officer under the old regime and in the security police, he had known all along that his days were numbered.

But it had been impossible to arrange an escape for his entire family which consisted of nine people. The news about his imminent arrest, however, forced him to move quickly. He and his brother made an agreement that Manh would leave with three sons and a nephew, and his brother would try to make arrangements later to bring out his wife and other children.

Manh made it to a camp in Thailand. The others weren't as fortunate. A passenger on the refugee boat from the city where he formerly lived had brought the crushing news that three months before, his brother and entire family had been caught in an escape attempt. The whole group had been thrown into jail.

"It makes me so sad," Manh said. "With my past occupation, I think it will be a long time before my wife and children are released from jail. A lot of nights I wonder if I should have left them."

Then he asks of no one in particular, "But what else could I do?"

"We All Fight to Live"

Many of the boat captains wrote brief reports of their escapes and experiences, just to make sure something was on record about what happened to them. Even though many use poor English, the words communicate the agony through which they went.

Here are excerpts from one report:

"We leave 31 May but get lost after three days. Pirates robbed us twice and one boat hit us hard so our magnetic compass got broke and engine no run. A Thai boat tossed us to Malaysia. We live on beach twenty days.

"Next Malaysians put us on barge to go to island, they say. Three barges. But on way they told us to hand over gold and money or be abandoned in open sea. Being very fright we hand over everything, but captain not satisfied and come back second time demanded more money. Some people give more so he get mad and come back third time. Now all lose everything. . . .

"But he still no take us to island of Bidong. He went to ocean and cut all barges loose. We drift apart but some engine not work. . . . Next we look for island to get water. We have nothing and many are died, but when we get back into local, Malaysian navy tow us away again.

"This time tow very fast. Many start singing and cried getting ready for death. Water was coming in fast. We all fight to live when we think we come to end. But this boat toss us to Indonesian waters and we stay two days on little island called Mankai where lighthouse was. Now was 7 July. We had died fifteen people.

"Our journey was miserable and bitter one. Everybody fight against death. We have to give away all our gold, money and belongings to save our lives. We came here with only our bare hands. Oh, yes—and our life."

"Blood Came Out Everywhere"

One small boat left Vietnam in early June, 1979, with only eight people. On board were five brothers and three other relatives—two old men and a girl. They encountered both pirates and men of compassion.

"The first pirates couldn't speak English and we didn't know Thai language," says one of the boys on the refugee boat. "After a time, fifteen of them armed with knives, axes, screwdrivers, steel bars and one gun came on our boat. They beat us bad. The old men and girl fell down unconscious. And for the part of our five brothers, they reserve for us a frightening beating. Blood came out everywhere from our bodies. We let them do whatever they wanted to.

"They stripped us naked and made us come over to their boat. Then they tore our clothes apart looking for gold. After an hour of searching our boat, they beat us again, asking for more dollars and gold but we answered that they had taken all we had.

"Then they started to take pieces off our boat to see if gold was hidden. They asked us more questions. Finally, they angrily poured over oil and fuel into the sea—100 liters of fuel and ten liters of oil. They tore our navigation chart. Water, fishing net, medicines all went into the sea. They tried to break our magnetic compass, but fortunately did not manage to do so.

"We lost maybe ten ounces of gold, $500 and some jewels. We continue on our course and ran across same boat. When we saw them, they laughed and left. About nine o'clock there was another Thai boat. It came alongside and they also

searched us and threatened us. I told them everything had been taken by the other Thai boat.
They laughed and fled.

"Late that day we saw a very big boat nearing us.
They stopped for about five minutes and went on.

"But two days later when we were in bad shape,
another Thai boat visited us and they were more
human. We got from them fuel, rice, fish, beans
and oil for our boat. We learned not everyone is
bad," the young man continued.

"Then on the 17 June we vaguely saw Malaysian
coast. We shouted happily knowing we were no
more threatened by pirates. We were happy too
soon, though.

"As we jumped from the boat and came to shore
in late afternoon, the Malaysians came out and
threw rocks and beat us. Two were hurt on the
head, one was beaten and his left arm broken. We
rushed back to our boat and started to go away
when the engine stopped completely. We were
drifting off land at midnight when Malaysian
soldiers used searchlight and make us come to
shore. They sent five young men to swim and
pull our boat.

"They searched for gold but could find nothing.
They took us along shore for maybe two kilo-
meters and let us stay at a camp. About 800 of us
were there for twenty days."

The rest of the young man's story has the same
sadness of so many others. There is abuse, rape of

a young girl, deception, broken promises—and, finally, the fast ride in a fragile boat at the end of a tow rope.

It was a ride to Indonesia, now regarded as the safest halfway stop for so many on their way to begin new lives.

323 Unaccounted For

A horrifying story was recorded by the captain of boat number PT MT 909. It is a long, rambling account which soberly tells of the same terrible ordeals as virtually all the others, including pirate raids, storms, rapes, Malay deception, family separations and drownings.

The PT MT 909 left Vietnam on June 9, 1979, with 491 passengers. When it arrived in Indonesia exactly one month later, only 168 people could be accounted for.

The Lone Survivor

On October 13, 1979, an exhausted Vietnamese refugee was washed up on the shores of Kuala Terengganu province on Malaysia's east coast. The story of Nguyen Van Voc is so incredible that it might not have been believed if others had not made the treacherous journey and told their horror tales, too.

"I was the sole survivor among forty-eight refugees who left Vietnam in a twenty-seven-foot wooden boat on October 1. Our boat was attacked by Thai pirates in the first week, and on October 8 it encountered bad weather and rough seas and capsized.

"All but seven of us drowned immediately. The survivors floated about, holding on to various items. But one by one, they all slipped beneath the waves until after twenty-four hours, only I was left," says the twenty-year-old man.

"For the next five days, I clung to a plastic tube until the sea carried me to land and gave up its hold on me."

Voc's companions are now among the many human victims in the Gulf of Thailand—a toll so great that veteran Asian correspondent, Keyes Beech, reported in the *Los Angeles Times* that those normally rich fishing grounds are now being avoided by fishermen because their nets were bringing up too many human bodies.

7

A Boat Called Christian

As I looked down the list of refugee boats which had arrived at Kuku camp on the Indonesian island of Jemaja between June and August, 1979, I saw that most of them were identified only by numbers. VT 903, for instance, meant the boat had come from Vung Tau, on the coast of Vietnam, and this was the official number by which it was registered in Vietnam. A few of the boats, however, were identified by names. One among them immediately captured my attention and imagination—a boat called Christian.

There had to be a story behind that name. I decided to learn how it got its name. I wasn't sure how difficult it would be, considering I had only a

83

short time and I was looking for the captain in a jam-packed refugee camp which then housed over 11,000 people. And the dirt paths didn't have names and the thatch huts didn't have numbers!

But I hadn't reckoned on the resourcefulness, thorough organization and tough discipline of my host, the camp commander, Colonel Nhu. An officer retired from the Army of the Republic of Vietnam, the diminutive but dynamic colonel issued a couple of terse orders to younger men standing nearby.

Nguyen Van Thieu, the object of my curiosity, was soon standing before me in the camp headquarters building.

The man I met was an ex-navy corporal, twenty-seven years old, who had been captain of the boat called Christian. Thieu was a Roman Catholic who brought with him an older man, the leader of the small group of twenty-eight who had escaped in the boat. Pham Duc Long was thirty-nine and he was a Protestant. I was eager to hear their story.

"When the boat slipped away from the coast of Vietnam just after midnight on June 8, 1979, it had neither a name nor a number," recounts Thieu. "It was so small and unimpressive that it scarcely seemed worthy of the dignity of either. It was not a pleasure craft or even a regular fishing vessel. It was just a boat. Like most similar boats in Vietnam, it was powered by a three-cylinder

Yangma diesel engine. It was thirty-three feet long and six-and one-half feet wide.

"The boat had never been fitted with a compass or instruments for ocean sailing because I couldn't afford them. Sometimes I had used it to fish a little in the inland waterways around my hometown of Vung Tau. Now and again I would take the family for a short excursion down the coast.

"Occasionally, I would seal the cracks between the timbers and touch it up with some paint. No major overhaul. It was . . . just a boat," says Thieu, a former Coast Guard navigator.

"As the pressures began to build against me my little boat began to look more and more as if it might provide an answer. But the problems were many. I was against Communism, and the new government in my country accused me of being an agent of the Americans whom they had left behind when the U.S. forces withdrew.

"This was not true, but I certainly would have participated in anti-Communist activities if the opportunity had presented itself. That's why I was arrested," Thieu says.

"I was in prison from July 16, 1977, to September 23, 1978. On my release, I discovered that not only had I lost my citizenship, but my property and all my other possessions had been confiscated.

"Somehow, though, the authorities had overlooked my boat.

"After I was out of jail, the Communists tailed me all the time," Thieu recalls. "I couldn't find a job and there was no way to support my family. Day and night, I was obsessed with fear and terror. I made up my mind to seek freedom as soon as possible."

Since Vietnam has no land borders contiguous with any free nation, he turned to the sea, as thousands of others have done. It was the only way out, and his little boat began to look—in his eyes—like Noah's ark. It would take him and his family to safety.

But the vessel needed lots of preparatory work and some additional equipment, and he had no money. So Thieu began looking for financial help from old and dependable friends.

"It took me a long time because I had to be extremely careful," he says. "I needed people who had good will, firmness, courage and a thirst for freedom to match my own."

His first recruit was Nyuyen Van Hai. Hai had been a lieutenant in the army and had served as a security officer. Considered by the Communists to be "politically unreliable," the thirty-one-year-old ex-ARVN officer had been sent to a re-education camp where he stayed three years and seven months. When Thieu met him in March, 1979, Hai had just escaped from the camp and was looking for a way out of the country.

Hai was given the job of finding some people who could help pay for the venture.

Pham Duc Long was the first one who enlisted. His background made him the ideal leader of the little close-knit group. He had been an ARVN officer and had served as an assistant professor at the military academy. The Communists had put him in a reeducation camp where he spent almost three years, not being released until 1978.

Long's home had been in Dalat, but on release from his brain-washing experience, he was required to live in Saigon where the authorities could keep an eye on him. His wife and children continued to live in Dalat, for he had no job to support them. He could not even visit them in his native highland without a permit.

Long brought into the plot his brother-in-law, Tran The Hung. His wife, Long's sister, had been a former teacher in World Vision's educational program in Vietnam. She was now pregnant and they wanted their child born in freedom.

Hung was also a former military man, but his primary value to the party was that he lived in a sparsely populated area on the water. It was an ideal place to keep the boat and from which to embark.

Others were gradually added, including two ex-soldiers whose wives had previously escaped and were living in the United States. Two young university students were brought into the group.

Their parents helped finance the trip in order to get them out of the country. They were Buddhists, the only non-Christians in the party.

To round out the boatload, Thieu put on board six orphaned children who were relatives and acquaintances of his wife. Their future in Vietnam would have been too bleak to have left them behind, Thieu says.

After all the plans were made, the escape had to be delayed several times because of government surveillance. All the leaders were suspect and their movements carefully watched.

Thieu recounts the eventful day: "We heard that the acting chief of police had been accidentally killed by one of his men and we seized that opportunity to launch our attempt. We figured that the excitement of the police might distract them from close supervision of our group."

At midnight, June 7, the selected people were transferred to the edge of a forest near Hung's hut. From there, they were put in sampans and rowed to where the boat was hidden.

The operation went off smoothly with only one hitch which Thieu now tearfully relives: "I left my home with my family at eight-thirty. It was raining and dark, just perfect for an escape. Two of my younger brothers were rowing another sampan. I was rowing fast through the mangrove swamps to the landing site, and somehow my two brothers got lost. No one knew where they were or how they got separated from us. I was heartbroken, but for the sake of my companions, I determined to continue.

"But what a deep sadness for me! I still don't know their fate."

Thieu threaded the little boat through the inland waters of Rung Sat Forest and headed for the sea. When they arrived in open waters at about 2:30 A.M., he turned up the speed to seven knots and held it there in order to get out of Vietnamese waters as quickly as possible. As soon as he calculated they had reached international waters, he set the boat on a course they hoped would take them to Singapore.

Now there was time to make an assessment of their situation. He was dismayed and irritated to discover that all three basic necessities—fuel, food and water—were in very short supply. Additionally, there was only a single compass. No maps. No light.

He now says, "It was stupid! This was the result of our leaving in haste. Without proper sea instruments, the voyage would be very dangerous. We knew it, but we hoped God would watch over us and help us."

Not the least of Thieu's problems was that he was the only one who could run the boat. This meant virtual twenty-four hour duty for him, with only occasional naps when Nguyen Giang, who was also doubling as cook, would take the wheel.

"With no light by which to read the compass, I tried to steer by the stars at night. On cloudy nights, I had to guess my way and frequently we were lost," recalls Thieu.

"Early on the morning of the fourth day, we caught sight of flashes of light in the far distance and assumed it was some large ship. As we came closer, however, we saw it was a platform and rig for drilling for offshore oil. Not knowing how far we had traveled, we guessed it belonged to the Vietnamese and decided it would be safer to avoid it rather than to investigate," he says.

Disaster loomed almost immediately as the engine began to malfunction. Shortly, with a gasp, it stopped altogether. Now they were faced with the dilemma of taking their chances on a big ocean with no engine power or trying to signal the Communists whom they were sure occupied the oil rig.

As the wind and the current pushed them straight for the platform, it looked like the decision was going to be made for them—and their fears mounted. They saw a boat approaching and were sure it was flying the Polish flag! Now they were totally dismayed. Only as the distance narrowed between them and the boat and the rig did they realize that the flag was not Polish, but Indonesian—and that an American flag was flying from the oil rig!

"No doubt we had come to the right place," Thieu says. "God had truly led us here. Intending to go to Singapore, where we would surely have been turned away, we had come to Indonesia where we were welcomed. The presence of Americans after four years was for us a light of hope indeed."

The Indonesian and American crew manning the rig told them it was the drill platform, Runkerdoff, from San Francisco. The crew gave the refugees food and water, fresh milk for the children, and repaired the broken engine. They also drew maps for the captain and advised him to continue his journey to the Indonesian island of Jemaja where they would be placed in a refugee camp.

"We thanked them with all our hearts, but begged them not to send us away," Thieu reflects. "Our boat was in poor condition and we were afraid we would get lost since we still had no navigational instruments. They understood and said we could stay overnight. In the meantime, they would try to contact refugee officials by radio and ask for an official boat to come and pick us up.

"We were overjoyed! That night we had a good dinner and slept soundly. Early the next morning, a United Nations boat arrived carrying other refugee women and children. They allowed us to put our women and children on board, while the men and boys stayed on our little boat and attempted to follow. However, the U.N. boat went much faster than ours. We tried to keep up, but the heavy water was splashing onto our deck and down into the engine compartment," Thieu recounts.

"We desperately signaled the other ship and it stopped. Realizing that our poor boat could no longer make the journey, they told us to abandon it and get aboard with our wives and children.

"As we sailed away, we watched sadly as our small but noble boat slowly sank under the waves."

When Thieu and the others registered at the refugee camp, the Indonesian authorities asked for the number of their boat.

Thieu and Long looked at each other.

It had no number.

Name?

Then and there they decided on the name *Christian*.

"We did so in order to remember the miracle of our salvation and to thank our Savior," they say.

Perhaps the name was more appropriate than they realized at the time. The little boat had saved others and had given its own life in the rescue.

PHOTO SECTION

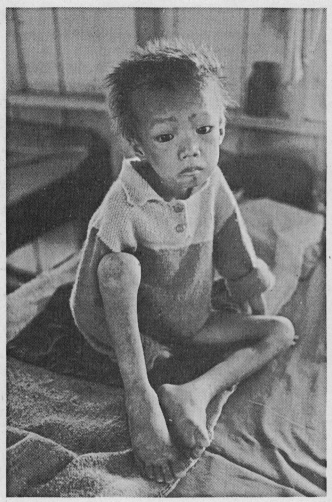
Cambodian baby in Thai border camp.

Stanley Mooneyham on the *Tung An*.

When Chin's family was rescued, this seventeen-year-old girl was one of the first to be brought on board and rescued.

Refugees boarding *Seasweep*.

Refugees sleeping in hold of *Seasweep* in October, 1979.

Nguyen Van Thieu, captain of the refugee boat *Christian* and his wife, Nguyen Thi Hoa, in Kuku refugee camp.

Refugee boat drawing near to *Seasweep*.

Galang refugee camp in Indonesia. World Vision provides medical and food service here.

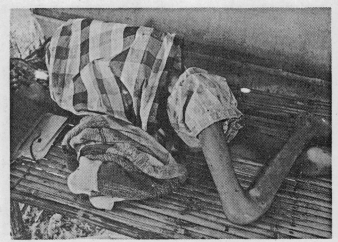

An emaciated Cambodian refugee at a Thai border camp.

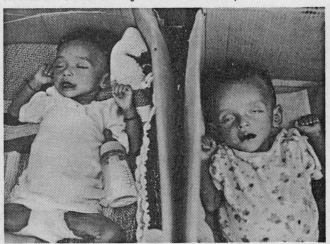

Dying Cambodian babies in a refugee camp in northern Thailand.

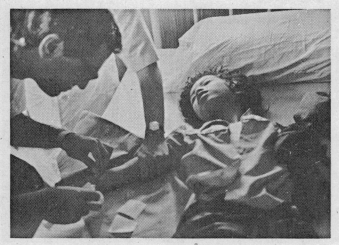

Emergency medical care for rescued refugee girl aboard *Seasweep*.

World Vision nurse, Rosemary (center), distributes malaria medicine.

Stanley Mooneyham with Cambodian refugees in a Thai border camp.

Hmong family at Ban Vinai camp—a husband, his two wives and children.

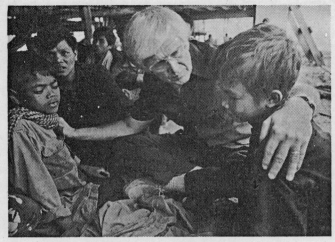

Stanley Mooneyham ministering to Cambodian children.

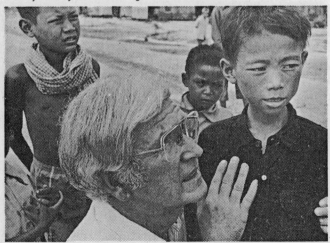

Stanley Mooneyham with a fifteen-year-old Cambodian boy.

World Vision-sponsored school for Hmong refugees in Ban Vinai, Thailand.

Stanley Mooneyham with American missionary and Cambodian Christian leaders in front of their church.

Refugees' thanksgiving worship aboard *Seasweep*.

Standing from left to right: Hung Quoc Nguyen, My Phuong Thi Nguyen.
Seated from left to right: My Lan The Nguyen, My Tran, My Hanh Thi Nguyen.

Stanley Mooneyham interviews Tinh Van Phan (center) and Au Tran (left).

PART II

THOSE WHO CARED

8

Don't Give Us Your Tired, Your Poor

Malay soldiers and Thai fishermen are not the first people to have treated their fellow human beings with contempt and brutality. Nor will they be the last.

The chronicles of man's inhumanity to man began between two brothers—Cain and Abel. It has continued unabated to the present moment.

America's treatment of its own native people is not a record of which we can be proud. Our national closet includes the skeletons of My Lai.

But only occasionally in history does a nation set out on a course to make brutality, terrorism and murder a national policy. Flagrant examples in recent memory could be cited from the Soviet Union, Nazi Germany, Cambodia under Pol Pot and Uganda under Idi Amin.

I would now have to add Malaysia to that list.

The fact that its cynical policy was directed against refugees seeking a haven on its shores rather than against its own people is not a mitigating factor at all. If anything, it makes the crimes more heinous.

Many other countries engage in oppression, violation of human rights, torture and even murder. However, they cover it neatly with a veneer of quasi-legality and pious rhetoric that talks about the need for internal security, protection against subversion, preservation of the motherland, and on and on.

Always, there is the need for self-justification. For Malaysia, it was done in the name of political stability and economic burden.

But by common understanding, refugees have generally been treated as a different category. Usually the objects of religious or racial persecution, or civilians fleeing a war, they have traditionally been given asylum by other countries. Even before a United Nations code, this was a kind of unwritten universal law. For example, African nations always have been awash with refugees trying to escape the ebb and flow of tribal conflicts. Even dictators and murderers have been protected by the principle of asylum. In 1971, India permitted nearly twelve million Bengalis to find refuge behind her borders while the civil war raged in Bangladesh.

History has no direct counterpart, though, for

what has been happening in Southeast Asia for the past five years. In addition to those Vietnamese, Laotians and Cambodians who left their countries voluntarily so they would not have to live under Communism, hundreds of thousands of Chinese have been literally thrown out of Vietnam simply because the government wanted them out. It is not surprising, then, that neighboring governments have asked the question, "Why should our own overpopulated countries be burdened with these people simply because Vietnam doesn't want them?"

It is not an easy question to answer. Indeed, if political considerations are allowed to take precedence over the human factors, the question has no answer.

As the numbers of refugees began to mount in Thailand, Hong Kong, the Philippines, Malaysia, Singapore and Indonesia, these countries closest to Vietnam and Cambodia urgently looked to the United Nations and the developed world for economic assistance to care for the refugees and commitments to resettle at least most of them outside of Southeast Asian nations.

It was a reasonable request.

Only China, which has absorbed up to 250,000 ethnic Chinese leaving Vietnam, has not complained. It would hardly have been appropriate, since most of these are third- and fourth-generation sons and daughters coming home, although not always happily.

But in response to the crisis of Southeast Asia, the Western world initially gave only token commitments. It didn't take much prophetic vision to see an apocalyptic situation developing.

Numerous pleas came from the capitals of the affected countries, asking for emergency action. But not until the largely unheeded pleas turned to threats, and threats escalated into brutal action against the refugees did the West, including the United States, begin to respond with significant resettlement programs. Even then, the arriving numbers continued to outpace the departures. Consequently, the camp populations continued to swell and the concern of the governments grew.

Although hard statistics are impossible to come by, the exodus has now reached well over one million from the three countries of Vietnam, Laos and Cambodia. Over 600,000 have been resettled outside the region, including the 250,000 who went to China, but there are still over 400,000 waiting in the camps of Southeast Asia.

Thailand has borne the brunt of the "invasion." Primarily, it is because the country shares land borders with Laos and Cambodia and these are relatively easy to cross. Additionally, from Vietnam, Thailand is a reasonably short sailing distance. Almost half of those awaiting resettlement are in camps in Thailand. Some of them have been there four years, although an effort is now being made to move out those who have been there the longest.

Even as this is being written, however, new fighting in Kampuchea (Cambodia) between the two Communist factions of Heng Samrin (backed by Vietnam and Russia) and Pol Pot (backed by China) has caused 70,000 starving Khmers to stream across the Thai border. An additional 60,000 desperate people are reported to be massed on the Cambodian side, just waiting for the right moment to cross.

Despite the heavy burden which the influx of refugees has placed on Thailand and the fact that it is fighting its own Communist guerrilla war in many parts of the countryside, the Thai government has generally taken a benevolent attitude toward these refugees. Some Vietnamese boat people have been pushed away from various landing points, but they usually managed to beach their boats elsewhere along the coast.

There is one black episode, however, which tarnishes an otherwise good record. It happened in June, 1979, when the first large masses of refugees since 1975 started to come across the border. The Vietnamese army had invaded Cambodia and the iron fist of the feared Khmer Rouge was forced to relax its grip on the people in order to fight the invaders. Thousands of refugees streamed toward the border, taking advantage of this breakdown in control.

While the Thais have never approved of the Khmér Rouge brutality against their own people, this situation presented them with a grave dilemma. The Thais possess an historic and well-founded fear that the Vietnamese have ambitions to dominate all of Southeast Asia. A victory in Cambodia would put them right on the Thai border where they could escalate the already intense Communist guerrilla war. For obvious reasons, Thailand wants to keep Cambodia as an independent buffer state between themselves and Vietnam. For them, this meant making the odious choice of supporting Pol Pot as the lesser of two evils when weighed in the scales of their own national interest.

It was not in Thailand's interest to have these masses of Khmer people leave a vacuum in Cambodia which they feared the Vietnamese would rush to fill.

Against this background, the Thai army was ordered to start rounding up newly arrived Cambodian refugees for transport back across the border. They prepared 220 buses and carried out what the United Nations High Commissioner for Refugees called the "worst case of forcible repatriation" in the thirty-year history of that organization.

When the buses stopped rolling on June 11

after four days of twenty-four-hour operations, 42,000 Cambodians had been put back across the border. Foreign organizations and the Thai public were told only that they had been put back into a "safe" area, which meant no fighting was going on there. After being taken off the buses and given a two-day supply of food, the refugees were marched to the border and pushed across it at gunpoint.

The area, which had neither food nor housing, is one of the most inhospitable parts of the Cambodian countryside. The people had to follow a narrow trail down a steep ravine. The Khmer Rouge had earlier concealed land mines in this area and any who wandered from the path were blown to bits. Those who tried to climb back up the hill were shot at.

No one knows how many thousands died, but Thai villagers in the area reported that the odor of putrefying bodies was in the air for many days.

Since that time there have been no forced repatriations from Thailand, even with the massive influx under which the country is now reeling. But it is only fair to say that Thailand's benign posture may be creating horrendous problems for them in the distant future. More than any other Asian country, Thailand is likely to be left with a large refugee residue—the nightmare of every Asian government—when the crisis passes and the West slows down its resettlement efforts. The reason is that the country has more of the kinds of refugees not desired by Western countries. They want educated and skilled people who will fit into an industrialized society. Tens of thousands of Thailand's refugees are semi-literate rice growers and many are tribal people from the mountains who are primarily slash-and-burn farmers.

Unless someone is found who will take these people into an environment comparable to the one from which they came, or unless a long-range training program is started, Thailand will have to make permanent space for them. The United Nations High Commissioner for Refugees has just announced a $200 million program of assistance to developing countries who will agree to take these unskilled workers.

Unless some solution is found, this residue left in Thailand could prove to be a politically unstablizing factor in a part of the world beset with political upheavals.

Singapore has solved its problem by closing its port, one of the busiest in the world for commercial shipping, to boat refugees. Any stray boat which happens to make it through the straits past the marine blockade is given supplies, told about the glories of Australia and Indonesia and put back to sea. This policy is rigidly carried out with minimal exceptions.

The government does permit a maximum of

1,000 refugees to be in transit if a local embassy will guarantee to have them out of the country within ninety days. They must be provided for by the UNHCR or local private organizations. The people of Singapore have shown themselves to be generous and sympathetic to the refugees, but the government applies its policy strictly.

Although the small city/state has only 225 square miles of land for its three-and-a-half million citizens, its policy toward refugees seems unduly harsh in view of the fact that it has had to bring in 20,000 migrants—called "guest workers"—to add to its labor force because of an industrial boom.

Hong Kong, too, has its peculiar problems. The modern city is virtually made up of refugees from China's mainland, many of whom came thirty years ago when the Communists came to power. It, too, has a limited land area and is vastly overcrowded. Illegal immigrants continue to find their way into the British crown colony from China. In 1978, Hong Kong had to absorb 200,000 legal and illegal immigrants which put a severe strain on its social services.

In spite of these problems, Hong Kong has turned away no refugee boats, although it has adopted strong measures to discourage their arrival. The small colony has received over 75,000 refugees, of whom two-thirds are still awaiting resettlement.

The makeup of this refugee population has an interesting aspect to it in that refugee officials estimate that 10 percent of them are Vietnamese from North Vietnam. Hong Kong is a closer port for them than Malaysia or Indonesia. Interviews with some of these disaffected northerners reveals a great deal about the situation in the country.

They picture life there as being so totally bleak, so despairing as to be without hope. Their view of the leaders who have led the Vietnamese Communist Party for thirty years is that they are ruthless old men obsessed with waging war against their neighbors while the people go hungry.

Hunger, they say, is the primary problem. One man gave an illustration of how severe the problem is:

"If a soldier deserts," he said, "his family loses its rice ration. I had a friend whose son came home from the army. His father made him go back because the family would lose its rice ration. Later, the son was killed and his family grieved—not for him but for their rice ration."

The refugees from the North say the credibility of the Hanoi regime is in shambles among their countrymen. It began to come apart after the liberation of the South. They had expected to find the South Vietnamese miserable and half-starved. Instead, the northerners found them living in what seemed like luxury.

"They even had color television sets," one former locomotive engineer says. "It was after people saw Saigon that they began to wonder why it had to be liberated."

Another man who was a former antiaircraft gunner said almost the same thing. He had shot down American planes, he said, and had no regrets "because they were bombing us." Later he became a propaganda officer in charge of giving psychological preparation to soldiers going to fight in Cambodia and Laos.

"I was doing something I believed in," he told a newspaper reporter. "We felt we were in the vanguard of world revolution. Then I went to Saigon and saw what conditions were really like there. It was then that the mask slipped."

Farther to the north of Hong Kong in Asia's richest country, the Japanese demonstrate what is probably the most selfish attitude of any country in the world. Rich from its exports all over the world, Japan has resettled only eleven refugee families thus far and is likely never to reach its announced goal of 500 places for the boat people.

The reason is the strict entry requirements laid down for the refugees. To be admitted, a refugee needs proof of a well-to-do sponsor, a guaranteed job or a close relative in Japan, fluency in Japanese and a year's residence in

Japan or employment abroad with a Japanese firm.

An American resident of Japan for the past seventeen years explains it this way: "The Japanese are so busy pursuing narrow national interests that they seem incapable of weighing the good will value of a humanitarian gesture."

One Japanese official said: "We are a small, poor, homogeneous country. Acceptance of the refugees would cause unemployment."

One might feel sorry for the poor Japanese, if the statement were not so blatantly hypocritical.

Down at the other end of Asia's section of the Pacific Ocean, there is a country where the unemployment rate is so high it isn't even reported. That nation is Indonesia, and it is truly poor. Yet no other Asian nation has been as open with its doors and as generous with its space.

If nations got medals or awards for having heart and compassion, I would submit a nomination for Indonesia.

In all my interviews, I have not heard of one boat which was turned away or one case of brutality involving Indonesia. That doesn't mean it couldn't have happened in some isolated instance, but the government has adopted a very benevolent attitude to allow temporary refuge to all who arrive there.

Many of them come by way of Malaysia and

Singapore, where they have either been towed away or sent away. The Indonesians know this, but don't seem bitter that their neighbors are sending these unwanted people on farther south.

When the first refugees arrived at the isolated town of Letung in the remote Anambas group of islands, they were treated as guests. The local residents welcomed them and invited them to stay in their homes. As the influx has continued and the refugee count in the Anambas has soared to 36,000—six times the local population— tensions have started to rise and some of the relationships have turned sour. One reason is that the huge numbers of new arrivals put a strain on the local economy and drive prices up for scarce commodities.

However, the situation has now improved as the refugees are moved into camps away from the towns.

I spoke to one senior official in Jakarta about the Indonesian attitude toward the refugees as contrasted with the attitude of some other countries. He didn't think his country should get any special credit for doing its humanitarian duty. He said: "These are our fellow human beings whose lives are precious. How could we mistreat them or send them to their death?"

Of course, he was right, but it was the first time I had heard words like that from an Asian participant in the problem. My heart was warmed.

Indonesia now has over 50,000 boat people on their islands and a huge processing center to be run by the UNHCR is under construction on the island of Galang. All the refugees are being transferred to this camp as the project moves toward completion. Because the people now live in such scattered situations across thousands of miles of islands, such a consolidation will make it easier for the United Nations to supply them and begin the resettlement process.

Next door to Indonesia, the Philippines is doing a similar thing. The problem has never been as large for this island country because it has had fewer refugees to deal with. It is farther from Vietnam and a boat trip across that part of the South China Sea is more hazardous. However, the Philippines has received between 5,000 and 10,000 refugees.

The largest number came on the *Tung An*, an old cargo vessel that was loaded with 2,200 expelled Chinese along with Vietnamese who had managed to buy forged identity papers changing their nationality. It was a typical syndicate operation which was arranged outside Vietnam in collusion with the government. These operations were very profitable and both the government and the organizers made millions of dollars from them by charging fantastic amounts of gold for passage, and then packing the ship mercilessly.

Large ships like these—the *Hai Hong, Skyluck, Tung An* and others—which trafficked in human bodies, were treated as the pariahs of the South China Sea.

Like Malaysia and Hong Kong, which also received such vessels, the Philippines wouldn't allow the people to leave the ship for months. While this may have taught the captains and crews a lesson about bringing in illegal immigrants, the treatment caused enormous physical and psychological suffering among the people.

I was on board the *Tung An* two months after it had sailed into Manila harbor. The conditions were appalling. It was unbelievably crowded, with not even room to lie down for sleeping. Manila's tropical climate turned the ship into an oven during the day.

Down in the hold, some 1,100 people were living on top of cattle feed which had been put aboard to provide ballast. However, during the ocean voyage, a storm had dumped sea water on top of the mixed grain and it had turned sour. In addition, it had become a breeding ground for bugs and worms by the millions. Never in my life have I seen worse conditions for human living.

I made several unsuccessful appeals to the Filipino government to permit the people to land. I even said World Vision would build the camp and pay for running it. But the government demurred when signs began to indicate that resettlement for these people would be a slow process. Eventually, the refugees were dispersed on other vessels in the harbor to relieve the crowding, but they were not permitted to touch land until August, 1979, an incredible eight months after they left Vietnam. They were taken to the island of Tara, a small 1200-acre plot which is seventeen hours by ship from Manila.

The *Far Eastern Economic Review* reported: "The refugees, though not visibly overwhelmed by the prospect of staying here, certainly found the new environment a pleasant contrast to their virtual imprisonment aboard the *Tung An.*"

The island is being readied for as many as 7,000 refugees. They will live in prefabricated buildings. A school, a clinic, and water and drainage systems are also under construction. It is estimated it will cost seventy-five dollars per person a month to keep the people there, but the figure will be reduced as they are able to grow some of their own food.

Foreign Minister Carlos Romulo had earlier promised a bigger processing center which could take up to 50,000 refugees from crowded camps elsewhere in Asia. This is now being readied on Bataan, a peninsula on Luzon Island made famous during World War II. The United States government has contributed $190 million for the construction of transit centers like this one and those on Galang and Tara.

Even though the centers are intended to be temporary, no one believes they can be closed out short of three years, at the present slow rate of resettlement. And even that optimistic prediction is based on present numbers, not future ones should the exodus continue unabated.

Malaysian response to the exodus deserves a more extensive analysis, both because it has made rejection a national policy—although it does allow exceptions on an ad hoc basis—and because the reasons for that policy are both interesting and important.

It must be said in all honesty that at first the Malaysians received all the refugees who came to their shores. True, they were never happy about the strangers in their midst, but they did not send them away. At the outset, the government seemed to try to apply a humane policy. Undoubtedly, they thought the rest of the world would come quickly to the aid of those countries which granted first asylum to the refugees. When the West appeared to be dragging its feet and when the steady stream of refugees became a flood, the Malaysian attitude turned bitter.

Deputy Prime Minister Mahathir Mohamed was quoted in the international press as saying that harsh treatment awaited any refugees who attempted to come to Malaysia.

"We will shoot them on sight!" he said. It was a

shocking statement which produced much negative reaction throughout the world. The prime minister of the country, Hussein Onn, was forced to try to remedy the damaging remark. He did so by explaining that his young deputy had been misquoted, lamely asserting that what Dr. Mahathir had actually said was that if any more refugees attempted to land, Malaysia would "shoo them away."

What his deputy actually said was what he had been quoted as saying. He also announced that Malaysia would tow out to sea 76,000 refugees already in the country.

"If they attempt to sink their boats, they will not be rescued," he added, explaining that Malaysia could not be held responsible for their death. "Their drowning will be because they sank their own boats, not anything else."

First of all, the small Malaysian navy was ordered to blockade the coast to prevent more boats from landing. Many boats were intercepted and turned back to sea, but some managed to slip through the net. These refugees were not permitted to go into camps, but were detained on the beaches by the thousands.

While they waited without shelters in barbed wire enclosures for up to three weeks, the government went about procuring dozens of small boats—some refugee boats, but also Malay fishing boats in all stages of decay.

Then the towing exercise began. It was an exercise in officially sanctioned murder. No amount of excuses and explanations can ever make it anything else. That it was also accompanied by robbery and rape on a massive scale should not be surprising. The earlier words of the deputy prime minister only fueled a vicious prejudice and served as a license for the soldiers and sailors to do anything they wanted to do and get away with it.

When scores of documented reports of the robberies and brutality began to surface, Malaysian officials were incensed. Home Minister Ghazalie Shafie assured the world that "our fine and brave lads" would never be guilty of anything like that and accused both the refugees and the press of trying to slander Malaysia.

He is the same one who earlier had suggested that the best solution to the problem was to ship most of the refugees to the United States. "Who could better appreciate the problems of the boat people," he asked sarcastically, "than the descendants of the *Mayflower*?"

It is difficult to sort out how much of the official position was based on philosophical belief and how much on practical politics. Certainly, politics played a large role. The attitude of the Malaysian people on the east coast, where the brunt of the refugee influx was borne, is as prejudiced and xenophobic as you will find anywhere in the world. Most of the people there live in *kampongs*—small, poor fishing villages which dot the coast. They were hostile to the refugees from the beginning. Huts were built on the sand to serve as guard posts against any Vietnamese landing. The locals even wrapped sarongs around scarecrows and planted them along the beaches.

Several hundred miles of swamp and mountainous jungle separate the east coast from the rest of the country, adding to the feeling of isolationism. There is a revival of Islamic fundamentalism here that almost equals that in Iran. Some women have recently adopted the *chuddar*, the long black covering with which they drape their entire bodies. Islamic moral codes are enforced with a vengeance by local religious vigilantes. They patrol the beaches at night looking for unmarried couples. Offenders can be arrested and are often roughed up.

A friend of mine from Singapore was visiting in the town of Kuala Terengganu. He and a young lady were sitting in a car on the street one night when the car was approached by these religious police. They questioned the girl, but did nothing because she was Chinese. The rules apply only to Malays.

The state of Terengganu has 430,000 people, most of them poor. Most live along the coast, in wooden houses built on stilts under tall coconut palms. They raise a little rice, and they fish. They have an antipathy toward the Chinese which goes back a long way, even though the Chinese make up 35 percent of the 12.5 million population and they have lived side-by-side for generations. Since Moslems eat no pork, they reserve their lowest insult for Chinese by calling them "pig eaters."

This age-old hatred is easily transferred to the refugees, since about 60 percent of those leaving Vietnam are ethnic Chinese.

There is another reason why the Malays do not trust the Chinese. The Communist insurgency in Malaysia which has ebbed and flowed for more than twenty years (but has never died), has its base in the local Chinese population. The Malays see the Chinese from Vietnam as part of the Communist conspiracy against their country— scouts for a further invasion. Even the deputy prime minister was quoted as saying, "It may be quite possible that they may enter into guerrilla activities. We have to watch out."

This, of course, conveniently overlooks the obvious point that, apart from a few possible infiltrators, the refugees themselves are fleeing Communism.

Pointing out the hulks of boat wrecks on the beach, an eighteen-year-old Malay fisherman said, "This boat, a hundred people. That one, two hundred. All Chinese. All Communists."

A teen-age girl pointed to a spot on the beach near her home and told a visitor, "One boat landed right here. Two women came first. They wanted a little water. Then they all came, and they wanted everything. We went for the police. The government of Vietnam is sending these people and in our hearts we don't want them."

Her father, a hard-muscled fisherman, told his own story: "Once I picked up some Vietnamese at sea. I took them to the camp at Bidong. They pay well, but they could start something. They may have guns. We already have Communists in our jungle. They could join them. No, I don't like these refugees. They are a social problem."

So the people started pushing the boats away and stoning and beating those who attempted to land. To protect the refugees from the local populace and preserve political peace, the government put over 40,000 of them on the island of Pulau Bidong, twenty miles offshore.

From a distance, Bidong looks like a Pacific paradise. On three sides the jungles stretch right down to the sea. On the fourth, the mountainside slopes down to a crescent, white-sand beach around a turquoise cove.

But that description is where paradise ends. The living area on the island is no larger than two city blocks and every inch of it is covered with makeshift shacks of cardboard, plywood, palm fronds and blue plastic sheeting. Some of the huts are two and three stories high. There are no sanitation facilities and the stench of human feces is in the air all the time. The lagoon is filled with garbage.

When Phan Van Tinh and his family arrived, there were fewer than a thousand people on the island. After wading ashore, they piled their possessions on the beach and slept there for five nights before a tent was made available to them. Then a representative of the United Nations gave them some plastic for roofing and told them to build their own shelter. Tinh and his sons cut wood from the side of the mountain and constructed a ten-by-twenty-foot hut which would be home for ten of them for the next eight and one-half months.

With a spade also provided by the United Nations, they dug their own well. They were more fortunate than most, for they found fresh water—a rarity on the small island—at ten feet. This spared them the ravages of disease which periodically swept the camp because of the lack of sanitation.

Food was always scarce. The United Nations distributed rice, sugar, milk, flour and one can of sardines per person every five days, although many times the distribution would be delayed by five or ten days. Frequently the supplies had been shortchanged by the time they got into the hands of the refugees. Malaysian fishing boats came to the island at night to ply a lucrative black market trade. Tinh says he had to sell most of his possessions at half their value in order to buy food at ten times the market price.

The children built some crude furniture for their crowded shelter. Tinh's wife, Sarah, learned to cook over a fire on the ground.

It was a hard life. The situation has not changed for the thousands who are still there. The Vietnamese have their own name for the island. The Malays call it Bidong. The refugees call it *Bi Dat* which in the Vietnamese language means "miserable."

But the island suits the Malaysian purpose of keeping the refugees hidden and uncomfortable. If the Vietnamese had been Moslems instead of "Chinese," there is no question they would have been treated differently. In fact, when 1,600 Moslem refugees from Cambodia came to Malaysia, they were integrated into the population without a ripple. Another 92,000 Moslem refugees from the southern Philippines have been in the Malaysian state of Sabah in northern Borneo for years and not a word of complaint is uttered.

But a prominent landlord in an east coast *kampong* explained the problem of the refugees this way: "It doesn't matter that they are rich, or even that they are Chinese. What distresses us is that they are foreigners, maybe foreign agents."

He takes a thoughtful puff on his cigarette. "It

isn't really that they are coming from Vietnam," he concludes. "It's just that they are coming."

While he has been speaking, his television set carries the picture and sound of someone reading from the Koran, the Islamic holy book. The landlord himself is a *hajji*—a Moslem who has made a pilgrimage to Mecca.

After he finished philosophizing with his visitor about the problem of refugees, he asked to be excused because it was time for his final prayer ritual of the day.

He retired to an inner room for his evening prayers.

And the refugees remained on the beaches.

9

The Jolly Roger on the South China Sea

The sharp-eyed young sailor standing watch on the U.S. Navy oiler *Wabash* rubbed his eyes and looked again.

It *was* a human being lying on a piece of driftwood which was bobbing around in the water!

He alerted the officer on duty. The ship slowed and made a gradual turn to starboard. Then it stopped just a few yards away from a piece of wood about the size of a cot on which lay a human body.

From the ship, they couldn't tell if the man was dead or alive.

A boat was lowered.

The sailors found a young man clinging so tightly to the piece of wood that it took two of them to pry his fingers loose before they could bring him on board.

The Seventh Fleet ship found two bodies floating nearby. One was recovered and buried at sea.

After a few days of recovery, sixteen-year-old Nguyen Van Phuoc was able to tell a sad and familiar story. He was the sole survivor of a pirate attack on a refugee boat in the South China Sea.

He did not remember being rescued. "I kept waking up and thinking I was dead," he said from his hospital bed. Still weak from his ordeal and recovering from pneumonia, Phuoc spoke in a hoarse whisper and with obvious effort. Sometimes he tried to smile, but the effort was too painful. His lips were covered with scabs. His skin was spotty from exposure to sun and salt water and his eyes were sunken.

He told about the ordeal. His boat containing 130 refugees was rammed and sunk by "dark-skinned men" believed to be Thai pirates.

In Vietnam, Phuoc had been a fisherman like most of the others who set out from Vung Tau about July 19, 1979. He couldn't be exact about the date because he was "still trying to remember what happened." He said they met two ships, both of which he thought were flying the Thai flag, which stopped and gave them food, water, and fuel.

The third vessel looked like a fishing craft and

"there were women and children on board," he said. About thirty men came on the refugee boat, some armed with pistols and others with long knives. "They shouted at us in a strange language," he said.

All the Vietnamese, including the thirty women and twenty children, were forced to board the pirate ship where the robbers made all of them strip so their clothing could be searched. Other members of the pirate crew stayed on board the refugee boat and searched it totally.

"They took everything—watches, rings and bracelets. Then they put us back aboard our boat and went away," Phuoc said. "No one was hurt," he added.

It was another pirate ship the next day that brought disaster.

"They were trying to board us," the survivor said, "but the seas were heavy and it was difficult. That was when they rammed us. They hit us amidships and our boat split in half and sank immediately. People were screaming and shouting. I saw a piece of wood and grabbed it and hung on."

He was in the water for three days without food. Phuoc said he was so thirsty that he drank salt water. He believes he owes his survival to the fact that he is a good swimmer, having spent all his sixteen years close to the water.

For those who remember the swashbuckling

tales of pirate adventure in literature or who have seen Douglas Fairbanks, Jr., in a late-night television film, pirates seem to belong to another time and place. But they are a very real twentieth-century menace in Southeast Asia and it is hard to romanticize their cruelty with visions of Captain Kidd.

Pirates in that part of the world come in two varieties. One is the professional whose vessel comes equipped with high-powered engine, radar and modern weaponry, including automatic rifles, machine guns, M-79 grenade launchers and even anti-tank guns. Their easiest prey is the thousands of fishing trawlers, ferries and small trading boats that sail throughout the inland waters.

However, they are not afraid to challenge the big ships. Recently, a Panamanian freighter ran aground after pirates had shot out navigational beacons in the shallows of the Sulu Sea off the southern Philippines. The disabled vessel was surrounded by pirate boats in such numbers that the Philippine air force had to be called in to drive them away.

In the same area, two small armed boats sped out of a cove to pounce on the 4,837-ton Liberian freighter, *Rio Colorado*, and blew out its portholes with automatic rifle fire and hand grenades before it got away.

In late October, 1979, a pirate vessel attacked a coastal freighter and ferry on a run between two

Borneo ports and kidnapped more than forty passengers. Seventeen of them were later found on an uninhabited island where they had been cast off, but the rest were still being held captive, presumably either for ransom or rape.

One Japanese cargo line is said to consider southern Philippine waters so dangerous that it has ordered its ships bound for Indonesia to detour westward into the well-traveled shipping lanes of the South China Sea.

The pirates will take whatever commercial cargo is on board. They also will rob fishing boats of their catches. As seafood prices have tripled, some of the fishermen have found it is easier to hijack fish than to catch them. A Malaysian official says, "The greed of the pirates is unbelievable."

Few people live to tell of their encounters with the pirates. One man who did is Kimheng Phonsawat, skipper of a small Thai fishing fleet. Two of his boats were trawling off the southern shore of Thailand on a moonlit night when the fishermen spotted two dark silhouettes speeding toward them across the water.

Skipper Kimheng didn't even wait to identify them, but ordered his boats to slash their nets and make for nearby Ko Kut Island at full throttle.

"I could tell by the sound that the other boats had 300-horsepower engines," he recalled. "As one of them came alongside, we came under rifle fire."

Three of Kimheng's crew were killed, but then the pirate boats suddenly veered off, apparently chasing the other trawler, and Kimheng's boat made it safely to shore. However, when he went to search for the missing boat, it had vanished into the sea, along with four crew members.

The organized pirate gangs have made their trade into a big and profitable business. During a six-month period during 1978, a gang operating near the Thai/Cambodian border captured twenty-six fishing boats and killed 450 fishermen.

Three senior officers, including a police colonel, were sent from Bangkok to investigate the pirate ring. Posing as fishermen, they joined the crew of a trawler. Around midnight, a much larger vessel loomed out of the darkness obviously intending to ram the fishing boat.

The police opened fire with their rifles and the pirate craft responded by raking the trawler with fifty-caliber machine gun fire and ramming it. The policemen were killed, but three members of the crew survived to testify against the pirate leader.

"We learned then why these pirates always killed everybody in sight," a police officer said. "The leader was a respected and influential man who owned a grocery store, a filling station and sold supplies to local fishermen. He couldn't afford to be recognized."

"The professional pirates are like wolves," an

official of a Thai company operating 100 fishing boats said. "They circle around until they find a target of opportunity."

"Usually they will hold the boat and crew for ransom," the fishing company executive said. "Usually they don't ask for much—maybe $2,500, so we pay it. We've paid ransom on one boat five times in two years."

The company's large ships are armed, but when asked why they did not arm all the boats, the managing director said, "Because if you give them all guns, they may turn pirate. We had a case where the chief engineer of one of our boats turned pirate and killed the captain and eight members of the crew."

The fishermen who are victimized are not very helpful to the police. "The fishermen are like your Mafia," one official told a reporter. "They don't talk. Either they have something to hide or they are afraid of reprisals."

One of the areas of most concentrated danger is the water off the Thailand provinces of Chantha-buri and Trat in the Gulf of Thailand. It is here that the second variety of these twentieth-century brigands are found. They are the part-timers—the pirates who most of the time are merely fisher-men. However, throughout history Thai fisher-men have turned to small-scale piracy whenever the opportunity presented itself.

Today that opportunity comes daily in the form

of the defenseless Vietnamese refugee boats which provide easy marks for the pirates. The rate of piracy rises and falls in proportion to the number of boats leaving Vietnam.

Because they know most of the refugees are carrying gold, they cruise the sea lanes in search of prey. If the refugees are lucky, they escape with being only robbed and raped. At worst, they drown when the boats are sunk to make sure there are no living witnesses. Only God knows how many thousands have died. The Thai pirates are known as pitiless killers. One pirate confessed to having murdered twenty-six people.

Pirate attacks on refugee boats have become so routine that refugee officials have given a name to this specific category of information about each boat. It is called "R and P"—rape and pillage.

During a recent four-month period, of slightly more than 100 refugee boats which had arrived in Indonesia's Anambas Islands, 160 miles east of the Malay Peninsula, ninety-six had been attacked by pirates. The average number of attacks on any one boat is four, but one vessel had been hit twenty-three times, long after it was clear that nothing of value remained except the women and girls.

"The pirates start with those as young as ten and rape systematically," a relief worker reports. "If the father tries to intervene, he is killed out of hand. Then the frenzy starts."

Attacks by these Thai fishermen-turned-pirates have reached such dimensions of frequency and ferocity that one magazine reports, "Cheers go up in the refugees' camps when a boat arrives unscathed." It is quite a feat, considering the heavy odds against the refugees ever making it.

There is a growing suspicion that the fishermen have unofficial approval from the local and regional authorities to operate as a kind of vicious vigilante coast guard. Pirate attacks discourage the refugees from coming, and one aid official said, "If the refugees don't come, the authorities are happy. So this gives the pirates a kind of carte blanche."

Although the Royal Thai Navy issued a directive in mid-1979 to all units to "prevent piracy at sea," there is little evidence that anything significant is being done to stop the attacks. In fact, a key naval officer in Thailand's coastal provinces was candid enough to say, "Why should we try to protect refugees? We don't want them to come here."

Anyhow, the captain said that he had never received the anti-piracy order.

The carnage continues.

A twenty-eight-year-old woman told her story to relief workers at a refugee camp in Thailand. Four boatloads of fishermen had rammed the small boat in which she and 100 other refugees were floundering off Thailand's Songkhla province. More than half of them, including the woman's husband and two-year-old son, were drowned when the boat sank. The survivors were taken aboard one of the Thai boats and stripped of their gold and their few other possessions. The women were locked below decks while the thirty men were systematically killed.

Then the women were raped repeatedly and thrown overboard, along with any children who had survived the ramming. But the captain of the Thai pirates took a liking to the young woman and decided to protect her. When they were near land, he handed her a life preserver and sent her overboard to save her from his crew.

Because the pirates are elusive and don't fly the black "Jolly Roger" any more for identification, trying to stop the traffic is probably an impossible task short of using decoy vessels which none of the countries seem ready to do. One recent robbery and rape episode was broken up by the appearance of a U.S. Navy search plane. However, regular air patrols of the whole South China Sea are an impractical solution.

"There is nothing new about piracy in the Gulf of Thailand," a fishing fleet operator said. "The jungle has its tigers and the sea has its pirates. It's something we live with."

Maybe that's true for fishermen.

But for refugees, it's something vastly different.

It's something they die with.

10

The Saga of Seasweep

"Well, what are you going to do about it?" Dr. E.V. Hill asked me straight out.

I wasn't sure.

I didn't know why I should be the one asked to do anything about it at all. I hadn't even heard about the Vietnamese boat people until this pastor of Mount Zion Missionary Baptist Church in the Watts section of Los Angeles had thrust a story clipped from the *Los Angeles Times* into my hands ten minutes before.

The clipping was a picture of a terrified Vietnamese refugee and her little girl sitting in a boat waiting to be pulled back to sea from the coast of Thailand where they had landed. The agony expressed on the woman's face wrenched my heart.

Somehow while traveling, I had missed the story. It was early December, 1977, and I had spent much of the year in Africa. Asia, my normal habitat, had been neglected in order to give attention to our growing programs on the other side of the world.

Consequently, I had been unaware of the beginning of what turned out to be one of the most dramatic human struggles since the exodus from Egypt. That newspaper clipping and the pointed remark of my friend Ed Hill turned out to be the catalyst that had me fully and emotionally linked with the Vietnamese boat people in less than three months.

I had gone to Dr. Hill's church that night to speak to his congregation. Instead, I was spoken to by God.

Everything I said was turned back to myself. I spoke about the call of Moses at the burning bush. In describing His relationship with His slave people in Egypt, God said He both saw and cared about their suffering: "I have surely seen the affliction of my people . . . and have heard their cry . . . I know their sorrows" (Exod. 3:7).

The face of that Vietnamese mother I had seen in Pastor Hill's study before the meeting kept coming up before me. It was comforting to know God was taking note of what was happening on the sea of heartbreak.

But God said that He did not stop His concern

with just seeing and hearing and feeling. He told Moses: "I am come down to deliver them" (Exod. 3:8). He was a God of action and He would deliver His people. I desperately wanted God to reveal His deliverance out on the South China Sea.

Then came the crushing verse: "Come now . . . and I will send thee . . . that thou mayest bring forth my people" (Exod. 3:10).

"What are you going to do about it?" Pastor Hill had asked me.

"Come now . . . and I will send thee."

"What are you going to—"

"I will send—"

"What are *you*—"

". . . thee—"

Driving home that night, I knew I had to do something. God would come down and deliver, as He had brought His people out of Egypt, but He needed somebody to send. I had not seen a burning bush like Moses nor heard voices like Joan of Arc, but my heart had surely been seized by God and I could not get away.

But I still didn't know what to do.

Or where to go.

First, I started reading everything I could find about the mushrooming problem. The media were not giving it too much attention back then, but I found out that the numbers of refugees were beginning to increase dramatically to several thousand a month. It was estimated that half of all those attempting to escape died at sea, a figure which I still support.

It was evident that the problem was going to be around for a long time and equally evident that the world's wish that it would simply go away was unrealistic.

There had been one or two earlier attempts to put a mercy ship out on the water to rescue the refugees. I studied those efforts and learned they had failed because of poor planning and management as well as a lack of cooperation by governments.

As I analyzed these previous attempts, I became convinced that such an operation could be done successfully if some government would simply agree to accept any refugees picked up at sea. The logistics of the operation could be handled with adequate planning.

I knew many lives could be saved by launching such a venture and it seemed to me that everybody ought to be intensely interested in that objective.

So with considerable enthusiasm and a moderate amount of hope, I went off to Washington to discuss the plan with officials in the State Department. I also arranged to meet with some friends in the Congress. I wasn't asking for money. I only wanted some help in thinking through the problems. And I needed a commitment that any refugees we picked up would be guaranteed resettlement in a Western country so we could land them temporarily at some Asian port.

Everybody was friendly and courteous.

Even sympathetic.

They listened patiently and interacted honestly as we discussed the problem and our plan.

Then, without exception, they advised me to do nothing.

It would mean only trouble, they explained. Trouble for me. For our organization. Trouble for the governments. A mercy ship out on the South China Sea would only generate more hostility from the governments in the region. Nobody wanted the refugees and no one would guarantee their resettlement. There were already enough people in the land camps to keep the immigration teams busy for a long time.

Why should the boat refugees jump to the head of the immigration lines just because they came out by boat? Why didn't I forget it? Do other things, I was told. Just don't get mixed up with these refugees. It was definitely a non-win situation and if we had a fiasco, which was likely, World Vision stood to lose a great deal of credibility.

I left Washington shaken. All the appeals to logic, to reason, to political reality were right. These friends had given the best advice they could with a far better understanding of the situation than I possessed.

However, they agreed on one thing. People were

dying and no one was doing anything about it. Commercial vessels had begun to pass up the refugee boats because of the resettlement difficulties. The shipowners felt compelled to go along with what they couldn't change.

Why couldn't I do the same? You can't fight city hall, they said. Or words to that effect.

"Yes, it is true that people are drowning," they said, "*but—*"

I determined to go to Southeast Asia and see for myself. My next stop was the refugee camps which dotted the shores of the countries of first asylum—at that time, principally Thailand, Malaysia and the Philippines. Here I confirmed everything first-hand as I talked to scores of victims in the camps.

In fact, it was worse than I had imagined and I came away convinced that the status quo had to be challenged.

Now that I had more factual data and could support my arguments with interviews and first-hand observations, I made the rounds again.

Washington.

Geneva.

Canberra.

Ottawa.

Bangkok.

Kuala Lumpur.

Singapore.

The response was widely varied, ranging all the

way from personal sympathy to derision to official hostility.

But still the unanimous advice was: *Do nothing*.

It was now certain no one was going to help us. Even if they personally wanted to, the policies of their governments made it impossible for them to support our plan. And I didn't see how we could run a search-and-rescue operation without the good will of some government which would allow us to land the refugees.

I left the office of the U.S. Ambassador to Singapore, John Holdridge, almost in total despair. He had been the most personally sympathetic, but he could offer no way around the official impasse. We had been thwarted at every turn, it seemed, and I was ready to admit defeat and give up. If the drowning refugees were going to be saved, it would have to be by somebody else.

Suddenly, my colleague, Hal Barber, had a flash of inspiration. If we couldn't put out a rescue vessel, there was no one to stop us from launching a supply mission. "We could equip a ship to give basic supplies to the refugees and even repair their boats so they might be able to reach shore under their own power," he explained.

My despair lifted. That was it! I had been so attached to the rescue idea that I hadn't allowed myself to think more broadly. The supply mission might be a second-best solution, but it allowed us to do something while at the same time accepting the realities of what we could not do.

However, we decided that if our supply ship came across any refugees whose lives were in peril, we would take them on board our ship whether or not we had guarantees, regardless of the consequences. We wouldn't let anybody drown if we could save them.

So it was in a taxi in Singapore, between the U.S. Embassy and the Shangri-La Hotel, that "Operation Seasweep" was born.

John Calder, from New Zealand, was named project director. Burt Singleton, from our U.S.A. staff, volunteered to run the shipboard operation. An Indian doctor and two Chinese nurses from Singapore were recruited to form the medical team. A Filipino captain and a mixed Asian crew were found for the ship.

The ship itself was an old War War II flat-bottomed LST, named the *Cal Loader*. Chartered from a Singapore company, it had made many runs to Saigon and up the Mekong River to Phnom Penh during the Vietnam War. As it wallowed out of Singapore harbor for its first mission for World Vision in mid-1978, it was outfitted with a two-room medical clinic and supplied with food, water, fuel, medicines, spare parts for the small diesel engines which power the refugee boats, and every other necessity of life for refugees who had been at sea for a long time and might have to remain there for some days in the future.

The first boat encountered was a serious test case for the mission. It was leaking and in danger of sinking. Nonetheless, we decided to play by the rules which had previously been announced to all governments which might be affected by our operation.

We took it under tow and our mechanics tried to repair it. When night came and the boat still was not fixed, we took the women and children on the *Cal Loader*. The six men, however, remained on the refugee boat. At midnight, without warning, the boat sank. The six men were thrown into the sea and our ship had an authentic search-and-rescue mission on its hands.

Five of the men were found and brought aboard quickly, but the sixth one—the son of a woman on board—couldn't be spotted by the searchlight after several sweeps around the area. The distraught mother attempted to throw herself overboard, but we restrained her. Finally, we found the son, barely clinging to a plastic water can we had put on board the refugee boat.

Now we had twenty-one people on board the ship with no place to land them. Negotiations with Malaysia proved fruitless. They would not permit them to come ashore. After two weeks, Thailand agreed to take them if the UNHCR would arrange for their resettlement.

So the passengers were disembarked, but the

ship had been out of operation for two weeks while we negotiated the arrangements. Obviously, a better way had to be found.

We decided to try a plan. John Calder went to the town of Kuantan on Malaysia's east coast and bought a good fishing boat, capable of taking 100 people, for $3,000. We took title to the boat and left it sitting at Kuantan until we might have use for it.

That time was not long in coming. Shortly thereafter, on his daily radio check with the office in Singapore, Singleton told Calder, "We had our devotions this morning from Psalm 73." The project director knew there were seventy-three more people on the *Cal Loader* who had to be off-loaded as quickly as possible.

It was time to try out the new plan.

After additional radio conversations, a rendezvous point was established almost directly east from Kuantan outside the Malaysian twelve-mile limit in international waters.

The transfer on the high seas took place without a hitch. All seventy-three climbed into the sturdy fishing boat which was well supplied. They now had a chart and compass, something they didn't have on the original vessel. They could go anywhere they chose. We learned later they selected Malaysia because of its proximity and that they were accepted for placement in one of the refugee camps to await resettlement.

The *Cal Loader* continued to sail on its mission of mercy. The ship had been out of operation for only two days while the transfer was made, not two weeks as in the previous instance. Thus we judged the new system to be very successful, although we never had an opportunity to use it again.

The ship stayed out on the South China Sea until the monsoons drove us off. The vessel was not suitable for operations during the treacherous storm season because it was not heavy enough and did not have enough draft. Consequently, in late 1978, we temporarily suspended "Operation Seasweep" and made an assessment of the entire mission.

We had helped a total of five boats and 230 people. Of those, certainly the people in the two boats which sank would not have been alive without us.

We had demonstrated our ability to run a credible mission, had gained the grudging respect of the governments and had brought life and hope to despairing people. Later we were told by many who left Vietnam that the mention of "Operation Seasweep" on the shortwave broadcasts of the Voice of America, Radio Australia and BBC had given them fresh courage.

But we were not happy about at least two aspects of our 1978 mission. The first was our inability to take refugees into a port and off-load them, with assurance that they would be resettled. The second was having to suspend the operation for several months because of the monsoon season. At 345 tons, the *Cal Loader* was just too small. We needed a heavier ship and we needed a guarantee of resettlement.

Another trip to Washington provided what appeared to be an answer. I learned that earlier President Jimmy Carter had sent a message to all commercial shipping interests stating that any refugees picked up by U.S.-owned or U.S.-registered vessels would have guaranteed resettlement in the United States if the refugees chose that option and were not given resettlement in some other country.

I specifically inquired if World Vision would qualify under that order if we were to purchase a ship in the name of the American entity which was a part of our international partnership. Official word came back from the U.S. State Department that indeed we did come under the presidential order, since there were no qualifying clauses.

This was good news!

Our other World Vision partners in Australia, Canada and New Zealand approved the purchase of a ship in the name of the U.S. organization— and the hunt was on.

We found a 1400-ton freighter for sale which was being used to haul copra from the Solomon

Islands to Singapore. For $200,000, we took it out of the copra business and with another $100,000 for a complete overhaul and paint job, made it ready for our work among people drifting on the South China Sea.

Then we started looking for a country in which to register the ship—looking for a flag to fly. Although the vessel was owned by a U.S. corporation, it was impossible to get registration in the United States because the ship couldn't meet Coast Guard standards. It was too old. To bring it up to specifications would have taken a lot more money and time, and we were running out of both. Also, if we flew the U.S. flag, we had to employ all U.S. citizens as crew and we simply weren't budgeted for American labor costs.

Singapore wasn't interested in registering the ship. Several other countries weren't interested either.

So we started looking around for what is known in the shipping trade as a "flag of convenience." Five small countries have adopted a less strict code for registration of ships in order to make it easier for many vessels to sail which otherwise would not be approved.

First, we tried Panama, whose flag is on a multitude of ships around the world. After serious explorations with the Panamanian Ambassador in Washington, we were assured registration would not be a problem. So we processed the papers, waited a month—and got a turn down. An appeal for reconsideration also brought a negative response. Although we were seeking registration as a cargo vessel, we were careful to explain the humanitarian nature of our mission and this apparently scared off the Panama Marine Department.

Honduras was next on our list. Our application was approved and we were notified that temporary registration had been granted. Permanent registration would be issued in about three months. We rejoiced at this answer to prayer and made preparations to start our first 1979 mission on July 3, a three-month delay because of the registration hassle.

The ship had been appropriately given the name of the project itself—*Seasweep.*

I went to Singapore and made plans to sail on her maiden voyage as a relief-and-supply ship, but disaster struck on the day before we were to leave port. We received notification from the Honduras representative in Singapore that our registration had been canceled.

Just like that.

Then the agent left the country.

We couldn't even find out an official reason why the registration had been canceled, although it seemed obvious the agent had either been approached by local authorities who didn't want us registered or else he moved on his own because he was afraid our humanitarian work would jeopardize the Honduras flag in all Southeast Asian ports.

From conversations with people in the agent's office I am inclined to believe the former, but could never confirm it. Anyhow, it was evident somebody was out to stop us.

We now had a ship without a flag. The Singapore port authorities could not clear us without a registration, and even if they could, we would be extremely vulnerable because a ship on the high seas without a flag is subject to takeover by anyone who wants it. It is a derelict vessel and under international marine law can be claimed for salvage.

The situation was serious.

Then began four mad, frantic days. We could make no headway in Singapore, so I called the World Vision regional director in Guatemala City and asked him to go to Honduras immediately and plead our case directly with the authorities there. Telephone calls and telexes flew between our base in Singapore, our international offices in Los Angeles, Washington and Tegucigalpa, Honduras.

In the meantime, our Indonesian captain and his Asian crew were being subjected to subtle but strong pressures from marine sources in Singapore. Captain Samudra was threatened with the blacklist if *Seasweep* brought any refugees into port. His career might be in jeopardy and he was unnerved by the prospect.

More pressures were being exerted on the Singapore members of our team. Dr. T.N. Chander, our two Chinese nurses, Rosemary Ng and Regina Loh, and our sixteen-year-old mess boy, Allen, were warned by immigration officials that if *Seasweep* attempted to bring any refugees into Singapore, the ship would not be allowed to enter the harbor and they would be marooned with it.

Allen, who had come to us from a Salvation Army orphanage, was a little shaken, but none of the others quavered.

I confess, however, that I was beginning to weaken.

I was ready to agree with some of my earlier advisers that it was impossible to win if the establishment wanted to stop you. I was weary of having to fight to do good. I couldn't understand how anybody could be against saving human lives.

I wasn't getting much sleep.

I was tired.

And I wanted to quit.

In my discouragement, I turned to the Scriptures for help and comfort. I was reading the Psalms one morning when God gave me a special word from Psalm 20, which I really needed.

In your day of trouble, may the Lord be with you! May the God of Jacob keep you from all harm. May he send you aid from his sanctuary in Zion. May he remember with pleasure the gifts you have given him, your sacrifices and burnt offerings. May he grant you your heart's desire and fulfill all your plans. May there be shouts of joy when we hear the news of your victory, flags flying with praise to God for all that he has done for you. May he answer all your prayers!

Psalm 20:1-5 (TLB)

I took great comfort from those words. As I read them, they seemed more like a promise than merely a prayer. Verse five promised total victory.

We had no flag, but God would give us one.

We had no assurance that Singapore would allow any refugees to land from *Seasweep*, but God was promising there would be shouts of joy over the news of our victory. I knew this meant total success for God's glory. We would not have to drop refugees off somewhere in the dead of night or unload them in secrecy. These words promised total, open vindication of the mission.

I telexed these verses to our international offices where much prayer was going on and urged them to begin to rejoice with us.

The next day I received a call from Honduras telling me our registration had never been revoked there. It had all been the work of the local representative and the Honduras Marine

Department was notifying him to transfer the registration papers to us immediately.

This was done the next day.

Port clearance was secured.

In the late afternoon of July 6, 1979, I took a launch from Clifford Pier out to where *Seasweep* was anchored.

We would sail before midnight.

As I walked up the gangway, I looked at the chalkboard attached at the top containing data for the immigration and customs officers who would come on board to give us final clearance. It had certain standard information such as the name of the ship, tonnage, date, etc. The last line called for the port of destination. It read, "Sailing for—" Since we had no special port in mind, the team had filled in the blank. I read it with tears in my eyes: "Sailing for—God's greater glory."

They were so right.

And a few days later, I would even know at least one of the reasons why He had delayed our sailing for four days.

11

Search and Rescue

On July 3, while *Seasweep* sat in Singapore harbor waiting for the registration matter to be cleared up, two other boats in different parts of the world put out to sea.

No one on any of the three vessels could anticipate how the events of the next few days would bring their lives together.

Besides *Seasweep,* one of the other two vessels was a sailing craft which the Jeffrey Klein family used for family cruises around Chesapeake Bay. In the twenty-nine-foot boat with Klein were his wife, Chin, and their two children—Linda, eight, and Rick, twelve. Chin remembers it as being a rainy, gusty day.

The family agreed they had seen better sailing

weather, but they had fun anyway.

Meanwhile, on the Malaysian coast, seventeen members of Chin Klein's family who were refugees from Vietnam, were forced at gunpoint to wade out into the water and climb aboard a little fishing boat. Almost the same size as Klein's sailboat—thirty feet long, eight feet wide—it was going to be home for Chin's family and seventy-six others for the next week.

They were part of a larger group of some 800 refugees who had been rounded up by soldiers and marched to a beach near Kuala Terengganu. There, two Navy patrol boats were waiting for them. One had four small boats secured for towing and the other had six. The boat onto which the Quach family was forced had the 1979 Malaysian marine registration still nailed to the wheelhouse, although the numbers on the bow had been painted out to prevent identification.

Seasweep was still riding easy at anchor, waiting for the powers-that-be to decide her fate. John Calder and I were rushing around Singapore, trying to break through the unfathomable maze which surrounded her unauthorized and unnecessary delay.

Meanwhile, up the Malaysian coast about 300 miles, fourteen-year-old Ngo Thi Tuyet Mai didn't know all that was going on, but it looked ominous and she was scared.

She hadn't kept track of the days since they had left Vietnam, but it seemed like a very long time. After their escape, there had come the encounter with the pirates. That had been terrifying for them all, especially the children. Mai's younger brother, Tuan, who is twelve, heard the pirates say that if they were not given jewels or gold, they would burn the whole boat.

"I thought we were all going to die, and I was very afraid," Tuan says. He is not too old to admit he cried.

The children's mother, Quach Thi Hiep, reassures her son, "We all cried, adults as well as the children. The pirates waved crescent-shaped swords as they swooped down on our helpless boat, and it was very scary.

"The robbery lasted two hours, but they did not hurt us," says Mrs. Quach. They stripped jewelry off everyone and stuffed it into their pockets and mouths. "When the pirates left the boat, they looked like walking jewelry stores."

As with so many other boats, the pirates' final act was to ram it amidships, weakening the timbers and making it susceptible to sinking.

Two days later, the disabled boat made it to the Malaysian shore. Since the timbers were cracking above the water line, they turned the boat toward the beach and abandoned it.

Now for the second time in four days, they

were subjected to fear and abuse. This time it was from the Malaysian soldiers. As the people got off the boat, they were beaten by those who should have been their protectors. The women and children were hit with sticks, while the men were beaten with rifle butts.

"The children were begging them to stop," Mrs. Quach says, but the soldiers responded with cries of "Gold! Gold! Come here!"

A rope enclosure was formed and the people were forced to stay inside it on the beach that night. After dark, other Malaysians came with flashlights and demanded gold, jewelry and money. There was little left to give after the two previous robberies, but this time they gave everything, including $300 in cash.

One of the men was apparently a customs officer of some kind, for he carefully wrote a receipt on plain paper for each family who gave him something and legalized the document with his official stamp. Everywhere in the world, the bureaucracy is nothing if not efficient, even when it cheats people.

As they were being taken away the next morning, the refugees saw the soldiers ripping their boat apart looking for any hidden valuables. On the pretext of moving them to a refugee camp, they were transported to another beach about six miles away where they joined a group of 500 more refugees.

They stayed there for eighteen days. The only shelter they had from the daily sun and nightly rain was the plastic sheeting they had brought from their boat, which they tied to sticks picked up along the beach.

People got sick and two elderly refugees died on the beach. "When the people asked for medicine," Mrs. Quach says, "the commander of the guards told us, 'If you have sick people, throw them out, and if you are hungry, cut up your children and eat them.'"

The only water they had was from a hole dug in the sand, about thirty feet deep, from which they drew brackish water with a rope and a bucket.

For ten days, the only food they had was what they had salvaged from their boat. Then the Malaysian Red Crescent Society—the Islamic equivalent of the Red Cross—brought food packages. Each person was given a package which was to last one week. It contained two bags of rice and one can each of chicken, beans and sardines.

On July 3, the day Mrs. Quach's aunt, Chin Klein, went sailing on Chesapeake Bay, the entire Quach family of seventeen persons left Malaysia by boat—unceremoniously tied to the end of a rope and towed at high speeds by a navy patrol boat.

Mrs. Klein had no way of knowing what was happening half a world away.

She had left Vietnam in 1970, the wife of an

153

American helicopter mechanic named Jeffrey Klein. He had met her when she worked at the Sac Trang PX and had been impressed not only with her beauty, but with her accommodating sincerity. He had bought a watch from her, but wanted to change the band. Since she was not permitted to do this as a part of the sale, she agreed to buy the kind of watchband he wanted in the local Vietnamese market.

He gave her about four dollars in local currency. The next day she was back with the band—and more than a dollar in change!

Klein was overwhelmed. He says: "This was a special person—somebody who would not only buy it for you cheap, but actually give you back the change. What honesty!"

Chin didn't know why it was such a big deal. Says she: "I wouldn't take money just for a favor."

Love blossomed.

At least within Klein.

As for Chin, she wasn't sure.

"Every day when I took time off, Jeffrey would come and invite me to the officers' club to play Ping-Pong. Then one day he said, 'I love you.' But I didn't trust him. I told him, 'I've heard every GI say that.' But I knew he was a very honest man with a very good heart. Because of some family problems, I asked my boss to transfer me to another PX near my home so I could be with my widowed mother.

"When I went to tell Jeffrey goodbye, he cried and asked me not to go. He said he wanted to marry me. He talked to me for a long time and I knew he really loved me. I kept my job in Sac Trang, but I still didn't marry him."

Klein offered to stay in Vietnam after his discharge from the Air Force in 1968 if Chin would marry him.

"I told him, 'No, you have been here a long time. Your family misses you, your mother worries about you. You have to go home. If you really love me, you'll be back,'" Chin recalls.

Then she continues enthusiastically: "In eighty-three days he came back! He really came back!"

Klein had managed to get a job selling cars through the PX.

They were married and stayed in Vietnam until 1970. Then Klein brought his bride to Baltimore where he was needed to help in his father's real estate development business.

The adjustment for Chin was very difficult.

"I was sad and really homesick," she says. "I listened to music from my country and cried all day, and then fought with Jeffrey when he came home at night. He is really a strong guy and I love him for that. But it was a horrible time. You know, when you go away from your country and you come here, you don't know anybody yet and you have a lot of problems. Some Americans would look at me like, well, with a dirty look, and look at me from head to toe. I was really upset, but now I don't care. I got used to it."

Chin went back to Vietnam for visits before 1975.

Then the curtain fell.

Both Jeffrey and Chin became extremely active in the resettlement program for refugees coming to the United States. This seemed to be one way they could work out the grief which they felt for a closed country and separated relatives. Klein worked in his own Jewish community through the Hebrew Immigration Aid Society. Since 1975, he and Chin have helped resettle over 100 refugee families.

When the big influx came in 1975 after the fall of Indochina, Indiantown Gap, Pennsylvania, became a major transit point on the East Coast for refugees coming to the United States. The Kleins put thousands of miles on their car helping refugee families with everything from acquiring Social Security numbers to finding housing.

Chin says: "Sometimes they don't speak English, and sometimes they need a job and I have to drive them from there to here. I remember one lady. She was in a camp and she was pregnant. I had to take her every time to see the doctor because she didn't speak English at all. I stayed at the hospital with her the night she had her baby."

And that's the way it's been for Jeffrey and Chin

Klein since 1975.

Back at Vinh Loi in the Bac Lieu province of Vietnam's delta country, Chin's eighty-two-year-old mother and six brothers and sisters kept in touch with her through the mails. Life grew harder, but Chin's aged mother put a strict censorship on the family's correspondence.

"Chin is all alone in the United States with her husband and we really must not cause her to cry about what is happening to us here," the matriarch would say.

Certainly no one dared write of a planned escape attempt. When Chin learned that two of her nephews escaped to Malaysia rather than be drafted to fight with the Vietnamese Army in Cambodia, she still could not picture her own family as being boat refugees.

Back in Vietnam, the family saved everything they could for two years. Then at the end of 1978, planning for the escape began. They recruited a total of 290 people, comprising sixteen families for the trip, paid off the government and hired a man to start building a boat. It was more than sixty feet long and about twelve feet wide. Besides a wheelhouse on top, there was one long hold below the deck for passengers.

When the people got on board, there was only room for sitting. There was no space to lie down. Seasickness had to be handled with a plastic bag and bodily functions had to be kept to a minimum.

It was this boat which left Ca Mau on June 12, 1979, and was torn apart on a Malaysian beach a few days later. Among the 290 passengers, it carried Chin's older sister, Chau Thi Lang, and her husband, Quach Thoai Tai. With them were three daughters, three sons, two daughters-in-law, five grandchildren and two other relatives.

These were the ones towed away from Malaysia while Chin was sailboating and we were sweating out *Seasweep's* registration.

The refugees were told they were being taken to an island. This story seemed to be a favorite ploy of the Malaysian military. Once in the boats, however, the towing never stopped for twenty hours. At times the speed was up to fifteen knots and a lot of water came into the boat. The refugees kept bailing, afraid the boat would either capsize or sink.

Finally, the rope was cut and the four boats which had been tied together for the towing were set adrift. They were given about two-and-a-half gallons of diesel fuel (which later proved to be contaminated with rust and water) and no drinking water.

When the captain pled for water, a gun was fired into the air and then leveled at him.

The patrol boat sped away and the four little boats with nearly 300 people took stock among themselves. They agreed to pair off and try to stay together as they made their way toward the south. Each boat towed another in order to conserve fuel, but after a few hours the engine in the Quach's boat stopped altogether and their companion boat kept moving on.

That was on July 4, 1979.

Alone, lost, and with their boat dead in the water, the family leaders rigged up four ponchos to try to catch the wind. Apparently, they had been towed to somewhere in the vicinity of the Anambas Islands, but with no power and the winds blowing northeasterly, the boat was moving slowly but inexorably back toward Vietnam.

They were without water for the first three or four days and it was sheer hell. The adults drank sea water and the children drank the urine of the adults.

The only food was uncooked rice which they had brought from the Malaysian beach.

They prayed for rain and an occasional squall would give them temporary relief, although these also brought chilling winds and there was no shelter. The corneas of one man's eyes were being scarred by the terrible dehydration.

While this life-and-death struggle was going on just a few hundred miles from Singapore, *Seasweep* was moving closer to sailing time. Prayers were being prayed in many places and inevitably the obstacles were giving way one by one.

Finally, on July 6, the registration papers were handed to us, and with great rejoicing we moved out through the Strait of Singapore toward the South China Sea on our mission of mercy.

As soon as we hit the Singapore/Hong Kong shipping lanes, we took a slight northwesterly heading that would bring us up the Malaysia coast without intruding into territorial waters. Watches were posted in four-hour shifts night and day. We saw oil tankers, automobile carriers, container cargo ships, freighters in abundance and hundreds of fishing trawlers.

But not a single refugee boat.

Since Malaysia was still in the towing-away process, we scanned the western horizon carefully. Now and again we would change course to check out a small craft which couldn't be identified through the binoculars.

In the early days, each episode like this would build the excitement level of us all, but eventually we stopped giving false alarms. Every morning during our devotional times we prayed for God to guide us that day to those who might need us.

We watched. And we prayed.

Second day.

Nothing.

It was on this day, however, that the powerless and drifting Quach boat had a heart-stopping encounter. Two Thai fishing boats came upon the helpless craft and decided to play a game. Attaching a rope between the two fishing vessels, they put the refugee boat in the middle and tried to capsize it with the rope.

Mrs. Quach Thi Hiep says, "The adults were praying and the children were crying, but the fishermen laughed and laughed as if it were great sport."

She thinks it is a miracle that the rope broke before the boat overturned. The refugees held up empty cans to signal that they needed water, but the only response was that one of the fishermen lowered his pants toward them before the boats sailed contemptuously away.

Mrs. Quach says this is when despair really set in.

"If the people whom we met on the ocean wouldn't help us, what chance did we have of living?" she asked logically. "That is when we gave up."

One twelve-year-old girl said, "I knew I was going to die. I prayed only that my death would be quick and merciful."

Third day on *Seasweep*.

Nothing.

On our third evening out, we moved close enough to the Malaysian coastline near the Thai border to take a reckoning from a beacon because the night was cloudy.

We headed northeast toward Vietnam.

On the refugee boat drifting almost due north, there was much prayer.

"We prayed to our ancestors, we prayed to Buddha, we prayed to Jesus. We prayed to anyone up there who would listen to us," one of the refugees said.

On *Seasweep*, we were also praying. Every prayer was concluded, "In the name of Jesus."

Personally, I find it very gratifying that it was Jesus who heard and who answered those elemental prayers for survival.

Fourth day.

July 9.

We were headed straight up "refugee alley." Boats coming out of Vietnam usually came directly south and then turned toward Malaysia as soon as they were out of the dangerous Vietnamese waters.

The watch was intensified as we moved through the swells at roughly seven knots. I had the noon to four o'clock watch. For three and a-half hours I had been studying the horizon through my binoculars. I could see clearly for approximately six miles ahead.

We were roughly 106 degrees east by seven degrees north, about 120 miles off the south coast of Vietnam.

Burt Singleton had gone on top of the bridge, the highest point on the ship except for the crow's-nest on the forward mast. From there he could add another mile or two to our visibility range. Shortly he motioned me to come and join him. Without alerting the others—for we were all weary of false alarms—he pointed to a small object on the port side of the bow.

It was a boat and we studied it intently for about fifteen minutes. It did not appear to be moving. We could see no mast. It was bobbing about crazily, with first the bow and then the stern coming up out of the water as it rode the waves. A boat did not act like that.

Still we waited, but quietly told the captain to turn the ship in the direction of the floating object. It did not appear to be moving across our bow as a vessel under power would do.

Now we were pretty sure the boat on which our eyes were riveted was a refugee craft.

At one mile away, there was no question about it and the team sprang into action. Five-gallon cans of water, which had previously been fortified with glucose, were brought on the deck from the cooler below. Tins of biscuits were put on deck. From previous encounters, we had learned the people were always thirsty and the glucose gave them a quick shot of energy. Handing the water around and eating something light also provided activity while we could have a conversation with the captain on our deck.

As we moved closer, my binoculars focused on

a devastating sight. The little boat was indeed dead in the water. The stern was damaged. I could see the ponchos which had been rigged to catch the wind. Little soiled white flags were fluttering from every stick and pole on the boat.

Everything on *Seasweep* was in readiness. The team was poised for instantaneous response.

The sight that came into view when we were a few hundred yards away unnerved me for a short time. I couldn't continue for a few moments when the producer for a BBC documentary television film who was on board asked me to describe the scene for the cameras. It was too heart-wrenching.

From bow to stern, which was no more than thirty feet, bodies lay stacked against each other. Other bodies were on top of the wheelhouse which stood above the deck about four feet. I could see babies and little children. One or two old people. A few hands waved feebly at us.

The boat was pitching in the swells and we had to be careful not to come too close or it would have been smashed against our steel hull. As we slowly circled, our interpreter told them through an amplified bullhorn that we were friends and had come to help them. This announcement was greeted with smiles and applause.

But there had been some apprehension on the little boat at first. Mrs. Quach says, "We thought it was a Russian boat and that maybe they would ship us back to Vietnam."

But someone then saw the word, *Seasweep*, on the bow and began to yell, "Our savior! You're our savior!" Several had read about the mercy ship in a Vietnamese-language magazine which had been brought into the country from the United States.

It was a high moment, packed with emotion, for the passengers on both vessels. It was a miracle we had found them, undoubtedly led by the hand of God. If we had been ten miles off in either direction, we would have missed them.

A line was thrown to the drifting boat and gradually the strong hands of the *Seasweep* crew pulled it alongside. Water and cups were lowered over the side. Biscuits were passed around. The leader of the group was brought up by ladder and while Burt talked with him, the rest of us set about bringing up those who were sick.

The basket stretcher was lowered four times. Only the desperately ill were brought aboard. First, we brought up a seventeen-year-old girl who was only semiconscious. Next, an old woman. Then, the man who would be partially blind for the rest of his life because of scarred corneas, also a victim of dehydration. Finally, an old man.

The clinic and deck alongside looked like a hospital ward. I.V. bottles and tubes ran everywhere as Dr. Chander, Regina and Rosemary brought all their professional training and experience to bear on the emergency situation.

Burt had learned the basics of their story from the young leader whom the refugees had elected their captain although he had had no marine experience.

In keeping with our policy of supply and service first, with rescue coming only if the former were not enough to guarantee survival, Burt sent *Seasweep's* chief engineer over the side to look at the boat's engine.

On the little boat, the people waited with mounting fears. Would this be another hoax? One more disappointment piled on top of all those they had already received?

"We were afraid of being left on the boat," Mrs. Quach recalls. "After seven days and nights of drifting on the ocean, we didn't know if we could take any more. Where would we go? We didn't even know where we were."

Mr. Choi, our engineer from Hong Kong, tried to calm them. "Don't panic," Mrs. Quach remembers he told them. "If the engine can't be fixed, then *Seasweep* will pick you up."

It seemed to her an eternity while the decision was being made. Mr. Choi came back up and reported to Burt and me that the engine could not be repaired. The block was cracked and the engine was filled with water.

"Could the refugees have cracked it when they

166

saw us coming?" I asked, since I had read charges that some refugees disabled their boats deliberately when help approached. At this time, I did not know that they had been drifting for seven days.

"No," the engineer said, "it's an old crack."

"Then, basically, what you've got down there is a floating coffin," Burt responded.

Mr. Choi nodded his head.

Burt and I looked at each other. "Do you want to give the order?" he asked.

"Commodore," I said, "you're the mission chief and I wouldn't want to deprive you of the privilege."

"Bring 'em aboard!" Burt said, and the team and ship's crew burst into feverish activity.

When the news was signaled down to the refugees, they shouted and clapped their hands.

By now it was nearly 5:30 in the afternoon and we had not much more than two hours of light left.

Tarps and planks were removed from the number-two hold which had been prepared for such an event. Ralph Lewis, a retired Los Angeles fireman who had volunteered for the *Seasweep* team, climbed onto the refugee boat to supervise the operation from that end. Ted Agon, who had formerly operated barges and ships throughout Vietnam and up the Mekong and is now *Seasweep's* operations chief, brought his muscles and experience to the deck side of the operation.

It was "all hands on deck." Burt's wife, Ellen, was a comforting presence to the women and mothers as she moved among them with her gentle touch. My seventeen-year-old son Mark proved himself to be an experienced, able-bodied seaman. Even the media personnel on board—the BBC television crew and its producer, Christine Fox; the CBS television news team; *Toronto Star* reporter Gerald Utting; and World Vision's Kenny Waters—not only covered the event, but participated in it.

Seasweep's cook, Quan Du Tran, himself a refugee with a wife and two sons still in a camp in Malaysia, put the galley's biggest pots on the stove in order to prepare dinner for our newly arrived guests.

The babies were brought up one by one in a pillowcase to which a strong line had been tied. Ted Agon lifted each of them over the side. A rope sling was used to help the children and the weaker ones who didn't have the strength to make the long climb up the ladder. Ralph Lewis brought up several women. Some children came up clinging to the backs of their fathers.

The operation wasn't over until the sun had set and the deck was illuminated by searchlights.

Mrs. Quach recalls: "I couldn't stand up when I got on the ship. I was dizzy because I had been sitting for so many days in one place."

As the hectic pace began to subside, a larger

problem loomed before Burt and me. Captain Samudra and the crew of *Seasweep* had begun to take stock of their own situation and faced us with their dilemma. If they sailed into Singapore, they had already been told their careers were in jeopardy.

Where, they asked, did we propose to take the refugees? We considered several options. Hong Kong's Marine Department had already notified us by cable that the vessel would not be allowed in that port, and that if we attempted to enter, both owner and captain would be subject to a $20,000 fine and up to five years' imprisonment. Although we had never considered going to Hong Kong, that cable was a little disquieting to me since I was officially listed as one of the owners.

A port in Thailand was considered as a possible option, but it was low on the list. We looked at Guam. The advantage presented by this island was that it was an American port and we were an American-owned vessel. There should be no problem. The disadvantages, however, were (1) it would be a fourteen-day trip; (2) we would have to pass through stormy waters during the typhoon season; (3) we would have to bunker in Manila for fuel and supplies; (4) our ship was registered for operations only within Southeast Asia; and (5) our crew was not licensed for the high seas.

That brought us right back to Singapore and the definite possibility of a mutinous crew.

Negotiations went on for a delicate two hours. I saw tears in the eyes of our Indonesian captain, Mr. Samudra, himself a Christian, as he agonized and wrestled within himself. He was risking his own career and the jobs of the crew who had signed on with him.

Yet his conscience told him he could not put these people back in that boat. Finally, a compromise was reached. The engineers agreed to try to repair the engine when it was daylight. I agreed to consider all other alternatives during the three days before we would get to Singapore. I also promised I would not allow any crew members to suffer economically as a result of my actions.

About midnight, the rescue operation was over, the impasse with the crew had been temporarily resolved, the big engine was started after nearly eight hours of quiet, and *Seasweep* turned in a southwesterly direction toward Singapore.

Things on board went smoothly. The refugees were fed and bedded down in the hold. They slept the sleep of exhaustion. Treatment of the sick went on well past midnight. The next day they showered on the deck and spread out hundreds of pieces of clothing to dry. Down in the hold it looked like a Chinese laundry!

We gave out Vietnamese magazines published in the United States and collected by Vietnamese college students just for our mission. They were literally devoured as they were passed from hand to hand. Vietnamese Bibles were also offered to all who desired them.

During our daily radio check with John Calder in Singapore the next day, he learned that "our devotions for the previous day were from Psalm 93." Actually, we were only two chapters off, for they had, in fact, been from Psalm 91! Immediately he set in motion the procedures earlier agreed on.

Life aboard ship gradually assumed a degree of routine normalcy. Three engineers worked for hours on the engine of the little boat before giving it up as a lost cause. We still continued to tow it, however.

On shore, John was getting half-promises but no firm commitments. I knew we didn't dare sail that ship into harbor without agreements all around as to just what would take place. We slowed our speed to give John more negotiating time.

Finally, on the fourth day of the return voyage, we anchored in the straits just outside Singapore harbor near Horsburgh Lighthouse. I waited for a launch to come and take me ashore so I could join John in the negotiations.

Since both Indonesia and Singapore share the straits, the waters are patrolled thoroughly by ships and planes of both countries. After about two hours we were spotted at anchor and it wasn't long until *Seasweep* was the center of quite a bit of attention. We were checked out by an Indonesian customs boat, three Singapore patrol boats and two patrol planes which kept us under constant observation.

The refugees got used to it and went about the necessary chores of life. Ellen Singleton and my son Mark organized games and activities to relieve the boredom of the children. They also began some rudimentary lessons in English.

An uneventful weekend passed.

Meanwhile, in Singapore, things began to fall into place. The American Embassy provided to the Singapore government a letter of guarantee for resettlement of the refugees. This was accepted by the Foreign Ministry as adequate for granting permission for the refugees to disembark temporarily. At that point, the local UNHCR office would take over.

As soon as John Ratigan from the embassy called to tell me that agreement had been reached, I radioed Burt on *Seasweep* and told him, with a sigh of relief, "Bring her home!"

When the ship sailed into the harbor on July 16, God was as good as His Word had promised me earlier. There were "shouts of joy when we hear the news of your victory, flags flying with praise to God for all that he has done for you"!

The refugees came ashore and were cleared

through immigration for a temporary stay at the local transit camp.

Another search-and-rescue mission was over.

For the Quach family and seventy-six others who had been rescued, a new life was about to begin.

For Chin Klein in Baltimore, the momentous news had not yet arrived. She was about to sit down for lunch with a couple of friends when the mailman came. Chin picked up the mail and took it to the kitchen. She hastily checked through it until she came to the letter from Singapore.

Her nephew, Quach Van Loi, had written it the third day after rescue. I had mailed it with dozens of others when I first arrived in Singapore. When Chin saw her nephew's name on the envelope, her hands began to shake.

"I was nervous and scared," she later reflected. "I wondered if something had happened to my family. I never connected my family with being boat people. They are business people."

Chin read the letter and began to cry. It told of the escape, of the suffering in Malaysia, of the abandonment at sea.

Then it continued: "Everyone was so hungry. There was no water. No food. We just had rice. A lot of children cried. Grown-ups cried. And we really prayed. Everyone laid down, closed their eyes and waited for time to die. We were very sad.

"On July 9, we saw a very big ship—the ship

named *Seasweep*. We are very lucky. Everybody on the boat was saved.

"This ship takes very good care of us. They give us a lot of food and everything. They make us happy. Please send telegram back to Vietnam to tell grandmother that everybody is safe. Maybe the family is worried about that.

"Everybody in my boat thinks they are reborn."

The letter spoiled Chin's lunch, but it made her day.

Not even bothering to wipe her tears and with hands still trembling, she dialed Jeffrey. He took the rest of the day off and drove home.

"I almost had to pull the car over to the side of the road because I couldn't see very well," he comments.

Less than three months later the family from Singapore landed at Baltimore's Friendship Air port. There were long, tearful hugs and whole nights of exchanging family news and catching up on events long past but not yet shared.

Jeffrey made a down payment on a house for them. He doesn't know quite how he will manage since the family has more than quadrupled virtually overnight. Chin's brother-in-law has tuberculosis and will require long treatment. They all need extensive dental work.

But Jeffrey Klein shrugs and says simply, "We'll work it out."

On the third day of July, 1979—three boats in

three different harbors, far removed from each other.

Less than a week later, the lives of the people on each had become involved with each other in ways that perhaps would last forever.

The secularist would say: "What an amazing coincidence."

To which George Mueller, a great man of faith from another century, would reply, "All I know is that when I pray, the coincidences happen; when I don't pray, they don't happen."

12

The Trail of Tears and Terror

She was only five yars old, the report noted.

It had taken her months to walk with her family to a refugee camp in Thailand, across the border from her homeland of Kampuchea.

It took her only thirty minutes to die while doctors fought to find a vein in order to give her a blood transfusion. They were unsuccessful. Her arms and neck were too withered from malnutrition.

While they struggled to find some flesh between skin and bone, she was gone. Her mother began to sob quietly, but could not bring herself to pick up the body of her dead child.

Medics carried it away.

This little one was another victim of the trail of

tears and terror—made up of many paths and roads across the once green and fertile land of Cambodia into camps of sickness and death. With her family, she had come to Thailand trying to escape the starvation and war which now devastate her country.

When she arrived where help was available, it was too late. She was too ravaged, too weak even to know where she was. She only stared with unseeing eyes at the people who tried to help her until death ended her life before it had even begun.

She was one of twenty people who died that day in late October, 1979, at a refugee camp housing a thousand Cambodians near Aranyaprathet, Thailand.

Since 1975, when the world has thought anything at all about Southeast Asia, its attention has been centered on Vietnam and the plight of its boat people. Theirs have been the most dramatic cases of uprooting and upheaval which characterized the entire region after the Communist takeover.

But the tragedy which has been happening in two sister countries, also under Vietnamese control, has been largely unknown and ignored.

These countries are Kampuchea (formerly Cambodia) and Laos. And it is impossible to know the extent of the suffering throughout the region unless you know something about what has taken place in these two countries in the past five years.

From April, 1975, until April, 1979, Kampuchea went behind a curtain of silence. Only sporadic reports by a few refugees filtered out, and much of the world either refused to believe or ignored their stories of genocide, which included the murder of virtually all the educated, the skilled and the supporters of former regimes.

What was taking place behind the curtain of silence was legalized insanity.

The chief "crazy man" of the whole country was a revolutionary named Pol Pot, who with a handful of fanatics inspired by the manic Red Guards of China's "cultural revolution," enslaved over six million people. The country fell to him and his Communist Khmer Rouge (or *Red Khmer*, Khmer being the cultural name for Cambodians) on April 17, 1975.

The *Angka*—for that is what they called themselves, meaning "organization on high"—intended to turn the calendar and history back to year zero. That is how they designated the calendar year of 1975, the year of their takeover. It was to be the first year of a revolutionary "pure" rural society with no ties to the past, except the ancient Khmer empire of the tenth century which had produced the spectacular city of Angkor Wat. They said that the new Kampuchea was going to be "classless and glorious."

To carry out this feat, Pol Pot estimated he would need no more than one million Cambodians. This meant that, in his program, at least five million were expendable.

The new regime was less than twelve hours old when Pol Pot began the systematic murder that in four-and-a-half years would eliminate between two million and three million of his fellow countrymen. He was well on his way to reducing the population to the one-sixth he wanted when the Vietnamese army marched into its next-door neighbor in early 1979 and put the Khmer Rouge forces to rout.

The madness is still not over, for the fighting yet rages across the land. But I was back in Cambodia for four days in October, 1979, for the first time since April, 1975, and can vouch for what happened during those four years.

In his efforts to erase all evidence of the twentieth century in his country, Pol Pot turned the cities into ghost towns and the countryside into one giant funeral pyre.

When the victorious Khmer Rouge peasant army marched into Phnom Penh on April 17, 1975, they ordered an immediate evacuation of the entire city. The conquering Communists arrived at 7:30 A.M. The order to abandon the city came at 1:00 P.M. There were no exceptions; every person had to go.

A few foreigners who had stayed behind to

report on the collapse were eyewitnesses to one of the most grotesque sights ever seen. The hospitals were emptied at gunpoint. Doctors were not even permitted to finish operations already underway. Dying patients on their beds were wheeled out by relatives. I.V. bottles and tubes were swinging crazily from the beds as they were pushed through the streets.

The sick and the dying were left beside the road. In all, more than two million people were sent away from their homes and their businesses, and the streams of people leaving the city by the six major roads lasted around the clock for two days and two nights.

Most of them marched to their deaths. Simply having lived in a city was itself a death sentence, for this meant you had been corrupted by the twentieth century. Teachers, office workers, students, businessmen, civil servants, technicians, anyone speaking a foreign language, anyone knowing a foreigner, Buddhist monks, Christians—all these and more had an immediate death sentence.

Of the two million who lived in the city, probably not more than a few tens of thousands survived the holocaust.

Around the city today, there are pyramids of automobiles, pianos, refrigerators, sewing machines, generators and scores of other kinds of devices which were smashed and simply piled up as an act of contempt for anything modern.

The beautiful Gothic cathedral, built nearly a century ago by French Roman Catholics, was leveled and every stone removed. Five years ago it had dominated the skyline of the peaceful city. Now it looks as if some giant had put down his finger and simply erased it from the lot which is overgrown with grass.

It was an eerie feeling to drive through the streets and see block upon block of empty buildings with their doors standing open. John Pilger of the London *Daily Mirror* wrote, "In the silent, airless humidity, it is like entering a city without people, as if in the wake of a nuclear war which spared only the buildings."

But the greatest tragedy is what happened to the people. I talked with scores of them and every single person had horrible stories to tell of the loss of whole families. One young soldier in the army of Heng Samrin shyly came up to me in a quiet corner of Phnom Penh's airport. (Since there is only one commercial flight a week into the airport, there are many quiet corners.)

He told me of the death of his entire family through various means of torture. He was so moved by his feelings of being alone that when he finished, he reached out and embraced me—a most difficult thing for the shy Khmer to do. He wept on my shoulder and said, "Be my father."

I asked him his age and he told me he was

twenty-three. I gently drew him away and took his face in my hands.

"My own son in America is also twenty-three," I said. "Now I have another son the same age."

I held his hand as we walked toward the door.

I visited what had once been the Tuol Sleng High School. Pol Pot had turned it into a murder factory. I have never seen anything more like a Nazi concentration camp. The former classrooms had been turned into interrogation rooms and torture chambers. Blood and tufts of hair were still on the floor. The instruments of torture were still in the rooms.

Some rooms had been divided into small, crude cells just large enough for a man to sit down and have his feet put in irons and his hands chained. One room was filled to the ceiling with clothes and shoes which had been taken from the dead prisoners. Articles of children's clothing could be seen in the pile.

It is said that between December, 1975, and June, 1977, approximately 14,000 prisoners died here. It is not difficult to document this figure. The sadistic guards took "before" and "after" pictures of their prisoners, apparently to prove their deaths. One of the most terrible experiences for me was to walk from room to room where these enlarged photographs are on display. I scanned every row to see if I might find the face of a friend.

There were none that I could identify, although I hoped I might be able to confirm the status of some of those with whom I had worked. Perhaps it is just as well for me that they remain among the "missing."

Now that Pol Pot is on the run and war between the Communist Vietnamese and the Khmer Rouge has disrupted the normal tight security, thousands of refugees are coming down the trail of terror to cross into the freedom and safety of Thailand. It is still a perilous journey. Fighting is taking place all along the Kampuchean/Thai border and the Khmer Rouge forces hold many civilian hostages.

For those trying to escape, jungle trails that lead to border-crossing areas are planted with land mines. Many make it, however, and over 200,000 have crossed since 1975. If the fighting continues, it is expected the number will increase to 400,000 before the end of 1979.

Many of those who make it look like the walking dead. Malnutrition, dysentery and malaria have reduced virtually all of them to mere shadows of their former selves. People are boiling bark and leaves for nutrition, and I have talked with those who said they ate grass because there was nothing else to eat.

Inside the country, starvation faces another two-and-a-half million people. The disruption of war has allowed only 10 to 20 percent of the arable land to be cultivated. Hunger among children is 100 percent, with severe malnutrition affecting as many as 80 percent of them. There is an epidemic of malaria.

Orphans roam the countryside. No one has made an estimate of the number of children without parents, but there are likely to be up to 50,000 of them.

At the Thai border late in 1979, I talked with a group which had just arrived from inside Kampuchea the night before. Out of seventeen, two of them were young orphan lads. Each told me he had seen his parents murdered. There were no family members with them. They had simply observed some people walking toward the border and the boys joined them because they had no other place to go.

When the group started out from Kompong Speu, a town about forty miles from the capital city of Phnom Penh, there were sixty of them. It took them twenty days to reach the border and by the time they arrived, their numbers had been reduced by forty-three who died along the way. Most of them just lay down on the roadside because they could go no further, I was told.

For them, every road is a trail of tears and terror.

Now and then someone comes down the trail whom we have known or who worked for World Vision prior to 1975.

Just four years after we were forced to abandon

our work in the country, one of our former staff members showed up in a refugee camp in Thailand, much to our delight and surprise. Since Ly Lorn's story carries in it all the elements of thousands more, I want to share it with you as typical of what has happened in a gentle land and to a gentle people.

Before the capital city fell to the Khmer Rouge, both Ly Lorn and her brother Ly Hy worked for World Vision. As with all the others, her family was ordered to leave the city and go to the forest.

"In my family were my parents, five brothers, two sisters, a boy cousin and myself. My eldest sister, Phan, who is with me now in America, had a baby boy and a sister-in-law. (Phan's husband was taken off by the Khmer Rouge and was never heard from again.) So all together, there were thirteen of us," Lorn says softly.

"A group of about 30,000 people, all from Phnom Penh, were ordered by the Khmer Rouge to live in the forest. This forest was very far away from any town or village. We were people of the city who did not know how to live off the land. The Khmer Rouge never gave us any materials for shelter; we lived in the open with the rain coming down on us. We had no beds to keep us off the muddy ground, so all night we had to squat. We could hear wild animals prowling and we were afraid. My sister's child was only twelve days old when we left Phnom Penh. We tried to make a shelter for her and the child with a cloth that we hung on a tree.

"The Khmer Rouge ordered the people to work in farms and they did not let them rest when they were tired. They gave them little rice to eat, no medicine and no hope for help of any kind. The people had to walk far to the farms, then work very long hours.

"After this went on for about a year, the people became sick, one by one, day after day. That's why from September to November, 1976, ten people in my family died. In some families, not one remained alive.

"The Khmer Rouge ordered all the children under ten years to go to school, but not a school for learning. The school was for working, whatever kind of work that children can do. So all the children had to live far away from their parents. It was a terrible hardship for them. They missed their parents; they did not have enough rice to eat, and they were tired from working.

"Three of my brothers stayed at a school like that. They did not get a daily bath, though everything around them was filthy. They had no beds, but had to live on the ground. After a year many children—including my three brothers—became sick and died.

"I was not with my oldest sister and brother

because the Khmer Rouge asked me to work far away. One day I heard that my brother Ly Hy had died. What could I do after I heard such bad news? I ran home to ask my sister how Hy died. Phan told me everything and how my brother had wanted to see my face before he died.

"My brother did not have sickness, only he was tired and very hungry. A few days before he died he could not walk, because he was so weak. He spoke only in a soft, weak voice. He looked like a dead body. My brother had been a tall, strong man. In Phnom Penh he had learned karate and judo and had won the black belt.

"My mother became very ill. She had swelling all over her body and could barely speak. She could not open her eyes. She asked my younger sister—who was eighteen—to go for medicine. This was during the month when the river is high. My sister had to cross this river to get the medicine. She did not know how to swim, but she loved my mother so much. She was afraid that if she did not get the medicine, our mother would die. She tried to cross the river. Someone told me later that they saw the water carry her away and saw her raise her hands for help, but she was too far away for anyone to rescue her.

"My mother did not send for Phan or me at the time because we were ill. Otherwise, I would have gone in my sister's place. This is how my youngest sister died, and it will always show how much she loved my mother.

"A few days after my mother heard about her youngest daughter drowning, she died as well. On the same day, Phan's baby also died. I, myself, with some help from others, carried their bodies away and dug a shallow grave. We buried them together with an old man.

"So in 1977, I had only one sister and one brother, who was seven years old. Since many children died in 1976 when they were taken to school, parents would not let the authorities take the children to school again. But in 1977 the Khmer Rouge made a new commandment, that all children must go to school again.

"At this time my youngest brother was among those who had to go; they would not give rice for him if he did not. In July, 1977, all the children became sick again and my youngest brother did too. When I heard, I went to the school to take him to the hospital. One week later, he died. He was the last of my brothers to die.

"So of the thirteen people in my family, only Ly Phan and I remained. From 1975 to 1979, all but 4,000 of the 30,000 people who were together in the forest died.

"On April 20, 1979, the Vietnamese won out over the Khmer Rouge soldiers. The Vietnamese told all the people to go wherever they wished. I was so happy to have an opportunity to look for my uncle and aunt and cousins. My sister and I went to Battambang Province, where my uncle and aunt were living. We were thrilled to find them all alive.

"My aunt gave us rice and food to eat, so in two weeks we grew strong. They were so kind to us; my aunt would tell us not to feel bad, that she would look after us as though we were her own children.

"One day I saw many people walking along the road. I asked them why, and they said they were going to Thai country because they felt that the Vietnamese did not have kind hearts, and there would be no good future in Cambodia. After I told my aunt, she agreed, and we left for Thai country on May 14, 1979.

"We stayed at a camp called Nong Chan. On our tenth day there, we saw a group of Americans come into the camp with some Cambodian men. After they took down the names of the people, they returned to Bangkok and three days later they returned to our camp with some buses. After they held up a list and called the names of refugees, they said, 'If your name has been called, please get in the bus.' I heard my name and my sister's name, but not the names of my aunt and uncle and cousins. I was very sorry. After we said goodbye to them, we got on the bus.

"About 400 families went on those buses to stay at Lumpini camp in Bangkok. In the camp, I studied the Bible, prayed every Sunday morning and sang God's songs with many people who know Jesus. There I met Paul Jones from World Vision, and he gave me a Bible and many other things.

"While we stayed at Lumpini camp, on June 5, the Thai government took all the people I knew at the Nong Chan camp back to Cambodia. My aunt and her family were among them.

"On June 18, we got to leave for the United States. But the news of my aunt made me have pity in my heart for them. You know, when the Cambodian people set foot in Thailand, they were so happy because they said, 'Now we have freedom.' For four years they had no freedom. I can't find words to say what happened in their hearts after the Thai government took them back to their country.

"They had hoped they would have a new life; now they were going back to the bad country that makes people die. How could they keep living without water, rice or shelter? I have just recently received bad news from a friend in Bangkok. He said that many of the people whom the Thai government took back to Cambodia died of hunger. I hear there is no hope that my relatives are still alive, for there is nothing to eat in Cambodia. If they are dead, my sister and I have no relatives any more.

"But we have relatives in Jesus Christ.

"So many Christians have shown us kindness.

They have provided everything we need. They talk to us about the Lord and take us to church with them. My sister, Phan, accepted the Lord as her Savior the first week we came to the United States. Thank God for our salvation! The Lord brought us here and I trust He will continue to look after us forever."

I have talked with many like Ly Lorn who have walked through the valley of the shadow of death on their trek out of the madness which gripped Kampuchea.

One conversation which stands out in my mind was held in the rain on the beach at a refugee camp called Ban Mai Rut. It was inside Thailand, but less than two miles from the Kampuchean border.

Lem Phana was thirty years old, old enough to remember the good and pleasant days in her gentle land. She struggled to ask me a difficult question.

"Does the world know about Cambodia?" she inquired.

She was referring to the genocide which had taken place in her country. I told her many people did. At long last the international media were telling the story of the death throes of a nation.

Then she asked: "Do they care?"

That question was harder to answer than the first one, for I have asked it myself so many times.

I told Lem Phana that some people cared, especially the ones I knew best, but that I was not sure it was enough.

I am haunted by a grim word of prophecy spoken twenty years ago by the Cambodian Prince Norodom Sihanouk, who is now living in exile. It was reported recently by Keyes Beech, veteran Asian correspondent for the *Los Angeles Times*.

During a discussion at the royal palace in the then-peaceful city of Phnom Penh, the prince turned to a group of journalists and said moodily: "We are all going to die."

When they protested that no one wished Cambodia ill and that certainly the world did not wish to see the death of the beautiful country, Sihanouk said almost angrily: "But you don't understand. There is no hope. We have to die."

If the world doesn't begin to care more—and care quickly—about those in Kampuchea who are walking the trail of tears and terror, Prince Sihanouk's bitter prophecy may become the world's next reality.

13

The Bitter End of the Hmong

Up in the high mountain vastness of Laos, where China and Vietnam surround the little landlocked nation on the north and east, the Hmong tribespeople have lived for generations.

Cut off from the rest of the world by geography and by choice, they grew their rice, raised their pigs and brought their children into the world. When the nutrients in the soil became exhausted on one mountaintop, they slashed down the trees on another, burned them and moved the entire village to the new location.

If their lives were not full and overflowing, they were certainly uncomplicated and pleasant.

It was a way of life which had been willed by their legendary chieftain, Sin Sai. Back in the very old days, when the whole world was no bigger than one mountain valley, the adults would tell each successive generation of children, the great warrior left his people to go off to another world and fight giants and evil spirits.

Sin Sai's last words to the Hmong were: "Don't leave the mountains; stay here in the high hills and wait until I return, for there may be many who will want to cause you harm."

Now they say bitterly that Sin Sai was right.

One international aid official working among them in the refugee camps in Thailand says glumly: "The Hmong have come to the end of the road."

The Hmong (pronounced "moan") themselves do not know for how many generations they have been running. Their history records constant battles and struggles, always to protect their way of life, never to conquer others. Although they are fierce fighters, they are not a warlike people. Rarely, if ever, have the Hmong been the aggressors.

Left alone, they would have lived out the rest of their generation in their beloved mountains and valleys.

The trouble is no one would leave them alone.

Their earliest history shows them being forced out of China. For many decades they tolerated the French colonial presence in Indochina, but barely. In World War II, however, they fought against the Japanese. Then they joined with the Vietnamese to help bring down France's crumbling Asian empire.

But the victory over the French was only the beginning of more sorrows for the Hmong. The Viet Minh, forerunner of the Vietnamese Communist Party, turned on their former tribal allies who stood in the way of the Vietnamese ambition to make Laos a part of their own territory. The Hmong had never supported Communism as an ideology. They fought alongside the Vietnamese against the French only as a matter of convenience.

Now for a quarter-century they have had to struggle against the efforts of the Vietnamese and their puppets, the Pathet Lao, to subjugate the Hmong. Acknowledged to be among the best fighters in Asia, they acquitted themselves well under their dynamic leader, General Vang Pao, during that part of the Vietnam War which was fought in Laos. Popularly called the "Meo," a denigrating term they dislike, the Hmong formed what some called "the CIA's secret army." They were the terror of their enemies.

In the debacle of 1975, the Americans abandoned them and left them with little more than their fierce independence and love of freedom. A lot of people are bitter about that. One is a former American pilot, Jack Blalock. In the middle of 1979, he left his importing business in the hands of a partner and went to Thailand to work among the Hmong in the refugee camps.

"The Hmong fought for us and were very pro-American," he says. "We lost the war, pulled out and left them holding the baby."

For him, helping them now is a matter of honor. While in Thailand he built a thirty-three bed hospital in one of the Hmong camps.

Left on their own, the Hmong still have put up the stiffest resistance to Communist rule in Indochina. They continue to attack government soldiers, ambush convoys and cut roads. The resistance movement, calling itself "The Armed Forces of the Sky God to Liberate Laos," fights with U.S. weapons and ammunition left behind during the pullout and with whatever they can capture from the enemy.

The Hmong tactic is to fight in small groups of fifteen to thirty men, moving fast among the familiar mist-shrouded peaks that rise as high as 9,000 feet.

But if the terrain is on their side, time isn't.

No one has come to their aid and it is increasingly difficult for them to fight against the Vietnamese and Laotians who have mounted a concerted attack to either break the spirit of the Hmong—a tough thing to do—or annihilate them.

Most objective sources believe they are doomed. Before the war, they numbered about

350,000. Knowledgeable people say as much as 20 percent of the population was killed between 1960 and 1974. Hunger and disease claimed many. Scores of their villages were flattened by massive American bombing on the Plain of Jars in central Laos in the face of the Communist advance.

With homes destroyed, the Hmong had to move again.

One man who has lived among them since 1960 is Edgar "Pop" Buell, an American farmer who went to Laos and spent fourteen years working with the Hmong.

Buell says, "It is going to be hard for the Hmong to survive as a group. Their leaders are gone. The tribal structure as I knew it will disappear."

Few will dispute his words.

It is not hard to see why they are a threatened people when you visit the Hmong refugee camp at Ban Vinai in Thailand, near the Laotian border. The camp now houses a population of over 40,000 people, but there are 53,000 Hmong refugees in all of Thailand. In four years, only 20,000 of the tribal people have been resettled in other countries, primarily France and the United States.

Hundreds more are arriving in Thailand each month, having been driven from their mountain homes by bombings, shellings and army raids. There have been reports for two years which are now being confirmed that the Vietnamese are also using poison gas against the diminishing tribe. When they leave their mountain homes, they must then deal with a veritable gauntlet of dangers before crossing the muddy Mekong River into the safety of Thailand.

One former district officer tells a typical story.

Every man in his village was a resistance fighter. The Pathet Lao sent spotter planes over the farming village, and these planes then called in artillery strikes. In addition to high explosive and shrapnel shells, they also shot poison gas into the village.

Following the artillery barrage, ground troops came into the village to finish it off. They burned homes, destroyed wells and burned rice fields. They also executed some of the villagers. The district officer, Wong Chong Lee, escaped by going into hiding. He decided, however, that he must take his family and flee into Thailand.

A total of eighteen people from two families started the trek of sixteen days through the mountains to the banks of the Mekong. The youngest was three years old. Mostly, they ate bamboo shoots and roots on the way.

Because of Communist patrols, they had to move at night. A young girl stepped on a land mine and was killed. A boy has puncture marks on his chest and shoulders from the same mine blast.

When they reached the Mekong River which forms the boundary between the two countries, they waited in the jungles until just a few hours before dawn. Scores of fleeing refugees have been shot while in the water by guards on the Laotian side.

Lee and his party made crude bamboo rafts and floated with the current across the river. They clung to the rafts, keeping their bodies in the water, and the children clung onto the backs of their parents. No one in the group could swim.

Safe on the other side, they sat down near the river bank and rested. Their feet were swollen and their legs were caked with dirt and dried blood from cuts and jungle leeches.

"If we had stayed maybe we would have died," a member of the little group says soberly. "We will have suffering now, but we will bear it."

A part of the suffering will be from the terribly crowded conditions at the Ban Vinai camp where they will be taken. Originally built to house a maximum of 10,000 people, the population suddenly exploded to 40,000 in mid-1979 when larger numbers started coming across—up to 4,000 a month—and other camps were closed.

Another part of the suffering is the fact that the refugees arrive in such a weakened state of health. This is especially true of the children. In the building that serves as a hospital, rows of tiny living skeletons lie motionless on wooden benches. A survey of the camp showed 3,000 malnourished children who had recently arrived from Laos. More than 1,000 under five years of age were suffering from acute maramus, a type of malnutrition caused by carbohydrate deficiency. A doctor says the reason is that the mothers of these babies have been living off nothing more substantial than roots and tree bark.

He calls it a "medical emergency" and explains that 50 percent of all the children in the camp are victims of third-degree malnutrition, the last stage before death from starvation or disease. He explains that malnutrition is a slow process that takes weeks or months to cause death.

"For these children," he says, "it all started in Laos."

During the month of July, 1979, residents of the camp dug fifty-five tiny graves.

Tribal lore as well as a shortage of medical personnel and facilities contribute to the high death rate. Most parents don't bring their children to the hospital until it is too late. The clapboard building with its intravenous fluids and modern medicines is usually the last resort, called upon only after the mother has despaired from her reliance on spirit doctors and amulets.

But the dying is not all happening in the camps. Back in their mountain homeland, the danger is even greater and that is why they flee. When the Pathet Lao took over the country in

1975 with the help of the North Vietnamese (who are said still to maintain between 40,000 and 50,000 soldiers in the country, twice the size of the Pathet Lao army), the first order of business was dealing with the independent and freedom-loving Hmong.

Families were broken up. Whole villages were moved out of the mountains so they could be more easily controlled. Former fighters were sent off to reeducation camps from which many never returned.

Some pilots with the Pathet Lao who defected in 1976 and 1977 said they had flown many missions against Hmong civilian villages as well as military targets. Lt. Bounmy Mekhagnomdara said he flew his last mission against a twenty-hut village some 6,000 feet up in the rugged mountains.

"I made two sorties, firing sixteen rockets in all. The village was suspected of having some rebels," he said. "Two days later I flew my plane out of Laos. I didn't want to kill Meo any more."

For two years, fleeing refugees have told of gas and chemical attacks by aircraft on their villages. Some have arrived in Thailand with what they said were chemical burns on their bodies, although many Western observers have been skeptical.

But in August, 1979, a group of refugees brought with them a yellow powder and leaves with yellow splotches which they say were caused by chemicals dropped from low-flying aircraft.

After analysis, Western observers are now inclined to believe that gas and chemicals are being used in central and western Laos. Refugees arriving from these areas say: "We are leaving because we are being poisoned."

Vang Sou Ying, an ex-soldier, explained why he left his homeland. "There are no birds or animals. They've all run away and died. The water is spoiled."

A leading Asian magazine reported that a senior Lao Communist Party defector told its editors that "he learned of the chemical attacks against Meo enclaves mainly from conversations with soldiers" who had fought in the Hmong area. He said the soldiers claimed it was released by Vietnamese aircraft flying from Vietnam.

The magazine also said: "U.S. intelligence reports indicate the Soviet Union has been supplying Hanoi with poison gas and that Soviet military officers have been taking a direct interest in its use. A Soviet major-general is reported to have recently visited one of the four sites in Vietnam where it is being stored" (*Far Eastern Economic Review*, August 24, 1979).

The article in the *Review* concluded: "There is a feeling in some quarters that Laos is perhaps being used as a testing ground because of its remoteness and the difficulties involved in furnishing proof."

So the people of the great warrior, Sin Sai, face what may be the last and final threat to their civilization and their culture. One man who had to leave his family in Laos because the Pathet Lao had taken them away, told me, "Sometimes I get so lonely, I write myself a letter and sign my wife's name. Sure, I know it is just pretending. We want our families with us because if we die in the camp in Thailand, at least we will die together.

"But if we die over there, we die apart. I don't know where I will go or what I will do."

The despair and boredom caused four Hmong to jump to their deaths from a bridge in mid-1979.

But not everyone despairs.

Pradith, a twenty-nine-year-old Laotian woman, has chosen a course of action. Twice a month, she makes secret forays across the Mekong River back into Laos. There she retrieves her M-16 rifle from its jungle hiding place and continues the hit-and-run war against the Pathet Lao.

She isn't worried about the dangers. Says she, "My hatred is greater than my fears."

In the camp, she tries to persuade the Hmong and other Laotians not to give up their country.

"They are wrong to go," she says. "They are discouraged and think we shall not succeed."

She is right about the dreary mood.

Vang Ying sums it up for most of the others.

Now thirty years old, he became a soldier in his early teens. He left his mountain homeland in June, 1975, and has been in a refugee camp ever since.

Ying, one of the leaders at Ban Vinai and resident chief for the World Vision development program working in the camp, says, "It's difficult for us because now we're like the Jews—we're dispersed to the whole world and our culture will die."

For Vang Ying and all the Hmong, after generations of running, it is a bitter end.

14

Refugees:
The World's Dilemma

From the time when Jacob and his sons went to live in Egypt because of famine in Canaan to the present exodus of tens of thousands of refugees from the Communist nations of Southeast Asia, much of the world's history has been the story of the movements of people across the face of the earth. Throughout recorded time, invasions, wars and conquests have been followed by large-scale movements of populations.

However, no period of history can match the twentieth century in either numbers of tragedies or displaced persons. Novelist Heinrich Böll has called it "the century of refugees and prisoners." Two world wars uprooted seventy million Europeans. The supposed years of peace since have seen almost as much misery and suffering as the years of actual war. More than forty million people have joined the ranks of the dispossessed at one time or another since World War II, causing this period to be called the "age of the uprooted."

Today, the Third World is awash with the homeless and dispossessed. Since 1960, the number has never been under eleven million while at peak periods, such as the civil war in Bangladesh, it has jumped to over twenty million.

Bona fide refugees are generally assigned to one of five categories:

(1) Refugees displaced by war. The military convulsions of this century have sent millions of tragic victims swarming over the planet.

(2) Refugees expelled or evacuated by political authorities, usually because they were ethnic minorities. These numbers are smaller and the transfer usually more orderly, but this does not lessen the trauma of being uprooted.

(3) Refugees from political oppression. Examples are numerous—from the million or more Armenians who fled Turkey more than half a century ago, to the Vietnamese who today board little boats and take to the open sea, to the Ugandan exiles who are returning home after five to eight years away when Amin was in power.

(4) Refugees from religious persecution, such as the Israeli Jews, many of whom are still trying to go home.

(5) Refugees from territorial alignment, the Palestinians being only one of many examples.

A sixth category—not generally recognized as bona fide refugees, but becoming increasingly troublesome—is composed of those who flee their countries in search of better economic opportunities, such as the Haitians who arrive on the shores of the United States in their own little boats.

While the UNHCR Convention of 1951 provides a comprehensive definition of a refugee (expanded by an international protocol in 1967), I personally prefer the more concise definition offered by author Elfan Rees in his book, *We Strangers and We Afraid.* He says that a refugee is "anyone who has been uprooted from his home, has crossed a frontier—artificial or traditional— and looks for protection and sustenance to a government or authority other than his former one."

The operative words in that definition are: (1) "uprooted," which indicates a coerced departure from one's homeland as distinguished from a migratory movement which may result from a population differential or economic hardship; and (2) "crossed a frontier," which distinguishes between a person temporarily displaced within his own country and an international refugee.

In making the distinction, I am not overlooking the misery and suffering of those internal refugees nor the need for urgent attention to their plight, but only pointing out that their situation is different from those who have been forced to leave their homelands.

An example of the confusion which sometimes results from unrealistic borders is the plight of the people in Shaba Province of Zaire. When I led the first relief survey team to that area in August, 1978, after the massacre at Kolwezi, we found thousands of people reduced to eating leaves. Large numbers were coming across the border adjoining Angola while thousands more were timorously coming out of the bush. They were in desperate circumstances, but governmental and international agencies in Kinshasa were delaying assistance until they could determine whether or not the "returnees" were legitimate refugees.

I was glad that, being a private agency, we didn't have to debate that technicality. People were starving and we launched an airlift directly from Nairobi, Kenya, to the Shaba provincial capital of Lubumbashi, bringing seeds, hoes, machetes and medicine for 50,000 families. Although they were returning to their homes, their crops and animals were lost and we considered them refugees from terror.

There was a time—not much more than a

century ago—when less rigid state boundaries and more porous frontiers made the refugee problem of less consequence. Although there were periodic waves of refugees, the movement from one country did not require passports and visas, and the right to asylum, which for a refugee is the equivalent of the right to life, was commonly recognized and honored.

Thus while there were *refugees*, there was no *refugee problem*.

But by the late nineteenth century, the era of open frontiers was over. National and ethnic homogeneity were elevated to priority positions by most governments. This resulted in complex systems of immigration quotas and restrictions making free movement impossible. At the same time, there has been an increasing tendency to single out people who are "different"—ethnic, religious and minority groups who are seen to pose some kind of threat to the ruling establishment—as the objects of discrimination and persecution. Totalitarian regimes sought to eliminate all dissent, either by imprisonment, harassment or expulsion.

The *Encyclopaedia Britannica* asserts that "By the 1920s and 1930s the long-standing tradition of political asylum had broken down completely, partly because of growing insensitivity to human suffering and partly because of unprecedented numbers of refugees." The respected reference source goes on to say, "Existing mechanisms of immigration and naturalization, which had been adjusted to a smaller, 'normal' influx of people, ground to an actual standstill."

That attitude, rightly or wrongly held, marked the beginning of the refugee *problem*. We would do well to remember that what we call the "problem" itself is of fairly recent origin and was created by the restrictive policies of government. I don't argue that policies are unnecessary, nor do I argue for a return to unrestricted movement or for the removal of all regulation. After all, one must deal with the political realities. I simply point out that these policies were made by men and do not bear the divine imprimatur from Mount Sinai.

Consequently, their very fallibility and existential nature opens them up to review and possible amendment in order to keep them current with both the need and a possible change in attitudes.

Personally, I have been distressed and saddened in recent years to see what I believe is a turning away from the common good of humanity to a preoccupation with more narrow, selfish interests. It is not all that surprising, however, in a world that rejects moral law as being transcendent. How is it possible to expect those who have never recognized or received the mercy of a gracious God to have a compelling inner motivation to demonstrate that mercy to others? That is not to say that unregenerate man is incapable of humane and compassionate feelings for other human beings, but he must struggle against even more powerful drives which arise out of an inherited selfishness. It is not necessary to point out which attitude most often prevails.

But while those attitudes may be natural for men and women of the world, it ought not to be so for the people of the kingdom. We are told to walk as children of the day, not as children of darkness. We should reflect the priorities of the kingdom, not those which belong to this world. Our words and our actions as Christians ought clearly to demonstrate that we march to the beat of a different drummer.

For that reason, I am personally compelled to identify myself with the world's outcasts, the dispossessed, the homeless and rootless, the hungry. I have not been called to join their ranks and share their lot—for what reason, only our sovereign God knows—but I have been called to plead their cause, to champion their hopes, to ease their suffering. I have met them in every part of the world and have watched their old die and seen their babies born, have wept with them over loved ones buried on the way and have raged inside at the bureaucratic delays that keep them in stagnating suspension between a past to which they cannot return and a future that lies beyond their reach. I have seen their human spirit die a little every day in those fetid, festering camps and I have felt myself dying with them.

For those reasons, I cannot view the problem from the clinical atmosphere of some remote ivory tower. A refugee is more than a statistic. Every number has a name and a face.

I have read three statements at various times in my life which have served not only to guide me, but also to motivate me in making my response to this tragic human problem.

The first is a Chinese proverb that bears serious thought: "Of all the precious things on earth, the most precious is people." No other resource on this planet is of such worth. I am not indifferent to the endangered status of the gray whale, the Bengal tiger, the black rhinoceros or even the tiny snail darter.

I simply ask—no, I shout!—"Who will make the emotional speeches and organize movements on behalf of a threatened humanity?" Is human life so cheap, especially if it happens to be black or brown, that it is no longer a cause worth championing? I find the embarrassed silence which surrounds the incalculable plight of the Vietnamese boat refugees to be one of the strangest acts of human behavior in my memory or knowledge.

Are these people of no value? Or of less value?

As Christians, we cannot believe that, but if we shut ourselves up half-a-world away, it is easier for us to forget it or to be indifferent to it. But when we come close—not necessarily in geography, but certainly in empathy—and open our hearts to *feel*, then we know the truth of G.K. Chesterton's lines:

We are all in the same boat
   in a stormy sea,
And we owe each other
   a terrible loyalty.

Every person has intrinsic worth because he is made in the image of God. The Marxist view of man is that he has value only so long as he produces for the State. That is why in some Eastern European countries, the government will allow the Church to care for the mentally retarded, which is the only social service religious bodies may perform. Those lives have no value in the eyes of the State because they are not productive. But with what tender care have I seen the loving hands of Christ's people care for those who are without worth or value in a materialistic society!

Maybe this is closer to what Jesus would be doing if He were among us today than all the high and mighty acts which take place in the corridors of power. I do not denigrate those acts when performed by dedicated public servants as a service to God and mankind, but I believe on Jesus' scale of priorities, a nation's Gross National Well-being would take precedence over its Gross National Product.

As a refugee himself when a baby, Jesus would not feel out of place today with those on the South China Sea or in the Gaza Strip.

I came across a book recently called *A Portrait of Jesus* by Alan T. Dale, published in England by Oxford University Press. I do not know if Mr. Dale would share my evangelical point of view, but he helped me greatly with one of his comments:

> Jesus made clear to me that the growing point of genuinely human society (call it God's Family, if you wish) is what we do for the fellow who is left out of the picture, whom nobody bothers with, who doesn't seem to belong, who is out of it. There can be no genuine human society if anybody is left out; if we leave anybody out we corrupt human society and destroy it. All this threw a new light for me on what, wherever I was, I ought to be concerned with; how I ought to look at whatever job I'd got (and where I should do it); and what I ought to press for, in

every way I knew how, in the public life of the world. The growing points of my world were to be where people were ignored, forgotten or in need—people in prison for conscience's sake, people who were the victims of starvation and the injustices of a world divided up into the haves and have nots. It came home to me that what Jesus was talking about was not just being kind and generous, but about how a world can ever be a world in any worthwhile sense of the word. When he talked about God being Father, he was not saying something about God, he was making clear what for him made all the difference to the way he lived and the way we must all live. . . . We can have a *world* in no other way.

For me that statement has profound application. The question now for me is not so much, "Am I my brother's keeper?" but "Am I my brother's brother?"

The growing point of my world is where humanity is being diminished by neglect or mistreatment. There is no place where this is more true than in the world of the homeless, the uprooted, the refugee. I saw in Malaysia in late 1978 what may be the world in microcosm. A refugee boat pulled in the shallow water along the east coast. A man jumped from the boat into the water and started to walk ashore. He was met at the water's edge by a local vigilante who slapped the man and knocked him down. As the refugee slowly picked himself up, the vigilante pointed him back to sea. The disappointed man turned and walked slowly back to his boat.

The experience filled me with an incredible sadness.

However, the next day I saw the exact opposite, demonstrating for me that individual action for good can be equally significant. At the town of Dungun, we were informed that a boatload of refugees had arrived in the night and were in detention inside the local soccer field. We could not see them without permission from the superintendent of police, the guard told us. We met a most gentle man. He was a Christian and compassion tempered his official attitude. He not only allowed us to buy boxes of food and personal items for the sixty-one refugees who had nothing, but went with us to the grocery shop and transported the goods to the refugees in his own Mercedes.

I thanked God that for some people, human beings still have immeasurable worth. Refugee status does not take away from a man his intrinsic worth as a creation of God.

As such, they are all worth saving.

The second statement that drives me back into

action when I want to quit because of the seemingly endless nature of the task and its sometimes apparent futility, is something I read many years ago from Aristotle. He was required reading during my freshman year at university and one day I stumbled upon something he said which struck me forcibly. I was so profoundly moved, I wrote it on the flyleaf of the first Bible I ever owned, for I had only recently become a Christian. What Aristotle said is both simple and very deep: "Where there are things to be done, the end is not to survey and recognize those various things, but rather to do them."

Somehow, I don't think God was offended to have Aristotle on one of the blank pages of my Bible. Since then I have found many verses in the printed pages of my Bible which confirm that God is the God who acts.

It is not enough to gather data, take survey trips, publish the results, enter into dialogue about it, analyze, synthesize and hypothesize when human life and dignity are at stake. That is not to say that all these things should not be done, but there comes a crucial moment when all those things must be finished and the nettle grasped, an action taken.

Did you ever vote on an issue or make a decision when you earnestly wished you had more information on which to base your vote or make your decision? Of course you have. The evidence is never all in. The time comes, in any case, when a judgment has to be made. After logic has done its best, there is still a gap that only the heart—or human sensitivity, or compassion, or love, or God—can bridge. History moves over that last gap not upon logic, but upon the risky action of a person who determines that, come what may, he must do right.

History's grandest moments have been history's moments of greatest risk. The great leader does not wait until advocacy is safe. President Anwar Sadat's dramatic trip to Jerusalem is an example of such courageous leadership.

A man does not become a leader by searching out a cause. He becomes a leader by daring to do what must be done.

I set this background in order to raise the question: Will God find someone whom He can raise up to champion the cause of the uprooted and dispossessed as William Wilberforce fought for the freedom of slaves in the last of the eighteenth century? Is it necessary to point out that the refugee cause today is no more popular an issue than was the abolition of slavery then? While a young member of Parliament, Wilberforce was converted to Christ in 1787 as he was on a trip to France. He returned to London, hoping to take holy orders. He was dissuaded by the hymn writer and former slave captain, John Newton, who urged him to serve his Lord in the House of

Commons.

Wilberforce determined to attack not only the slave trade, but the very institution of slavery itself. He was a leader in that fight for the rest of his life. It took twenty years of struggle, but when his vision was finally caught by the younger members of Parliament, the bill to abolish slave traffic was carried in 1807 by a vote of 283 to 6. It took another twenty-six years before 700,000 slaves were permanently freed throughout the empire and it didn't happen until a month after Wilberforce died.

But his name shines lustrous in England's history.

As the "Me Generation" approaches its peak in the 1980s, it may become even less popular to champion the cause of the dispossessed—whom many countries view as a "burden." Nonetheless, together with Third World poverty and injustice, this represents one of the greatest moral challenges facing the world today. A just and right cause languishes for lack of strong voices and committed leadership.

Another word I want to give you is one that keeps me from despairing in the face of insuperable odds. There are days when I would quit because my emotions are so bruised and the task is so great. When I went on board the refugee ship *Tung An* in Manila harbor, the conditions were some of the most deplorable I have ever seen. I wanted to do so much, but we were prohibited. Finally, we were given permission to put eight gas stoves on the ship to supplement the two already there so that mothers would not have to wait so long for boiled water to feed their babies.

Eight stoves in the face of such staggering need seemed utterly futile until I remembered these words of Jesus: "Whoever gives a cup of cold water in my name shall not lose his reward." Suddenly, even something small seemed worthwhile. Every single act of kindness is blessed by Christ to both receiver and giver.

I am comforted that Jesus didn't say it had to be a well or a gusher. He said just a cup of cold water. Sometimes we become paralyzed by the magnitude of the task. Perhaps it is time to think small—to give ourselves to doing what we can do.

That's what we have decided to do in World Vision International, even though sometimes the particular action may seem insignificant and futile. Sometimes we may not do things very well. We may seem amateurish instead of professional.

But we are not going to fail to do what we can do!

When we put our ship *Seasweep* out on the South China Sea, it seemed like a very small act. Tens of thousands were coming across that body of water; we might be able to help a few hundred. And the cost would not be small.

Why did we do it? Apart from feeling terribly responsible under God for the preservation of even a single human life, I also believe there is a fallout of good as surely as there is a fallout of evil. One act of kindness can inspire others to act.

In Grand Central Station in New York City, two sets of doors lead into the waiting area. It is interesting to watch people coming into the station during evening rush hour. Some hurry through—tired, self-centered, letting a door close in the face of the person following, not even aware of anyone else. This irritates the person who is following, and he or she tends to do likewise to relieve irritation. Eventually this pattern of selfishness is broken by someone who thoughtfully holds the door for the one behind him. That one, put under some kind of constraint by this thoughtfulness, holds the door for the one behind him, and this pattern, too, continues until eventually it is broken.

That is what I call the fallout of good. A cup of cold water—it is not just a futile gesture and it is more than symbolic; it has validity in itself. It is symbolic because it has validity; it is not valid because it is symbolic.

When we do what lies at hand, when we do what we can do, the symbolism will take care of itself.

A few years ago when the Bengalis were streaming into India out of Bangladesh to escape the civil war, I drove from Calcutta to the border over roads choked by the fleeing refugees. An estimated 200,000 were on the roads that hot, sticky day. As we moved slowly through the masses of people, I saw the crumpled body of an old woman lying in a ditch. Assuming she was dead, we drove on. When we returned an hour later, I saw that she was moving about and moaning. The thin cotton sari she had been wearing earlier had been stripped from her body.

I asked the driver to stop and I went down into the ditch. The woman was alive, but very sick and incoherent. In order to cover her nakedness, I bought a piece of cloth from another refugee who had an extra one. I wrapped the cotton fabric around her.

One of my companions joined me and we carried her across the road to a temporary camp where I tried to get the director to take her in. He refused, saying he had no hospital or medical facilities for one so obviously near death. I offered to leave money and pay someone just to bring her water and food twice a day until she died, but could find no takers.

In desperation, I got the camp commander to give me a little thatched lean-to which was empty. I bought a bamboo mat and we laid her on it in the shade of the little shelter. She ate a little bread and drank a few sips of water. After putting the water and some bread beside her, we had to leave.

There was nothing more I could do.

But I was haunted by that scene for a long time. We had done so little. Was it all an empty symbolism, meaningless in the face of such remaining awesome needs? Should those few moments and few rupees have been spent on someone with a better chance of survival?

And then the episode took on a whole new meaning in the light of our Lord's words, "Inasmuch as ye have done it unto one of the least of these my brethren, ye have done it unto me" (Matt. 25:40).

We had ministered to Christ.

I am not optimistic that the world will ever again be without refugees. However, if we can get enough people to replicate the caring act of giving a cup of cold water—in whatever form they are able to do so—I believe we could eliminate the refugee *problem*.

I know that for me, I cannot stop trying.

POSTSCRIPT

After a mission on board *Seasweep* into the refugee camps on the Anambas Islands, Dr. Kenneth Wilson wrote these words:

"Being a refugee is being a name and a number on lists. It is being in a mass of people shuffled from one point to another, not knowing what you have to do next or where you are going. It is being a child fearful you will be separated from your parents.

"It is being an elderly woman too weak to walk without help, but not too weak to smile luminously at a small act of kindness. It is having faith to believe that wherever you go will be better than where you have been.

"When you are a refugee, hope is the last thing

you dare let go."

For thirty years, World Vision International has been holding out hope to refugees, extending hands of help and kindness in Jesus' name to millions of people around the world.

If you would like to share in the ministries of caring and witness, which World Vision now has in 73 countries, you may send a tax-deductible gift to:

World Vision International
Department S10000
919 W. Huntington Drive
Monrovia, CA 91016